# COWBOY MILLIONAIRE
## —THE NEW AMERICAN PIONEER—

### BY LIEF SIMON
### AND THE STAFF OF LIVE AND INVEST OVERSEAS

Published by Lahardan Books

Published by Lahardan Books

Copyright © Live And Invest Overseas, 2024
All rights reserved

ISBN 978-1-958583-04-3

Book and Cover Design by Cristian Landero

No part of this publication may be reproduced, stored in, or introduced into a retrieval system, or transmitted, in any form, or by any means (electronic, mechanical, photocopying, recording, or otherwise), without the prior written permission of both the copyright owner and the publisher of this book.

The scanning, uploading, and distribution of this book via the Internet or via any other means without the permission of the publisher is illegal and punishable by law. Please purchase only authorized electronic editions, and do not participate in or encourage electronic piracy of copyrighted materials. Your support of the author's rights is appreciated.

# Acknowledgements

Publishing this book is another milestone on the journey my wife, Kathleen, and I began when we started our Live And Invest Overseas publishing business—based in Panama—in 2008.

This book has been thirty years in the making, taking into account all the years I've been living and doing business overseas and the lessons I've learned in that time.

More specifically, I started my *Simon Letter* monthly newsletter service in 2012, writing about and chronicling my journey in that letter. This book could not have been put together without the years of information and research built up in the process of publishing *Simon Letter*.

Work by numerous writers and editors at *Simon Letter* and Live And Invest Overseas has gone into this book, including work by Kathleen Peddicord, Victoria Harmer, Harry Kalashian, Kat Kalashian, Mónica Linares, Con Murphy, and Sophia Titley.

# About The Author

Lief Simon has lived and worked in seven countries on five continents and has traveled to more than seventy-five countries.

In that time, he has become the world's preeminent expert on overseas real estate investing and using the opportunities available to you internationally to protect and grow your wealth.

Lief's real estate investing experience began in 1995 with a multi-unit building in Chicago. After selling that building for a total return of more than one thousand eight hundred percent in just thirty months, Lief began to diversify internationally.

In the decades since, Lief has personally bought and sold property in twenty-four countries. He has managed multi-million-dollar developments, multi-million-dollar property portfolios, and more than two-dozen rental properties.

Over the years that Lief has been living overseas, he has also been actively engaged in doing business.

He has launched and managed business ventures in ten

countries, including local businesses, web-based businesses, and international franchises.

Lief has spent more than three weeks out of four on the road for the better part of the past two decades, traveling almost constantly in search of the world's top opportunities.

In recent years, Lief has also turned readers on to targeted investments suitable for the individual investor in Mexico, Nicaragua, Romania, Panama, Belize, Argentina, Brazil, Uruguay, the Philippines, the Dominican Republic, Colombia, Ireland, Portugal, Spain, Northern Cyprus, Montenegro, and Turkey. In every case, readers who took his advice made money.

Over the decades he's spent living and doing business around the world, Lief has learned many lessons about how to succeed in business (and life) offshore... and he shares those lessons and his ongoing journey with readers of his *Offshore Living Letter* e-letter and *Simon Letter* monthly newsletter.

Lief has built a network of reliable and expert contacts—attorneys, bankers, tax consultants, and other advisors—both stateside and in the jurisdictions where he spends time and money. With their help, he stays on top of the ever-changing world of offshore business and opportunities... as they happen.

Lief says: "You don't have to be a millionaire to take up the idea of banking, doing business, or investing offshore. There are different levels to this game. Only you will know what makes sense for your circumstances and what's within your comfort zone.

"Your strategy might be as simple as opening a bank account in another country. You don't even have to leave the United States to do this.

"Or you can get more complex and diversify into real estate or precious metals, form an offshore corporation, move overseas, and even acquire second citizenship, as I have..."

"Either way, *Offshore Living Letter* and *Simon Letter* will help get you started on your path to relying on yourself for your future's prosperity... not some government."

# Resources

Throughout this book, I reference charts, graphs, tables, and other infographics. To view these visual aids, visit this link: **cowboymillionairesecrets.com**, or scan the QR code below.

The maps on the two pages to follow show all the places around the world where Lief has "planted a flag" over the past thirty years. For new American pioneers, planting a flag refers to taking a step towards international diversification. Officially, there are five flags: residency, citizenship, asset protection, banking, and business. Lief has planted all five many times over. His life and assets are about as well-diversified globally as anyone's could be. More on the five flags theory of diversification in Chapter VII.

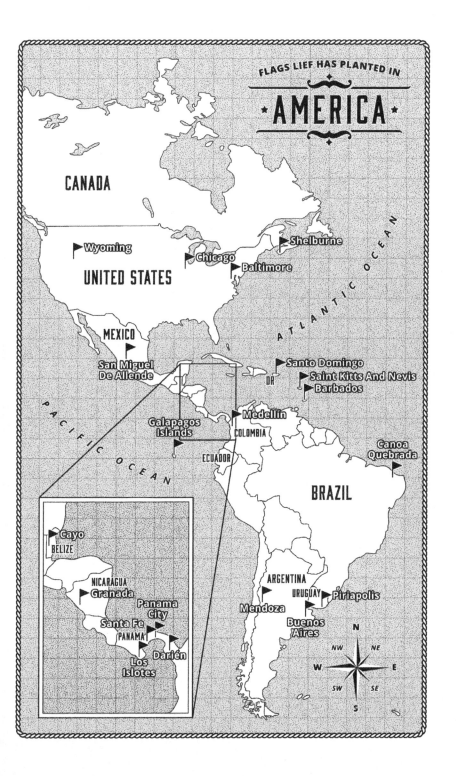

# Contents

Introduction: The New Frontier And The New American Pioneer …… 17

## PART I: CREATING YOUR FORTUNE ON THE NEW FRONTIER

Chapter I: The Secret That Will Save Your Financial Future …… 53

Chapter II: The Number-One Opportunity In The World …… 64

Chapter III: How To Build The Perfect Portfolio …… 86

Chapter IV: The Six Top Markets To Look At Right Now …… 101

Chapter V: Eight Things You Need To Know About "Frontier" Markets …… 135

Chapter VI: Three Hard Assets That Preserve Your Wealth …… 170

## PART II: HOW TO PROTECT WHAT'S YOURS (WHEN EVERYONE WANTS A PIECE)

Chapter VII: Five Keys That Secure What You've Built …… 197

Chapter VIII: Never Worry About A Bank Collapse Again …… 213

Chapter IX: Beat The Bureaucrats… Wipe Out Your Tax Bill …… 259

**COWBOY MILLIONAIRE—THE NEW AMERICAN PIONEER**
Contents

| | |
|---|---|
| Chapter X: Do This Before You Get Sued (And You'll Be Safe) | 302 |
| Chapter XI: The "Secret Of The Kings" That Keeps Your Money Safe | 331 |
| Chapter XII: The Three Most Important Things To Know Before You "Go Offshore" | 348 |

## PART III: THE ULTIMATE "BACKUP PLAN" FOR YOUR LIFESTYLE

| | |
|---|---|
| Chapter XIII: The "Master Key" That Allows You To Escape Lockdowns And Travel Restrictions | 369 |
| Chapter XIV: The "Inheritance Gift" You Never Knew About—That You Could Be Entitled To (Here's How) | 378 |
| Chapter XV: How To Live Anywhere You Want For As Long As You Want | 412 |
| Chapter XVI: The Easiest And Cheapest Way To Get Your "Master Key" | 438 |
| Chapter XVII: The Investment With "No Profits" That's Still A Good Buy | 481 |
| Chapter XVIII: The Fastest Way To Get Your "Master Key" | 498 |

## EPILOGUE: FROM PIONEER TO JET-SETTER IN THREE EASY STEPS

INTRODUCTION

# The New Frontier And The New American Pioneer

Americans used to be the great movers of the world.

Think of the pioneers who settled the West... traveling thousands of miles with nothing just to find a place where they could truly live free, far from the Old World governments that kept them down... looking for new opportunities on new lands because opportunities had dried up back home.

That was a hard life.

I remember the words of Captain Shea Brennan, one of my favorite characters in the "Yellowstone" prequel series "1883," about a caravan of migrants heading from Tennessee toward Montana and Oregon...

"You are pioneers, and that's all you are until you get there. You have no home. No job. No farm. You have the journey. That's it."

For the pioneers, the journey was worth it... because of the promise of what they would find.

## "Yellowstone" Is Wrong

I like the "Yellowstone" TV show because it's a modern cowboy story. There's edge-of-the-seat action, ruthless characters, and compelling twists.

But the series also has a lot to say about America—past, present, and future.

"Yellowstone" is in some ways just one more example of America's red state/blue state divide.

"Yellowstone" is the number-one-rated show in America… but a lot of people in big cities have never heard of it.

The *New York Times* called it a "conservative fantasy": "liberal audiences mostly ignore it."

In the original "Yellowstone" series, John Dutton (Kevin Costner) and his family—owners of a vast ranch in Montana bordering Yellowstone National Park—fight to preserve their cattle-rearing way of life against developers who want to turn the ranch into a vacation resort for rich New Yorkers.

Developers want to build a city and pave over the grazing land, rivers, and forests that the Duttons have made their home for generations.

I'm not a warrior on either side of America's "culture war." I call it as I see it. And I like what I like.

But it does not surprise me that "Yellowstone" isn't popular in America's big cities.

## COWBOY MILLIONAIRE—THE NEW AMERICAN PIONEER
*Introduction: The New Frontier And The New American Pioneer*

I think it might surprise a lot of people in big cities to learn that there are actually still cowboys in America today...

Dutton doesn't care about what's trending on social media or what's the "politically correct" or "woke" thing to say.

He prefers working with his hands to staring at a computer... and prefers riding his horse to driving his truck...

Dutton runs for governor of Montana because he wants to make it the state where "progress" goes to die.

That old-school American way of life—working hard, just you and the land; the spirit of adventure, the kind that settled the West—is what Dutton wants to keep alive.

But Dutton knows he's one of the last cowboys in America. That's why he's fighting so hard.

If you know anything about me, you probably know that I don't hold my tongue. I "shoot from the hip"... I also like my Stetsons and my guns...

So, Costner's character is my man.

Dutton fights by any means possible to hold onto the way of life his family sacrificed for, going back generations.

In a way, everything I do, everything I write about, is about building a legacy.

The opportunities I share with you... My views on maximizing your wealth by going offshore... It's all about setting you and your family up for the future. Protecting what's yours.

I've used the strategies that I recommend to build a legacy that my family can take over and carry forward into future generations...

I understand the mind of John Dutton.

But in a very important way, the hero of "Yellowstone" is wrong, and the pioneers of "1883" were right.

It's a noble thing to want to hold onto a way of life that's disappearing in today's fast-paced, tech-obsessed world.

But the real Duttons of history... the pioneers who settled the West and who built what Costner's character wants to preserve... they were driven by opportunity.

The opportunity to cultivate new lands. Build things where nothing existed before. They wanted to change their lives for the better. The freedom of open spaces and finding your fortune...

What made America great was that spirit of opportunity and adventure... that idea of freedom. Forging your own destiny...

## Opportunity Is Everywhere

Today, pioneering Americans (like me) can take that idea of freedom, find our fortune, and build our legacy even beyond the borders of our own country. Follow opportunity wherever it leads. That's an incredible thing.

The American West has been settled. Many people feel that the same opportunities that once existed in America no

## COWBOY MILLIONAIRE—THE NEW AMERICAN PIONEER
*Introduction: The New Frontier And The New American Pioneer*

longer exist there, and they're right.

But here's the thing: The whole wide world is your frontier, to find your fortune and build your legacy...

I've gone overseas to find opportunities. And I've found plenty... the kinds of wealth-building and wealth-protection opportunities I could never find back home. Thousands of other Americans have done it, too. And I can show you how.

Expats are forging their own path wherever it leads...

After years of investing overseas, I've found my personal "Yellowstone" on Panama's Azuero Peninsula, the "Sunset Coast." This is where my wife, Kathleen, and I are staking our claim and building a two-hundred-fifteen-acre community called Los Islotes to enjoy open space that stretches to the sea, with hiking trails, an equestrian center, two beaches, and much more...

I'm hoping this community will pass down through the generations and still be around in a few hundred years, just like the fictional Yellowstone.

We consider ourselves stewards of the land and protectors of the legacy we're building in the same way that John Dutton does.

But it's not a problem for us that we can't live the life we want in America anymore. There are plenty of other places where we can. Places where the living is slow (if that's what you want) and you can tune out whatever it is the keyboard warriors care about. The whole world is our frontier.

It can be yours, too. That's what this book is about.

## America Is Not Enough

Why should you be looking beyond the United States for opportunity?

I probably don't need to go into all the problems America is facing these days. Unsustainable debt. Useless politicians. Everybody angry at everybody else.

I started looking overseas for investment opportunities more than thirty years ago—and I did it because I wanted new adventures, not because I was running away from the States.

But every time I return to the United States these days, I want to leave again as soon as I can.

My takeaway is that, to borrow a line from Will McAvoy's opening monologue in the first episode of the HBO series "Newsroom" (I'm a TV fan, as you can tell), America isn't the greatest country in the world.

Stick with me…

In every way that you can measure quality of life, the United States doesn't rank number one. It ranks well in many categories, but not the best in any one that I'm aware of.

In the Global Peace Index, which measures murders and violence, the United States ranks one hundred thirty-one out of one hundred sixty-three countries. The country doesn't make the top ten in any health care ranking that I've seen.

This is a big place, and, even in categories where the United States excels overall, parts of the country lag far behind the developed world.

Take infrastructure, for example. Every time I'm in the United States, I'm struck by the poor quality of the infrastructure. The roads I travel every day in rural Woodstock, Illinois (where my mother lives), aren't in any better condition than the roads I drive anywhere else in the world where I spend time.

And they're far worse than roads in France, for example, where I've got a lot of experience behind the wheel.

This is true not only in the context of roads in northern Illinois.

The broken asphalt and potholes I bump over every day in Illinois are similar to those in downtown Houston and suburban Baltimore, two other places in the States where I've spent time in the last few years.

Cell phone coverage, likewise, is hit-and-miss. In Woodstock, my phone gets one bar at best, and most calls are going straight to voicemail. The internet service is maddening.

And it's not just infrastructure...

Health care in the United States is a factory experience. One reason I return to Illinois regularly is to help my mother with some health problems. The experience is eye-opening in the worst possible way.

Old people in America go to various doctors regularly for one ailment after another. The result in every instance, as far as I can tell, is for the doctor to prescribe a pill or an injection.

Two out of three commercials on television are for prescription drugs. "Ask your doctor about blah, blah, blah," every one of them recommends in the end. And many aging Americans do. They ask, the doctors write out a prescription, and the patient goes away to buy more drugs to take along with all the other drugs he's taking, feeding the health insurance and pharmaceutical conglomerates that run the health care industry in this country.

All those drugs come with long lists of side effects, countereffects, and potential complications.

And don't even get me started on the insane bureaucracy surrounding Medicare and U.S. health insurance and working out what's covered and what's not, what you'll pay out of pocket and what you won't...

In no other country on Earth is the health care bureaucracy so complex—or health care itself so expensive. In Panama, Kathleen and I pay $35 to visit an excellent, English-speaking doctor. In France—ranked by the World Health Organization as the best health system in the world—a family doctor visit costs 25 euros. And seventy-five percent of that can be reimbursed if you're part of the national health care system.

There are excellent private health care facilities all over the world that rival any center of excellence in the States...

Despite all the medicating in the States (or, I'd say, at least in part because of all the medicating), the health of the average American is critically low. I haven't checked the statistics, but my observational experience suggests that more than seventy percent of people in this country are overweight, and half of those are excessively overweight.

They go to their doctors with complaints related to being overweight. Rather than counseling the patient on lifestyle choices, the doctor, to make the point again, writes out a prescription.

It's not like that elsewhere...

I don't want to get into a debate about why people get fat (there, I used the word... not very "woke" of me). However, I believe that, in most cases, it's because they eat too much and exercise too little.

The poor eating habits of the average American are understandable. You have to work hard here to eat healthy. I estimate that more than two-thirds of the grocery store where I shop in Illinois is given over to nonfood items. For every aisle offering fresh fruit and vegetables, meat and bread, there are at least two selling candy, chips, cakes, doughnuts, soda, and a lot of nonfood that I've never seen before.

I've taken to reading the nutritional labels on each item I'm considering buying. Every processed product has sugar listed among the top five ingredients. It's no wonder more than ten percent of the population of the United States suffers from diabetes... and another thirty-five percent are considered pre-diabetic.

Enough about food.

Let's talk instead about attorneys!

Television commercials in America sell one of three things: drugs, charities, or lawyers. "Were you ever exposed to XYZ? If so, you may be eligible for a payout. Get in touch now to talk about filing a suit..." recommend the sleezy attorneys in bad suits.

Like prescription medications and sugary foods, lawsuits have become an American industry. We should all aspire to go our whole lives without one, but they are being pushed on us from all angles.

(Forty million lawsuits are filed in America every year... and no doubt many of them are frivolous.)

In northern Illinois, most people seem happy with the lifestyle they've been sold. I'd say that's because they're not aware of the alternatives.

Like Will McAvoy, I've undertaken a mission to civilize. Or, well, to expand the minds of my neighbors in Woodstock.

How's it going so far? Not so well...

"Where do you live?" one lady wanted to know.

"Part of the year in Panama and part of the year in Paris,"

## COWBOY MILLIONAIRE—THE NEW AMERICAN PIONEER
*Introduction: The New Frontier And The New American Pioneer*

I told her.

"But Paris is so dirty!" she said. "Everyone I've known who's been there says the French are filthy. How can you stand living like that?"

Funny, I thought. I'm wondering the same thing about you.

The anger in America has become too much to bear in person every day. It's in your face in the news and sometimes in person when you go out, but more importantly, it's just under the surface with so many people.

The vitriol from the two political parties in the United States only encourages the average man on the street to be angry. You're either with them or against them.

Standing in the middle, you get hit from both sides. That leaves most reasonable people to stay silent for fear of being shot, having their home or business burned down, or becoming a victim of cancel culture.

Maybe this anger was always there, and I just didn't see it growing up in the United States. At this point, I have been living out of the country for three decades.

Looking back through the decades since World War II, you can find riots and protests over civil rights, wars, and the economy.

Taking that perspective, one has to wonder why anything hasn't improved over the years…

Whatever the reasons for the current anger in the United

**COWBOY MILLIONAIRE—THE NEW AMERICAN PIONEER**
*Introduction: The New Frontier And The New American Pioneer*

States, whether it's just always been there to resurface in new ways today or because the politicians find it better to rule at the extremes of society, I'm ready to move on.

Fortunately, thirty years of internationalizing my life makes moving on from America possible.

And I'm finding more and more people continue to look at how to do the same for themselves, as the politicians seem to only taunt each other.

I'm not anti-America, and I'm certainly not anti-American. But I am anti the lifestyle that I see all around me in the States... and I appreciate the diversified lifestyle I've developed over the past thirty years more every day.

As I say, this is not about being anti-America or anti-American.

On the contrary, it's about rescuing that older, pioneering, adventurous spirit of America from the lifestyle I see around me every day in the United States.

We need to renew the spirit of the American pioneer. That's what this book is about.

## Why Should You Listen To Me?

You could say I've been writing this book for thirty years.

It brings together all the advice, lessons, and wisdom I've learned the hard way from three decades of exploring new markets and investigating opportunities outside my

**COWBOY MILLIONAIRE—THE NEW AMERICAN PIONEER**
*Introduction: The New Frontier And The New American Pioneer*

home country...

At age eighteen, I promised myself I'd be a millionaire by the age of thirty-five. And I achieved that.

But I had to take risks and be a pioneer along the way...

I grew up in a lower-middle-class home, the son of a single mother. There was no trust fund to give me a leg up in life.

I saved long to be able to pay for my first car, and I worked two jobs to cover college tuition... then grad school.

I tell you this to prove the point that you don't need to be born with a silver spoon in your mouth to take advantage of the kind of wealth-building strategies I've followed. The same strategies that I share with you in this book.

I had that pioneering spirit in me from an early age. I simply had an idea that I wanted more out of life than growing up, going to school, working, and dying in the same place.

I had that idea for the first time when I was in high school.

I could have achieved my objective—of not spending my whole life in one place—by moving to another state. But something in my head told me to push for something more than that. I wanted options... as many as possible.

Beyond-the-border options.

I heard about a school called, at the time, the American Graduate School of International Management. You might know it as Thunderbird. I decided in high school that that's where I'd go after college. The school has since merged with

Arizona State University, but it still offers one of the best international MBA programs in the world.

That was as far as my thinking went at the time.

After graduating college and getting into Thunderbird, my plan began to expand; my focus was on job opportunities overseas. Let someone pay me to see the world, I figured... so I could either find a job in another country or join the Navy, as my best friend had decided to do. I knew myself well enough to realize that I wouldn't be much good as a link in the chain of anyone's command.

I finished the program at Thunderbird and got what I thought was an ideal offer of employment from an international oil drilling company. Just as I'd hoped, they wanted to pay me to see the world... at least the world where they operated. The trouble, I found, is that oil seems to be in places where humans probably shouldn't hang out in the long term.

That drilling outfit sent me to work in Chad, the Tengiz oil fields in Kazakhstan (where it is minus fifty degrees in winter), and northern Argentina in a town so close to Bolivia that that's where we shopped for most things.

The experience was great. Unfortunately, the company wasn't. So I quit and returned to the United States.

But that initial international experience was all I needed to confirm that that was the life for me.

I spent the next four years living in Chicago (another place humans probably shouldn't be in winter... at least not this boy from Arizona) regrouping.

Finally, I felt ready to look overseas again.

I signed up for a tour of Ireland. I had an idea for a property development project... and, from my research, Ireland seemed like a good place for it.

That tour was led by Kathleen Peddicord, who, coincidentally, was also considering a move to the Emerald Isle. We met in June, were married in November, and headed to Ireland together two weeks later.

Whereas the jobs with the drilling company had been short-term gigs, that move to Ireland was indefinite. That meant obtaining legal residency, setting up a bank account, buying a car, getting a local driver's license, and all the other fun things you do when you move to another country.

Ireland became my first real experience at internationalizing my life.

In the more than two decades since, I've gone offshore completely and thoroughly. At this point, I've done just about everything one could think about doing in another country...

I have obtained residency (in four countries), opened bank accounts (more than twenty-five accounts in fifteen countries), launched and operated businesses (in seven countries), bought real estate (in twenty-four countries), educated my children (in four countries), and obtained a second citizenship.

## COWBOY MILLIONAIRE—THE NEW AMERICAN PIONEER
*Introduction: The New Frontier And The New American Pioneer*

I don't tell you all this to brag... but to show you that—unlike other "offshore experts" you may find out there on the internet—I have real-world, firsthand experience with the offshore world. It's my everyday life.

None of this happened overnight, and here's a secret: Much of it was not according to any plan.

Kathleen and I have built our offshore life organically, step by step. Each step has opened new doors and led to more options... and we've sifted and filtered and made choices, one after another, that have gotten us from where we were all those years ago to where we are today.

But you don't have to "play it by ear." Because you can learn from this book all the things that I had to learn the hard way.

And believe me, though the road I chose to take has not always been easy... it's been worth it.

What have I gained?

Well, as you'll read about in the chapters ahead, I've built my fortune overseas—primarily in overseas real estate.

But more than that, I've been able to protect my fortune through the international diversification strategies I've discovered.

A key to making money is making sure you're not losing it... and that's where my "offshore" expertise really shines.

I've worked for decades to increase my understanding of asset protection... The result? Not only has it helped make me money, it ended up saving me a fortune... three fortunes, actually...

This method allowed me to make money during the 2000 dot-com crash, the 2008 financial crisis, and even the global pandemic of 2020...

You know as well as I do that each of those events devastated millions of retirement plans and businesses across the United States. They forced a lot folks out of retirement... and many more out of their homes.

And I can tell you now that what I've learned—and what you'll learn in these pages—will keep us from losing money during the next economic crisis.

No matter who's pulling the strings in the White House... No matter how high taxes rise... Or how far the stock market falls... No matter when the next recession strikes—or how hard it hits... I am not worried.

And you shouldn't be either. Because none of that has to affect you.

## Freedom Means Having Options

In fall 2018, some residents of the Carolinas found themselves out of options.

Some Carolinians weren't able—for various reasons—to heed the mandatory hurricane evacuation announcements.

**COWBOY MILLIONAIRE—THE NEW AMERICAN PIONEER**
*Introduction: The New Frontier And The New American Pioneer*

Eventually, they had to be rescued.

It's the same story with many so-called "acts of God" that happen across the United States every year...

Very unfortunate situation... that always reminds me why I've worked so hard to organize my life the way that I have.

You see, when you look internationally, you're considering all your options.

And when you incorporate more options into your lifestyle, you're less likely to ever run out of them.

Your wealth and your lifestyle will be protected... against economic downturns, pure bad luck, and, yes, even "acts of God."

I prioritize options above all else... because, without options, you're vulnerable. You can find yourself stuck... and in need of rescue (literally or figuratively) from some third party... meaning you've got no choice but to give up control over your situation and your future.

For me, that's the worst situation imaginable.

Life is filled with complications, challenges, disappointments, downturns, and outright disasters. When an impediment presents itself, you want to be able to adjust your circumstances in a way that allows you to leap over or dart around the trouble... rather than having your life upended and finding yourself forced to scramble into the back of someone else's lifeboat.

**COWBOY MILLIONAIRE—THE NEW AMERICAN PIONEER**
*Introduction: The New Frontier And The New American Pioneer*

If you're all-in on one country's economy—that is, if you're living, working, doing business, and investing one hundred percent in one country—then you're more vulnerable to the fallout if something goes wrong in that country than you could be if your life and assets were better diversified.

You want at least some of your investments to be outside your home country... but don't stop there.

You need a backup plan for how to move money from one country to another (bottom line: you need more than one offshore bank account)... for how to get yourself from one country to another (this is where your backup residency and, best case, your second citizenship come in)... and for how to survive if and when global systems go sideways.

For me, the answer to that final challenge has been to create a home for myself and my family at Los Islotes in Panama where we could, if we needed or wanted, live self-sufficiently.

Doom and gloom aren't my thing, but our world today demands options and backup plans.

The good news is that, as our world grows more complicated, it has also become smaller. It's easier today to move both yourself and your money.

The most successful people I know all have one important thing in common: They've developed their own well-rounded ecosystems—global networks of friends, colleagues, and trusted advisors.

That—not the total amount of money that you have—is the key.

And it's easier to put in place than you might think... and quicker. Again, this book is your shortcut.

With a personal ecosystem in place, you'll find yourself much better able to adjust your circumstances as needed. Rather than reacting to crisis when it hits, you'll simply pivot to redirect your path.

And you and your alliance will carry merrily on your way.

## The "New American Pioneer" Enjoys The Best Of All Worlds

To be an American pioneer today, as opposed to in 1883, is not about a hard life of toil and migration in search of opportunities and freedom—but plucking from the best opportunities, freedoms, and wealth-protection strategies available to you all across the world.

It really is about availing yourself of and enjoying the best of all possible worlds.

To return again to my obsession with TV's "Yellowstone" franchise...

All the series—especially the prequels, "1883" and "1923"—are old-fashioned Wild West stories, with cowboys and Indians and lots of horseback riding and gunfights.

## COWBOY MILLIONAIRE—THE NEW AMERICAN PIONEER
*Introduction: The New Frontier And The New American Pioneer*

But the franchise is also a deep exploration of the American Dream... and what you might call a contradiction at the heart of the American Dream: the desire to be free versus the desire to live a comfortable life.

The American frontier, the Old West, was in many ways the perfect representation of freedom... the moment of greatest freedom in the history of the human race, in the minds of many...

For the American settlers traveling west and building lives for themselves, there were few laws, no government support—little interference, even from other people... just man and the land... almost endless landscapes waiting to be tamed.

The tension between a city and a country way of life is at the heart of the franchise—and, you might say, at the heart of the political divide in America...

In "1923" (set, of course, in that year), there's a funny scene where the cowboys head into town, and a vendor is selling some brand-new conveniences—washing machines and refrigerators.

The cowboys can't understand the purpose of these things. It will save time, the vendor explains, and then you'll have more time for leisure. The cowboys are more interested in sticking to their old ways of doing things—the way of life they know and love—than trading in their traditions

## COWBOY MILLIONAIRE—THE NEW AMERICAN PIONEER
*Introduction: The New Frontier And The New American Pioneer*

for convenience...

At another point in "1923," Harrison Ford's character imagines how wonderful life would be if there were no cities—just man free in nature. A businessman explains that cities are the future. In the countryside, you merely survive against nature—bracing winters and digging holes to use as toilets. In the city, man is the master of nature. Water flows from the tap, and light comes at the flick of a switch...

The voiceover in "1883" warns us that cities have weakened us as a species. In the city, there are fewer consequences to your actions... you won't sit down in the grass to pee and get bitten by a snake... you don't have to keep wolves away from your campsite... you become weak, and you can't fend for yourself.

These are the tensions "Yellowstone" sees in American life between freedom and comfort... urban versus rural... tough versus soft...

And it's true: Old-style rural life offers a very different set of freedoms than the freedom a city offers. In the wilderness, you have freedom from people... the freedom to make your own way and build something entirely new from the ground up. But you have to have the toughness and the skills to do it.

Rural freedom is the freedom to chart your own path as a pioneer...

The city offers a different kind of freedom... freedom of

## COWBOY MILLIONAIRE—THE NEW AMERICAN PIONEER
*Introduction: The New Frontier And The New American Pioneer*

choice. An abundance of choices for entertainment, food, and lifestyle... freedom from want, with modern conveniences like delis on your doorstep...

But that essence of freedom you feel when you stand on the edge of a mountain and yell into the void... that's not something you'll find in a city.

In many ways, this city-versus-country divide still lies at the heart of America's political divide: the liberal city dwellers who want freedom from want and need, to be free of the need to provide for themselves (as our ancestors did), thanks to modern conveniences and government protections... to live that comfortable life.

And then, that older American ideal of freedom that still holds sway in the heartlands... the individual fending for himself against the frontier.

Why am I delving into a popular TV show like this in the introduction to a book about offshore opportunities?

Well, like I say, I'm a fan.

But, I've got to say, when I think about the two ideas of freedom that the show sees in conflict... the sovereign individual versus the freedom of a life where everything you want is at your fingertips... with expat life today, you don't have to choose between them. Both of those freedoms are possible. Indeed, they're combined and fused together. The expat is both a pioneer and has the option to have every comfort at his fingertips...

For the characters of "1883," there is the grand adventure of pursuing a new life on the frontier—but with that comes the risk of death in nearly every moment: wolves, snakes, raging rivers, bitter cold, and beating sun (and little to safely drink)...

I think of today's expats and those of us who go offshore as the new American pioneers... we're looking for adventure and freedoms beyond those we had in our old lives...

But today's American pioneers (we expats and overseas investors) can enjoy the adventure of the pioneer lifestyle without the same perils—all of the good and none of the bad.

Take the life I live myself... I get to be a cowboy in Los Islotes in Panama, where we keep horses, and the wide open spaces rival anything in "Yellowstone"...

But I also enjoy city life and its conveniences and opportunities to enjoy culture and the best restaurants—and I get to enjoy that in Panama City or, especially, when we spend time in Paris.

For today's American pioneer, the whole world and all its opportunities are our frontier...

So, "Yellowstone" has got it right: This rural and urban divide is at the heart of political conflict in America...

But those of us who are true American pioneers today aren't constrained by one idea of freedom or the other—we want it all.

**COWBOY MILLIONAIRE—THE NEW AMERICAN PIONEER**
*Introduction: The New Frontier And The New American Pioneer*

We want to build something brand new (build up our wealth; create our own community, like I've done at Los Islotes), and we want to enjoy modern comforts—easy travel; cosmopolitan luxury...

Like I said, it's about having options. Investment options. Lifestyle options. Backup options. When you have options, not only are you prepared against disaster, you're also expanding your life in the most positive way possible... enjoying every kind of experience the world has to offer...

When you think beyond the divisive terms on which American life is lived today... when you decide you want more than that—you want it all... the world becomes your frontier... and the lifestyle described in this book is the life for you.

---

## You Can't Change The Weather... But You Can Change Where You Live

Paris can get hot in the summer. That's why the French take off for the months of July and August and head to the beach.

Medellín, Colombia, has eighty-degree weather all year, which can be great but can get boring.

Panama is hot and humid year-round.

**COWBOY MILLIONAIRE—THE NEW AMERICAN PIONEER**
*Introduction: The New Frontier And The New American Pioneer*

The Algarve in Portugal can get windy. Istria, Croatia (another of my favorite spots), can be cold and rainy.

In other words, you could organize your life around the weather. At one level, that's what my wife, Kathleen, and I have done. We've identified a handful of interesting places where we like the idea of being able to return regularly, year after year, over the very long term, and we've organized a plan that has us in each of these destinations during the best season each year.

We're able to spend better weather months in Paris (April, May, and June), followed by time in the Algarve and Istria during the summer if we want, moving back to the Western Hemisphere when it gets cold in Europe.

You don't have to include five destinations in your eventual retirement plan.

Kathleen and I have been working at this for a long time, and, still, even I find our plan ambitious some days. Our friends Paul and Vicki live nowhere and have no fixed plan to ever be anywhere indefinitely. They rent a small house or apartment wherever they land... or stay with friends... or find a long-term-stay hotel. They're open... flexible.

Paul and Vicki have been living this life since 1985, when Paul retired from one of the Big Eight accounting firms. I couldn't live indefinitely out of a suitcase, but it suits Paul and Vickie.

Other people I know do more of a snowbirding thing, spending time between two places to enjoy the best time of year in each. You could make either your current home or your new home overseas your base and bounce back and forth from there.

This go-offshore thing can be customized however you would like it to be.

The options for living an international lifestyle are unlimited.

You just have to decide where you want to spend time... where you want your investments and "centers of vital interest" to be... and then organize yourself.

## What Type Of "New Pioneer" Are You?

I don't need to remind you of the challenges of our time in history. Cable news has got that beat covered.

And in any case, I'm about finding opportunity (because I believe it can always be found) and organizing your life so you can enjoy what the world has to offer... even if you have to make a few adjustments along the way.

My job is to help you formulate a customized plan that allows you and your family to carry on safe, protected, comfortable, and prosperous no matter what the rest of the world gets up to.

As I see it, big picture, you have three options.

I suggest that these are your three possible "go offshore" paths:

- Path I: The Backup Plan
- Path II: An Integrated Lifestyle
- Path III: Total Paranoia

## How To Make Your Perfect Plan

Let's start with Path III—the paranoids.

This group is small but active and vocal. They want the government out of every aspect of their lives and invest in extreme measures to try to achieve what they perceive as total independence. Some go one hundred percent off-grid, vowing to be dependent on no centralized system for water or electricity.

Some operate on a cash-only basis… or, today, crypto-only.

Some denounce electronics or invest in bunkers and container loads of canned goods.

Few things in life are enjoyable at the extreme, including offshore diversification. Still, I understand that our world today can be interpreted as an end-of-days scene.

**COWBOY MILLIONAIRE—THE NEW AMERICAN PIONEER**
*Introduction: The New Frontier And The New American Pioneer*

The problem, though, is predicting how, exactly, the apocalypse will play out.

A television show about preppers I saw had each prepper participant lay out his plans and preparations for surviving the coming end of the world so the review committee could consider the plan for viability.

In the episode I watched, everyone's plan was deemed more or less viable... should the catastrophe each respective prepper was most paranoid about come to pass.

If doomsday took any other form, though, the plans were all insufficient for survival.

One guy was ready for the big earthquake in California, but he wasn't ready for a meteor strike... for example.

Most people don't subscribe to that acute level of concern or aren't up for such dramatic lifestyle transformations.

We can all agree that our world is rife with risk and danger. Metaphoric minefields are everywhere. However, not all of us are ready to reduce or restrict our lives to the extreme in an effort to avoid them.

Most of us want more options for how and where to live our lives... not fewer. And the Total Paranoia Path can lead to many fewer alternatives.

If your objective in diversifying your life offshore is to improve your lifestyle, expand your upside, and guarantee yourself and your family control in the face of chaos... then I'd say you're on Path I... in search of a Backup Plan.

You can develop a Backup Plan anywhere, including from wherever you're living right now. You don't need to move—not overseas or even around the block—to put a Backup Plan in place. You can achieve a solid level of global diversification from the comfort of your current home.

I began down Path I about thirty years ago. I knew from an early age that I wanted a Backup Plan that put me in control of my own future.

A funny thing happened at some point during the decades since...

My Plan B became my Plan A.

That is, my Backup Plan became my lifestyle.

I made a property investment here... opened a bank account there... then traveled to check in on them...

Another property investment... another bank account... residency in Ireland... then an Irish passport...

More property purchases... that doubled as both investments and places to enjoy time with my family.

The more time I spent in the locations where I'd planted flags, the more contacts I made... the more business ventures I staked... the more connected I felt...

Fast-forward to today, and I have home bases in four countries... residency in two (currently)... a second passport... and investments generating cash in five currencies.

**COWBOY MILLIONAIRE—THE NEW AMERICAN PIONEER**
*Introduction: The New Frontier And The New American Pioneer*

In addition (my wife would say more important), as a result of all this backup planning, I've developed a global network of friends that makes my life much richer than it would be otherwise.

When I'm in Panama... in Colombia... in France... in Portugal... I'm not a visitor. I'm at home. My wife and I stay in houses and apartments that we own and have furnished to be comfortable for us (while also suitable for rental when we're somewhere else).

We've become part of the local scene. We're residents, not tourists. And we prefer it that way.

Organically, over decades, we've built a Backup Plan that is also our ideal way of life.

I call this Path II: An Integrated Lifestyle. And it's this path, more than the others, that this book is about achieving.

In the past few years, Kathleen and I have entered what I believe is the ultimate phase of a lifestyle like this one. With the help of friends and business partners on the ground in the places where we regularly spend time, we've noticed opportunities for becoming connected in a new way.

We've begun investing not only for personal profit... but also in helping our adopted communities in small ways—providing scholarships, for example, and donating computers to schools that otherwise couldn't afford them. As we look ahead, we see this as an increasingly priority agenda.

Living an Integrated Lifestyle, you're a moving target for any disaster that might strike. You're not at the mercy of any one government administration... any single economy... any particular currency. If life should become unpleasant in the place where you are... you can easily go somewhere else and plug into another fully fledged life.

An Integrated Lifestyle doesn't emerge overnight.

Frankly, I've reached my limit, and Kathleen and I are now spending time consolidating and downsizing.

The point is that we're in control. We're deciding where we most enjoy spending time... which of our investments is worth the ongoing administration hassle and expense... and which aren't... etc.

That's the objective—being in control of your own destiny. And that's what the steps in this book are all about.

## How To Use This Book

The steps in this book are very simple. The book is divided into three parts.

First, I'll show you how—by looking beyond America—you could become far wealthier than you could ever be at home...

Second, I'll show you how to protect what you've built so you can secure it for future generations...

Third, I'll reveal my personal secret backup plan—which

can become your backup plan, too—so that, even if things turn sour in your new overseas life, you have a Plan B in place that means you're all good.

That's it—just three steps.

Put another way: build something, defend it, and have an insurance policy.

Those are the three parts to this book.

Enjoy.

*[signature]*
Lief Simon

**COWBOY MILLIONAIRE—THE NEW AMERICAN PIONEER**

## PART I

# Creating Your Fortune On The New Frontier

## CHAPTER I

# The Secret That Will Save Your Financial Future

In January 1994, I moved to Argentina.

By that time, I had already done short stints in Chad and Kazakhstan.

These aren't places known for their good living.

I contracted malaria within two weeks of arriving in Chad and was diagnosed with bronchitis after forty-eight hours on the ground in Kazakhstan.

Everyone in Kazakhstan had bronchitis. Temperatures fell to minus fifty degrees each night.

Every night before falling asleep, I had to set my alarm to wake me so I could go outside to start my car at 3:00 a.m. Otherwise, the battery wouldn't turn over the next morning.

In Chad, I was the only white guy for miles... in a village of mud huts.

Both moves were made based on the directives of the international oil drilling company I was working for back then.

Was I just a glutton for punishment? Not exactly.

I had an itch for adventure, yes... but, more than that, I realized, even at that age, the advantages of being an American offshore.

I was a twenty-five-year-old kid earning oil company wages that would be one hundred percent tax-free.

## Bad Times In Buenos Aires

Then, New Year's 1994, that drilling firm sent me to Argentina.

Arriving in Buenos Aires for the first time, my initial reaction was...

This isn't Chad... This isn't Kazakhstan.

The international airport was busy but organized... orderly. The drive to the domestic airport to connect to my in-country flight to northern Salta Province, where I was being posted, took me through a metropolitan area that I later learned holds a third of the country's population.

But, again, this wasn't third-world Africa. The people were well dressed, the men in suits, the women chic even... everyone going about their business.

This was before the internet, and I didn't know I was going to Argentina until the day I left Kazakhstan, so I had had no time to study up on the country in advance of my arrival.

### COWBOY MILLIONAIRE—THE NEW AMERICAN PIONEER
*Chapter I: The Secret That Will Save Your Financial Future*

I showed up and began trying to size up the situation as I experienced it.

At first, I thought that the prosperity I was seeing was the result of the country's vast natural resources. After a couple of weeks, however, the local economics became clearer.

Yes, Argentina was doing well... but not the typical Argentine on the street. They were struggling to make ends meet.

Stores didn't indicate sales prices on items but payment terms. Want to buy a shirt? You could make eight payments of $4. A television... that was twenty payments of $30...

Store owners were confused when I asked what the price would be if I paid in full. I was supplying a new office and camp for the drilling company. I had a lot of shopping to do, both immediately and ongoing. Paying over time would have been a nuisance.

Plus, I figured we should be able to get a nice discount by paying in full up front... and indeed, we did.

With the discount, prices were more reasonable—not cheap but OK.

Then someone told me about shopping in Bolivia. The border was only an hour from the town in Salta where my operation was based, and prices in Bolivia were a fraction of prices in Argentina for, in many cases, the exact same products.

So my assistant and I started traveling to Bolivia to do our shopping.

**COWBOY MILLIONAIRE—THE NEW AMERICAN PIONEER**
*Chapter I: The Secret That Will Save Your Financial Future*

## The Old Money Argentines Had A Secret

That got me thinking... Why was Bolivia so much cheaper than Argentina?

Locals would tell me stories about when the reverse had been true. They could remember, they said, when Bolivians came across the border to shop in Argentina, where prices were much lower.

What had changed?

The currency.

Argentina pegged its currency to the U.S. dollar in April 1990, eventually changing their currency from the austral to the peso and using a one-to-one peg between the Argentine peso and the U.S. dollar.

Pesos or dollars... the average Argentine on the street didn't know the difference and didn't care.

However, the more sophisticated Argentines... the business people and the old-money families... they did understand the difference... and they wanted U.S. dollars.

In fact, they were accumulating them and hoarding them... in bank accounts outside the country.

They knew that the situation created by the artificial currency peg was unsustainable, so they were squirreling away everything they could and storing it outside the Argentine economy.

**COWBOY MILLIONAIRE—THE NEW AMERICAN PIONEER**
*Chapter I: The Secret That Will Save Your Financial Future*

Prices for everything in Argentina rose and rose until, eventually, the country's manufacturing sector vanished. It became too expensive to produce anything in the country. Cheaper to import goods... so that's what everyone did.

I left the drilling company after six months in Argentina, and it wasn't until eight years later that the economics of what I had lived through during those six months in 1994 became much clearer to me.

In December 2001, Argentina removed the peg between its peso and the U.S. dollar. The government converted all bank accounts from dollars to pesos in one fell swoop overnight.

Same for debt. Whatever you owed was no longer repayable in U.S. dollars... but now in Argentine pesos.

People with savings in banks woke up one morning to find that their account values had been decimated.

Meantime, farmers with mortgages on their properties got big breaks as the peso fell in the wake of the decoupling. In 2002, the exchange rate dropped from one-to-one, where it'd been with the peg, to as low as four-to-one.

Banks closed, and real estate prices collapsed. It was a bona fide crisis investing opportunity and perhaps the best chance of our lifetime to buy property in this country.

Unfortunately, I wasn't able to get on a plane until October. Prices bottomed out in July, but I still managed to find some amazing deals in October. My friends and I bought

**COWBOY MILLIONAIRE—THE NEW AMERICAN PIONEER**
*Chapter I: The Secret That Will Save Your Financial Future*

three downtown Buenos Aires apartments over the next six months.

What surprised me during my property scouting trips and then during the time I spent in the country over the next two years, while the local economy was trying to stabilize itself, was that most of the Argentine businessmen I met with didn't seem concerned. They weren't struggling financially. In fact, they were doing quite well.

What's going on here, I wondered. What do they know that I don't?

And then finally, it began to sink in...

The businessmen and professionals I was speaking with were the ones who had been accumulating physical dollars and keeping as much of their wealth as possible outside their country. They could see the writing on the wall and had taken steps to prepare for the collapse they knew was inevitable.

Argentina's economic history is filled with dramatic ups and disastrous downs. I realized that Argentines, over generations of experience, had learned to diversify their wealth outside their own country.

It was simple and effective self-preservation.

That revelation in 2002 about the wisdom of keeping the bulk of your money outside your home country made a big impression on me. By this time, I'd already begun working to diversify my life and my investment portfolio, but watching this lesson play out in real life in Argentina compelled me to work harder and faster.

I wanted to be like the Argentine businessmen who were able to come through unfazed by what amounted to total economic collapse in their country... not like the average Argentine on the street struggling to pay his rent or buy groceries for his family because his life savings had literally disappeared overnight.

And, thanks to those Argentine businessmen, I understood in a real way the secret to making sure my family and I would be OK no matter what happened in the economy or markets of our home country... or of any other country for that matter.

For these Argentines, offshore diversification was not a theoretical exercise. It was the key to survival.

Protecting your wealth is, of course, one reason... and a very important one... for going offshore...

Unless you have this international mindset—looking at all your options, not just those closest to home—you'll be at risk...

Now, what happened in Argentina may not happen in the United States.

People have been talking about the demise of the dollar as the world's reserve currency for more than a decade now... I don't see that happening anytime soon.

But other things—even everyday things—that threaten

your wealth are happening and will happen.

Fluctuating currency rates, bank issues—look at the major banks that closed recently in America. You want international diversification just to stay safe.

Argentina was once one of the wealthiest countries in the world... but bad management by politicians ruined this once-great economic powerhouse...

Sound familiar?

I wrote a decade ago that America "is on a path of self-destruction that it's probably too late now to avoid."

That's because of unsustainable debt... government spying on its own citizens... and too many other things, large and small, to go into right here.

The country's course has been set... and will be very hard to change.

I wrote in that same article, published just before the 2012 election, that it didn't matter who won that election—or any other...

No politician, I wrote, "can change the course the United States is on...

"In an effort to maintain its position as the global leader as long as possible, the United States will put policies in place that run counter to the constitution.

"This has already begun... It will continue to ignore citizens' rights to privacy in the name of fighting terrorism, drugs, or whatever war du jour they can propagate, meantime sweeping long-term problems under the rug.

"That is why globalizing your life in a way to keep your family, your wealth, and yourself safe no matter what happens in the United States or anywhere else is so important.

"Organize your affairs so you don't have to worry… or at least so you can worry less."

Just like those old-money Argentines, you can sidestep economic conditions on the ground… and even "opt out" of the bad decisions made by the politicians in power… by looking beyond your own borders.

## Protect Yourself… And Profit

So, protecting your wealth is for sure a reason to look offshore and overseas for strategies that get you out of your home market.

I want you to keep that story of the old-money Argentines in your mind as you read through this book.

Nothing that you've earned or built in life is fully secure if it can be taken away at a moment's notice by a political decision or an act of God.

That's why you want your wealth spread out between countries—so you're not at the mercy of what might happen in one place.

I'll delve in much more detail into wealth protection strategies in Part II of the book. For now, as I say, it's important to know that going offshore can not only be the key to finding profit opportunities you won't find at home—but also the key to keeping your profits secure.

But going offshore is not just about protection... it's about profit.

There's another lesson I learned from Argentina's troubles in the early 2000s. When you're looking overseas, you'll find killer opportunities you'd have no chance of hearing about if your sole focus is your home country.

I'm talking about those three downtown Buenos Aires apartments that friends and I bought for a steal at Argentina's moment of crisis...

We put the three apartments up for short-term rental... fully managed by my local contacts. The result? Eight percent annual yields for a full six years... until I sold them for double my investment—one hundred percent profit.

I didn't just learn wealth protection from the Argentinians; I also found great opportunity to profit by playing the Argentine crisis...

The best opportunities in the world today lie on what I call the "new frontier" for Americans—i.e., outside the United States.

You will find opportunities overseas and in foreign markets that you never would at home...

And the remaining chapters in the first part of this book are all about finding those profits...

I call it "creating your fortune on the new frontier."

## CHAPTER II

# The Number-One Opportunity In The World

I didn't start my investment career overseas. My investing journey began at home.

I bought my first investment property in the United States.

It was 1995, and I bought a three-flat building in Chicago. I was renting an apartment in another three-flat, and the owners told us they were selling the building. Until that moment, I hadn't been thinking about buying a house, let alone a multi-unit building.

But I liked the apartment where we were living, so I began looking into whether it would be possible for me to buy the building. I started to educate myself, running numbers, speaking with mortgage lenders, checking the prices of other buildings, and trying to understand the market.

While the negotiations didn't work out for the building where we'd been living (that really was a great apartment... designed by Frank Lloyd Wright), the seed had been planted.

**COWBOY MILLIONAIRE—THE NEW AMERICAN PIONEER**
*Chapter II: The Number-One Opportunity In The World*

I found another building that met all my parameters...

Friends and family all thought it was a bad idea to buy. Too risky.

Why was someone as young as I was at the time—in my twenties—just starting out, thinking about making such a big property purchase?

With the help of a $5,000 loan from my first wife's parents, I put a down payment on that three-apartment building.

It turned out to be one of the best investments I ever made.

I sold the building less than three years later for a leveraged return of three thousand percent, turning my $5,000 down payment into $150,000 in profit after closing costs and commissions. I'd sold it for almost double what I'd paid.

I'd run the numbers and knew that building was a great prospect. There was some risk—for example, if the property lay vacant and we couldn't get renters. But for me, it was worth taking the risk because of the potential upside...

It worked out.

With that willingness to take that risk early in life, I was able to achieve my ambition to become a millionaire by age thirty-five, and my net worth has grown and grown since.

I've applied the same principles from that first investment to my investments since then.

I study the market... I run the numbers... and if the numbers stack up, I buy.

By looking overseas, I've been able to find opportunities to grow my wealth that I never would have found back home...

With that "nut" from my Chicago investment, I was able to purchase (along with Kathleen) a property in Ireland... which, thanks to Ireland's strong property market, we were also able to eventually sell for more than three times our investment.

My next real estate investment was in Spain. I bought a pre-construction apartment on the beach.

Again, I was looking for an opportunity where the numbers stacked up...

I spent ten days traveling the entire southern coast of Spain looking at real estate and speaking with a dozen developers and agents.

By the time I got to Estepona on the south end of the Costa del Sol, I had seen a lot of properties—most of them crap.

The developer I met in Estepona had released a new beachfront project the day before I'd arrived. His group didn't even have their sales office set up at the property yet. They were working out of their main admin office down the road.

We visited the site, I looked at the plans and prices, and I was ready to invest.

This was the best opportunity I'd seen on the entire trip... and because it was pre-construction, the initial capital outlay for the deposit wasn't much.

I called my wife, Kathleen. She's a fairly conservative investor. Her first reaction was to tell me I was crazy to be thinking about investing in Spain... in a pre-construction project. What did we know about buying pre-construction real estate in Spain?

While a ten-day trip couldn't be called an all-encompassing education in Spanish real estate, it was enough, as I explained to Kathleen, for me to know a good deal when I saw one.

She begrudgingly agreed to buy a unit because I was there and she wasn't. She had to trust my instincts.

And, in the end, she sure was glad she did.

That purchase falls into the top ten of my more than sixty real estate investments over the years. The developer sold the apartment for me before it was completed. The returns were almost one hundred percent profit over the less than two years that I held the property.

Other great deals I've invested in over the years include...

- Eighty percent profits in just eight months in Romania. Thanks to my legwork and my contacts on the ground, I spotted a market in Eastern Europe that was set to rise—before most anyone else was looking. Before I could begin the renovations I planned, a buyer came to me... cash in hand... and I almost doubled my money...
- Twenty percent net yields and one hundred percent appreciation In Panama. This home-run purchase at one

of the best addresses in downtown Panama City has provided double-digit cash flow as both a short-term and a long-term rental. Today, it is worth more than twice what I paid for it and serves as Kathleen and my personal pied-à-terre as we come and go for business and pleasure from the Hub of the Americas...

- Fifty percent appreciation in less than a year and a half from a coastal pre-construction buy in Cyprus. This recent investment is on track to bring me a greater return than my pre-construction win in Spain...

This, essentially, is how you make your fortune in real estate... how I made my fortune.

My personal research and my trusted contacts have helped me see more overseas real estate returns like that over the years...

As I wrote in my previous book, "Buying Real Estate Overseas For Cash Flow (And A Better Life),"

"How do you get rich investing in real estate overseas? You make one purchase in a market generating decent yields. Rent it, setting aside the excess cash flow each month, until the property's value has appreciated to a level where it makes sense to sell. Roll over the accumulated rental income and the capital gain into a next property in a next market. Do this until you're accumulating enough excess cash flow that you can afford to buy a next investment without selling one you already own. Continue in this way, on and on, until, in time, you're a bona fide global property baron earning enough cash flow to fund a life of travel and the retirement of your dreams."

This is the lifestyle of the New American Pioneer...

## The Most Valuable Stuff In Human History

I consider overseas real estate to be the most valuable commodity in the world and the number-one investment opportunity in the world.

After all... what's the most valuable stuff in human history? It's not gold... or oil... or even food... It's land.

Property is the basis for civilization. It's where you can base a city, raise a family, mine for gold, grow crops, breed animals...

The National Bureau of Economic Research published a study covering one hundred fifty years up to the modern day. Compared to equities, bonds, and treasury bills, real estate boasts the best long-term return of any asset class.

Real estate's value can almost never go to zero—unlike stocks.

Plus, you can actually enjoy your property when you're not using it for cash flow.

And real estate overseas?

Here's where you need to consider the opportunities of the frontier...

**COWBOY MILLIONAIRE—THE NEW AMERICAN PIONEER**
*Chapter II: The Number-One Opportunity In The World*

There are opportunities to be found in countries like Belize or Montenegro that will never, ever exist in America again. That's precisely why countries like these are on my radar.

I'm talking about the opportunity to get in ahead of the curve, to stake your claim in a particular location before it's fully developed, and to profit as it matures.

The United States and Canada are mature markets—that opportunity is gone.

But in Belize, Montenegro, and other locations that I keep my eye on…

Let's take Belize as an example. As a speaker pointed out at a recent conference I hosted for my Live And Invest Overseas business, Belize right now is in the "sweet spot."

Just a couple decades ago, it was a country only divers and fishermen had heard of. Then cruise ships began bringing tourists to Ambergris Caye, Belize's "paradise isle." It started to take off as a family destination…

I've seen Belize's construction boom firsthand…

Belize's development is on an upward curve. It's got all the appeal of Caribbean hot spots like the Bahamas, but its real estate is half the price. The opportunity is to buy now and profit as prices converge with other top-tier Caribbean destinations. Meanwhile, cash flows in from renting…

These are the kind of "sweet spot" opportunities that, as I say, you have to be looking in the right places to find.

But the benefits of owning overseas real estate go far beyond that...

A piece of property in another country could be your second home, a vacation spot, your escape hatch, or your ultimate retirement plan.

Real estate overseas also brings diversification—of currency, of market, and of asset type....

Plus, the IRS doesn't require you to report property abroad in your tax filings, though certain deductions are available if you do.

In short, the purchase of a piece of real estate overseas could bring you profits, privacy, and a tax break.

My expectation when investing in real estate—in the right markets—is to double my money in three to five years.

If I'm looking for cash flow, I'm usually not interested unless I know it can give me returns of at least five percent net a year...

You don't need to be rich to get started in overseas real estate investing...

I began my property investing career with just $5,000.

Today, I've turned that modest sum into a multimillion-dollar property portfolio... one diversified across multiple continents, markets, industries, and currencies.

If Wall Street collapses tomorrow, I'll be OK, thanks to my overseas property portfolio.

Even during the pandemic a few years ago, which devasted the holiday rental industry, I still made money thanks to my investments in farming and other essential services...

Real estate abroad boasts privacy, tax savings, and profits—plus, it's more affordable.

These are hard assets that go up and up in value over time...

Worst case? I can live in my property and enjoy it myself whenever I want.

Bottom line: Property overseas is an asset that every investor in the world must have in their portfolio.

## Don't Just Take My Word For It

"The major fortunes in America have been made in land." – John D. Rockefeller

"Real estate cannot be lost or stolen, nor can it be carried away. Purchased with common sense, paid for in full, and managed with reasonable care, it is about the safest investment in the world." – Franklin D. Roosevelt

"Ninety percent of millionaires become so through owning real estate. More money has been made in real

> estate than in all industrial investments combined."–Andrew Carnegie

## My Philosophy: Cash Flow Is King

While land has intrinsic value and real estate can almost never be worth nothing, it is true, of course, that real estate markets can crash and prices can plunge. The crisis of 2008 started as a real estate/mortgage crisis...

This is certainly a worry if you're primarily relying on capital appreciation... on real estate prices to go up so you can sell...

If your main concern is rental cash flow, the situation is entirely different.

You don't face the same challenges to your income...

With my property investments, at this point in my career, I'm primarily interested in the rental cash flow I can achieve rather than the value of the property going up.

The reason for this is simple: Rental cash flow is true passive income. And it's an income you can rely on even as the value of your property goes up or down or as economic conditions ebb and flow.

You may face other challenges, of course, in a recession (reduced rent payments, etc.).

But this is also why it's important to own in different countries and different markets.

There are parts of the world—Northern Brazil, for example—that were entirely unaffected by the price plunge across the Western world post-2008.

Invest for cash flow and passive income. And invest for diversification and to protect your overall net worth.

If you get capital appreciation, that's the gravy.

This is my personal investment philosophy.

## How To Be Your Own Central Bank And Make Your Own Reserve Currency

The reserve currency status of the U.S. dollar is in the news more right now than it has been for the last few years.

Several years ago, pundits were calling for the collapse of the U.S. dollar and its replacement as the world's reserve currency.

That isn't going to happen any time soon. No other currency has the chops to allow for a rapid redeployment of currency holdings to the central banks around the world, though other currencies have been gaining ground.

Today, the U.S. dollar represents about sixty percent

of total currency reserves held by countries. That's down from seventy-three percent in 2001.

The euro is the next largest currency held in reserve, at twenty percent. The pound and yen follow at about five percent each. The Chinese yuan is less than three percent of global currency reserves.

No other currency has the prerequisites to push the U.S. dollar quickly out of the top positions. That will be a slow shift over time that could see no single currency dominating the global markets.

The euro, as one colleague likes to say, is a "who owes you" versus the "I owe you" that other currencies represent in their respective countries.

Therefore, it doesn't have the international clout that the German mark or the French franc had before the euro. The euro is still young as far as currencies go, still in its twenties. You can still find chatter about the euro going away, though that scenario is unlikely as I write this.

The pound was the main global reserve currency until after World War II.

It's not likely to have a comeback. Japan doesn't want the job. Although Swiss francs are a popular currency to own for diversification purposes, the Swiss economy is too small for its currency to be a true global reserve. What's more, right now, the Chinese don't offer enough transparency to get far.

That leaves the world with the U.S. dollar.

Being the reserve currency of the world has its benefits... like cheaper transaction costs on the international currency markets and lower interest rates.

It also means you can carry U.S. dollars with you in many countries and spend them directly, without exchanging them for local currency, and get the same or better exchange rate than you would at a bank.

Tourist areas in Central America are a good example. Shops there either won't take euro cash or they charge a premium for taking it, unlike when taking dollars.

For someone living an international life, sticking with U.S. dollars is generally prudent for these reasons, but only while the dollar stays relatively strong against most currencies compared to its most recent lows. Exchange rates are difficult to predict long term.

For vacationers, the cost of the euro plays a role in whether or not they go to France for summer vacation or Florida. At a buck sixty, Europe is twice as expensive as when the euro is at eighty-four cents.

However, as a global citizen with long-term plans, you don't want to worry about exchange rate fluctuations, and you definitely don't want them dictating your travel schedule.

Take a page out of the central banks' playbook:

Diversify your currency holdings and hold investments in currencies for countries where you want to spend time.

That's what Kathleen and I have been working towards for a long time. In many cases, it's not easy because you want to time the movements of large amounts of U.S. dollars to when the dollar is strong against the particular currency you're looking to hold. You also have to find the right investment.

Timing exchange rates doesn't usually work. You have to make the investment when the investment presents itself. Long term, it won't matter what you paid for the asset in the other currency. The important thing is to generate passive income in that currency.

## Local Passive Income Is Priceless

Europe is an easy example because the euro has bounced up and down and today sits at roughly the same place where it started twenty years ago. Other currencies are more complicated... especially developing countries' currencies like Brazil or Colombia.

Your personal reserve currency may remain the U.S. dollar, but holding investments that produce cash flow in currencies you'll be spending when you travel or live outside the dollar world will reduce your long-term lifestyle risk.

How much to put in another currency depends on how much you'll need.

Make a budget. If you're planning on spending three months a year in Italy, for example, and your monthly budget is estimated at 2,500 euros, then you want to generate 7,500 euros in passive income in euros (let's ignore taxes to make it simpler). One rental property valued at 150,000 euros, throwing off a net return of five percent, would cover your time in Italy every year.

Buy a property you want to stay in yourself and visit in the off-season, and you can generate the passive income you need to live rent-free for your three months in the country.

Say you want to spend another six months a year in Colombia. Colombia could be cheaper or more expensive than Italy, depending on how and where you live in each country, but let's stick with a similar budget at the exchange rate at the time of writing, which would be about 9 million pesos a month or 54 million pesos for six months.

Let's say you can get a ten percent yield on your investment in Colombia (colleagues have some cash-flowing investments that produce in that range).

That means you need to invest 540 million pesos (about $175,000) to generate six months' worth of living expenses for your time in Colombia.

Perhaps the other three months of the year you want to spend in Ecuador.

Ecuador, like Panama, uses the U.S. dollar, so investments in Ecuador, Panama, or the United States can generate the cash needed for the time you'll spend there.

Ecuador remains a low-cost country and you can get by with a budget of about $2,000 a month, so you'll need $6,000 in passive income per year to cover your living expenses.

Assume a six percent yield on a rental property and you're looking at a $100,000 investment for your time in Ecuador.

Of course, your budget should allow for travel expenses, health care and insurance, and unforeseen expenses, but organizing your investments to match your cash flow by currency removes long-term currency risk from your lifestyle...

And you don't have to worry about when or if the U.S. dollar is going to lose its reserve currency status, thereby devaluing substantially and throwing a spanner into your long-term plans.

COWBOY MILLIONAIRE—THE NEW AMERICAN PIONEER
Chapter II: The Number-One Opportunity In The World

## The Best Way To Own Overseas Property

Before we get into where exactly you should own overseas—and what kinds of overseas real estate specifically you could be looking at... it's worth considering the question of how you can own overseas property.

This feeds into bigger questions about offshore structures and asset protection strategies... which we'll dig into more deeply in Part II of the book.

For now, let's focus on the narrow question of the best way to own overseas property.

How should one hold property overseas?

It's a question I regularly get at conferences... especially my Global Property Summit event each year.

The best option depends on the person, the property, and the country where the property is located... and even what funds you're using for the investment.

Use IRA funds, and, generally speaking, you should set up an LLC to hold the property. In fact, for some countries, you'll have to use an LLC because an American IRA isn't an entity that other countries recognize. They just don't know what to do to title a property owned by "XYZ IRA Custodian, Inc. FBO John Smith, Account #12345."

If John Smith is the buyer, why isn't the title going into his name?

Ironically, one concern is probably money laundering worries, which are a current focus of the U.S. government. The person who pays for the property should hold title to the property.

Outside of an IRA, the question of how to hold title can get much more complicated. Estate planning, tax filings and taxes, probate (part of estate planning but a separate issue to consider), and asset protection all need to be considered. One lesson I learned early on as I tried to streamline how my overseas properties were held was that one size doesn't fit all. You have to consider each property separately as you buy it, based on what makes the most sense for that property and that country.

For example, Croatia allows foreigners to hold property in their own names if their country allows Croatians to own property in that country. In addition, if you hold property in Croatia in your own name for three years or more, you pay no capital gains taxes.

Hold the property in a Croatian corporation, which would be required if your home country doesn't allow Croatians to own property, and you'll pay capital gains taxes when you sell.

For Americans, the complication of proving your home country allows Croatians to own property was something I couldn't overcome. The individual state laws govern real estate in the States, so I had to get proof from the last state I lived in that Croatians could own property there. The proof had to be positive proof, not a lack of a restriction on Croatians. In other words, it wasn't going to happen.

Fortunately, by that time I was also an Irish citizen, so I used my Irish nationality to get the title processed in Croatia.

This particular purchase fell well outside of my standard holding structure, which is a Nevis LLC. First, the options in Croatia at the time were either your own name or a Croatian corporation. Foreign entities weren't an option.

Second, the tax benefits of holding in my own name outweighed the probate considerations for the kids should I die before selling the property.

Europe in general is more complicated than the Americas when trying to use a structure for holding real estate. France has a special corporation you can use for holding real estate, which can be managed outside of France's inheritance rules if you're not French or living in France.

Portugal has a blacklist of countries. If you use an entity from one country on the blacklist, you'll pay more in property and other taxes in Portugal. That's how I ended up with an intermediary company to hold my Portuguese apartment.

Using an offshore LLC to hold property in most countries in the Americas is straightforward. Sometimes you have to register the foreign entity and get it a local tax ID number, but you can hold property with a foreign entity. Don't let your local attorney tell you otherwise.

A reader of my *Simon Letter* newsletter service once wrote in after she'd already completed the purchase of a property in Costa Rica and the Dominican Republic. She'd set up a holding company in Nevis after reading my recommended standard holding structure.

She thought she was set, and she was... until her local attorneys in Costa Rica and the DR told her she needed a local company from the country where the property was located.

Both attorneys told her the same thing in the same timeframe (she was buying both properties at the same time), so she figured it must be true, and she paid each of them to set up a local company that was owned by her Nevis LLC. The property titles were put in the names of the local companies.

Unfortunately, the attorneys she used were either liars or morons. I vote for liars.

You can hold property directly in the name of a foreign entity in both Costa Rica and the DR, so why would her attorneys tell her otherwise?

To sell her a local corporation.

Attorneys make money when they set up entities... and they earn an annual fee acting as the registered agent.

Use a foreign entity, and they only make money on their work for the real estate transaction.

Just retitle the property, you say? The costs of retitling

can be high thanks to transfer taxes. You can't just do a quit claim deed like you can in the States and title the property in another name.

So what's my recommended baseline holding structure and why?

It's an offshore LLC in Nevis that you use to hold as many of your offshore properties as you can based on the local situations where the properties are located.

Using a single offshore LLC keeps your costs low—one entity with one annual fee. More entities mean more fees, so only use intermediary entities when necessary, like I did in Portugal—but not like the woman did in Costa Rica and the DR, where they weren't necessary.

(It goes without saying that having reputable and trustworthy attorneys on your side in any country where you do business—and your home country too—is a must.)

Using an offshore LLC rather than a local company takes local probate and inheritance questions out of the country where the property is located and places it under the jurisdiction where the LLC was formed.

Own properties in several countries in your own name or in local entities, and your heirs will have to go through probate in each country, costing time and money.

Of course, if you are only buying one second home in a foreign country, you may just opt to hold the property in your own name and leave your heirs to deal with the local probate.

You have to weigh the ongoing costs of an entity against the future cost of probate and how much you care if your intended heirs actually end up with that property. Many countries have inheritance laws that dictate how assets are distributed to heirs.

The key is to keep things as simple as you can while still achieving your offshore goals. That will help you determine how to hold title to your properties overseas.

As I said, we'll dig deeper into some of those complex questions in Part II of the book...

Going overseas can seem complicated and scary compared to staying within the boundaries of your home country. But it really isn't. It's just about knowing what to expect and understanding the differences.

Overseas real estate is the best money-making opportunity I know of... don't be deterred by some of the quirks.

After all, we're pioneers. We tread where others fear to go.

CHAPTER III

# How To Build The Perfect Portfolio

How do you define "being wealthy"?

An offshore attorney I met years ago defined being wealthy as having enough passive income to cover all your monthly expenses.

That's an easy answer, but not as easy a goal to achieve...

Rental income can be the perfect passive income... but unfortunately, most U.S. investment professionals don't know much about investing in real estate.

And overseas real estate? Forget about it!

Investment professionals in the United States are all trained in financial products. As a result, the investment and retirement portfolios that most of them recommend include paper investments only, in three categories: stocks, bonds, and cash.

Depending on your age and your risk tolerance, most financial advisors will tell you to put some percentage of your investment portfolio into stocks (riskier and longer-term), another percentage into bonds (lower risk and medium-term), and the balance into cash (zero risk and short-term).

Some advisors focus on specific industries or domestic versus international offerings. Some throw metals into the mix.

Real estate is rarely, if ever, seen in an investment portfolio pie chart.

It's not because investment advisors, as a rule, think that real estate is a bad investment. They just aren't in the business of selling real estate. They have financial investments to sell you... so that's what they're going to recommend you use to build your portfolio. If you want some real estate exposure, they'll suggest a real estate investment trust (REIT).

That approach has never made sense to me, including when I was studying it in graduate school.

Historically, many of the world's richest people have had real estate to thank for their wealth. That fact alone should be enough to make the case that it's counter-intuitive to exclude real estate from your investment portfolio.

Real estate has always been my preferred investment class, and my investment portfolio has the reverse problem of the portfolios most financial advisors create—it's heavy real estate.

More than ninety percent of my investment portfolio is invested in property in some form. The few stocks that I have owned over the years haven't done well, and mutual funds are simply fee-generation mechanisms for the managers, in my view. Few beat the market over any period of time.

I'm not recommending that you put all your investment eggs in real estate.

What I am saying is that real estate is key to any diversified investment portfolio. Further, whatever real estate assets you invest in should be diversified as well, including and especially by country.

Real estate diversification comes in three parts: the location of the property (I'm referring to the market, not the street address), the currency the property is valued in, and the property type.

In each issue of my *Global Property Advisor* service, my team and I introduce readers to the best current opportunities for diversifying your real estate investment portfolio according to market (which, in turn, means diversification for political regime, current administration, economy, market cycle, population demographics, infrastructure development, and so on) and currency.

The advice I have for you in this chapter is drawn from that experience.

Note here that, in some countries with their own currencies, real estate is priced and trades in U.S. dollars. Nicaragua is an example.

Note, too, that, while I believe currency diversification is key to any well-strategized portfolio, it's also a risk as it exposes you to currency fluctuations... which can move in your favor or out of it.

Right now, if you're an investor with U.S. dollars in your pocket, you're riding high. The U.S. dollar has soared against currencies worldwide, including in some of the markets I think make the most sense for property investors. Colombia is a top example.

In addition to market and currency diversification, in *Global Property Advisor*, we work hard to make sure that our recommendations cover all the asset bases.

By asset diversification, I don't mean investing in a two-bedroom rental and a three-bedroom rental in different neighborhoods of the same city. You need to look at different types of real estate.

Visit this link **cowboymillionairesecrets.com** or scan the QR code to view my pie chart of the ideal portfolio. It's broken down by asset type as well as the percentage of the total portfolio that each asset type should consist of.

As my pie chart shows, broadly speaking, your options break down as follows:

- Rental property, short- or long-term, residential or commercial
- Land... for land banking or development
- Agriculture
- Indirect investment

In *Global Property Advisor*, we look closely at each of these asset types. I draw out the pluses and the minuses of each while also directing you to the best current markets for each kind of buy.

While you should see some appreciation on a rental investment to help boost your overall returns, your main expectation for return on investment in this case is the net yield from rental cash flow.

Non-agricultural land, on the other hand, doesn't generate a rental yield. In this case, you're looking for all of your return from the appreciation of the property.

Land banking (buying land and holding it) can have tremendous upside if you buy right. But also, one big benefit of owning land is that it has little downside if you buy right.

It is a store of wealth with minimal carrying costs (usually nothing more than property taxes). You may want to keep the land cleared, and you might have an HOA fee if the land is part of a development. Otherwise, little is required out of pocket to hold a piece of land, as long as you want to hold it.

The point of an agricultural investment is a cash return, annually from crops or productive trees (fruit or nut) or every twelve to twenty-five years in the case of a timber plantation.

You don't have to be a farmer to make money from agricultural land today. This is a breakthrough reality of our times for us global property investors... and turn-key agricultural offerings are a constant focus for me.

## Why "The World's Oldest Asset" Is Booming In The Twenty-First Century

Farmland is the world's oldest asset class... but it continues to be more and more attractive.

The world's supply of productive farmland is decreasing because of over-farming, the growth of cities—especially in China and the East—and events like the war in Ukraine. (Russia and Ukraine were major commodity exporters before the war.)

As reduced supply pushes up prices, food demand is increasing as the world's population grows and as more

> consumers in China and the East enter the middle class and eat richer diets (more meat and dairy).
>
> The uber-rich have bought up farmland around the world because they see the opportunity. Bill Gates, for instance, owns almost three hundred thousand acres of farmland.
>
> As legendary investor Warren Buffet put it, "Would you rather own all the gold in the world or all the farmland?"

The final asset category on my list—"indirect investment"—refers to any property investment where you don't own the real estate directly. This could be the REIT that your financial investment advisor suggested, or it could be an investment in a company that develops real estate or a hard money loan.

A hard money loan is when an investor lends cash to a real estate entrepreneur (a developer or someone who does renovation projects, for example). You lend the money for a short term at an interest rate that is much higher than would be typical for a bank loan.

The developer is willing to pay the higher rate of interest because getting a bank loan would be too complicated or simply not an option. You, as the investor, get the property (or a piece of the property, in the case of a big development) as collateral.

The risk with these options is that you don't directly own or control the asset (the property).

### Chapter III: How To Build The Perfect Portfolio

Some types of real estate can cross category lines. Pre-construction refers to an investment in a piece of real estate that is under construction or planned for construction. It could be a short- or long-term rental, residential or commercial, or maybe a condo-hotel.

## You Won't Find This In America... What Is A Condo-Hotel?

Condo-hotels are hotels in which each unit has an individual owner, as opposed to the case with a typical hotel, where a single company owns the entire building. A management company operates the hotel, and the individual unit owners share in the profits.

Condo-hotels give you built-in management while offering diversification offshore. You don't find these in the United States because most condo-hotels pool revenue and disburse profits to unit owners rather than tracking the nightly rental for each unit individually. Therefore, these would be highly regulated in the United States.

The benefit of pooling is that you don't run the risk of the management company playing favorites with any specific units. The downside is that you can't differenti-

> ate your unit to try to get better occupancy. However, most condo-hotels are professionally run hotels that offer management and branding that help you achieve good returns.

The advantage of buying pre-construction is a reduced price, meaning you should expect good appreciation during the construction period. A pre-construction investment can be flipped to an end buyer when the building is close to completion, or you can take possession of the unit and turn it into a rental yourself.

Renovation projects (fixer-uppers) offer the same choices in the end—to flip or to rent.

The upside appreciation potential of a renovation should translate to enough return to make the project worthwhile. Sometimes, though, even in a case of great appreciation, you find that you could get a great ongoing return on your investment by renting the property out.

The downside to renovations is the hard work and direct effort required on the investor's part to make the project successful.

I offer a table of all the sub-categories that a diversified property portfolio might consist of. View it at this link **cowboy-millionairesecrets.com** or by scanning the following QR code:

Don't worry if you haven't invested in all of these sub-categories, however. You don't need all of them to realize a reasonably diversified property portfolio.

I offer these categories as a guide.

An ideal portfolio might include them all, according to the percentages I laid out in my pie chart.

However, few of us are going to build The Ideal Portfolio… and you don't need to try. What you need to do at this point, as you set out to build not The Ideal Portfolio but the portfolio that is ideal for you, is to pin down the following:

- Your budget. How much money do you have available to put into your real estate portfolio?;
- Your level of risk tolerance;
- Your diversification objectives (currency, country, category). You may want or be able to invest in only one or two properties to get started. That's OK. That's the idea.

Let my Model Portfolio, detailed above, be your guide as you work through all the decisions you'll need to make as you consider each of the property investment options and opportunities you seek out.

Don't get too bogged down in the percentages. They should be fluid.

And don't be impatient. It'll take time to create a broadly diversified international real estate portfolio.

I've been at it for thirty years... and my portfolio remains a work in process.

And considering new opportunities remains a big part of the appeal and the fun.

## How A Seven Percent Return Can Beat A Twelve Percent Return

In 2005, I hosted a real estate investment conference in the Dominican Republic. The speakers were from around the world, and each was there representing a current real estate investment opportunity.

During the lunch break the second day, a young guy who was attending the conference with his dad came up to me to ask, "Why in the world would I invest in a rental property throwing off a seven percent yield when I can get twelve percent on my money all day long back in Iowa with our hard-money loan business?"

I'm guessing the answer became obvious to the kid when 2008 rolled around and the bottom fell out of the U.S. real estate market.

I was invested with a hard-money lender in the D.C. area at the time. My money had been with him for a few years, and he had been paying me thirteen percent on my investment annually in quarterly payments reliably.

Then, in late 2009, he sent his investors, including me, an email saying he was done. He'd been keeping up with the payments on the investment funds, but he couldn't do it anymore.

The majority of the hard-money loans he'd made were in default, and the likelihood of getting anything out of the properties that he held as collateral was small.

My capital was gone, and I'm guessing that if the young investor from the DR hadn't liquidated his hard money loans in Iowa in time, so was his. Fortunately, I had invested only a small amount of money, so the loss wasn't anything to talk about. It was a cheap lesson in the virtues of diversification.

I was reminded of this conversation in the DR when a colleague selling condo-hotel properties projecting yields in the eight percent range was told by someone who inquired about the opportunity that she could "make twelve percent all day long in San Francisco" and so wasn't interested in this eight percent offer.

In this case, it seems the returns are coming from rental properties.

Great, I'm in. Tell me how to make twelve percent with the same risk level as I'd have if I invested in the condo-hotel my colleague has available, and I'll invest all day long in San Francisco rentals, too.

Investing in San Francisco could be great diversification for me. I don't currently own anything in the United States, and I'd be very happy with a twelve percent return on my money.

Before I took the leap, though, I'd have some questions.

To get twelve percent all day long in San Francisco, I'm thinking leverage must be involved. Maybe the investor is talking about a cash-on-cash yield for a rental property where she's put twenty percent down, and the property cash flows well enough to give her a twelve percent net yield on that twenty percent.

Leverage can be an important tool for the property investor, but you always want to remember that leverage works two ways. It can boost returns, but it can also kill an investment.

The investor in this case (I'm guessing at this, I admit) seems to be chasing return without assessing the risk differences between her twelve percent investment and the eight percent investment she was inquiring about.

## The Trouble With Making Money "All Day Long"

Whenever someone tells me he (or she) can make me X percent "all day long," it worries me, and it should worry you.

High yields are possible but generally not sustainable in the long run, and they usually come with a higher-than-typical level of risk.

You have to consider return in the context of associated risk, investment to investment.

The kid in the Dominican Republic didn't understand risk or how to analyze it.

He was chasing returns and had come to expect twelve percent. If he couldn't get twelve percent, then he wasn't interested. Had any of the presenters told him that they were projecting twelve percent returns or better, he likely would have invested, potential risks notwithstanding... maybe not even understood.

Diversification disperses risk, but you still have to ana-

> lyze the associated risks, investment to investment.
>
> Chasing high yields without understanding the risks is dangerous… but so is dismissing lower returns without understanding the investment.

## Get Updates On The Model Portfolio

If you want my up-to-the-minute recommendations for rentals, agriculture, and more… specific investment recommendations with specific projected returns… then I urge you to become a member of Live and Invest Overseas' *Global Property Advisor* service.

Every issue of *Global Property Advisor* includes a running review of all *GPA* portfolio recommendations to date and how those fit into the ideal portfolio.

You can become a member of the service at the Live And Invest Overseas Bookstore by clicking this link, **bit.ly/GlobalPropertyAdvisor**, or by scanning the QR code below.

CHAPTER IV

# The Six Top Markets To Look At Right Now

Where is the best place to invest in property overseas?

At this point in my career, I'm confident I could go into pretty much any overseas real estate market and find a good deal. It's just a question of how much time, research, and exploration I want to put in.

There are, however, markets I know better than others from personal experience—and markets that I know are proven winners...

The real question you need to ask yourself is this: "Where is the best place to invest in property overseas for me and my portfolio?"

Years ago, I came across a compelling investment opportunity in pre-construction condos in a market that was generating fifteen percent net yields or more in existing, newly completed condos.

The expectation was that those yields would continue even

when the new construction that was underway came online for rental. (Note that I always look at the net yield... rather than the gross yield.)

The market was Ulan Bataar, Mongolia, where prices were affordable and everything lined up for the investment.

The commodity boom was in full swing in Mongolia, with lots of mining companies setting up and sending executives and other workers who needed places to live. Hence the demand and the high rental yields.

While the investment was compelling (and I have to say I have a romantic vision of Mongolia but have not been there yet), the idea of chasing fifteen percent rental yields in a country that is not on the way to or from anywhere did not make sense for many investors.

Even with proven yields that almost doubled the high end of my general yield expectation, the other risks were simply too high for any investor who could not afford to lose his entire investment.

It seems that that market is still generating good yields... rents are still high compared to prices, but prices have come down.

More importantly, traveling to check on the property could be fun once, but the trip would be long and expensive. Dealing with your management company with an eight- to twelve-hour time difference would be complicated.

Maybe an investment like that fits your portfolio needs and your risk tolerance, but probably not.

Chasing yields can prove profitable, but the property must fit the needs of your portfolio, which includes capital required, country risk, currency risk, and location. You need to be able to administer your entire property portfolio without stretching yourself too thin.

Another market that offered fifteen percent and higher yields when I first dug into it was Medellín, Colombia, more than a dozen years ago.

At that time, short-term rental owners were getting as high as eighteen percent net yields. Property prices were low in U.S. dollar terms, making the market enticingly affordable for investors.

However, there were very few short-term rentals available, skewing the supply curve and making nightly rental rates for apartments as high or higher than hotel rates.

The out-of-the-norm yields attracted foreign buyers, which added to the supply side. While the larger supply dampened the market, it was the short-term rental law limiting short-term rentals of less than thirty days that pulled yields down for most rental owners.

Property prices went up, knocking yields down based on the higher values of apartments.

The currency weakening over time did not help the overall

returns for dollar investors, but property prices kept up with the currency depreciation of the peso.

My apartment in Medellín is worth more in U.S. dollars today than we have in it, but not enough in annualized returns to write home about. The play in Medellín was the rental yields.

Buying a property for the rental yields should be your focus rather than expecting—hoping for—outsized appreciation in the short term. It is hard to predict that kind of appreciation, so relying on it for your profit is more speculation than investing.

The markets I'm looking at in this chapter have potential for appreciation, but that is not something we want to rely on. They all have rental yield stories that make sense, with net yield expectations ranging from four to ten percent.

Remember your portfolio and your risk tolerance.

Consider the risks (economic, currency, market location), and consider the required administration (do you need a local bank account or not, travel time to check on your property, maintenance management, and so on).

I have passed on excellent investments over the years because the property did not really make sense for my portfolio.

I did not invest in Mongolia, even though it was compelling for me, because I knew it would be a distraction… even if it did end up throwing off fifteen percent a year cash flow.

I have skipped investments that only required a small amount of capital due to the oversized administrative time required compared to larger investments.

Only you can decide what makes sense for your portfolio...

Take a look at my most-favored markets right now and see what you think...

## #1: Ceará, Brazil—A Hot Spot Getting Hotter

Beautiful beaches with white sand... huge rolling dunes... and sparkling waters fringed with palms...

Brazil's Ceará state sits on the country's northeast coast, just a couple of degrees south of the equator.

Responsible for Ceará's strong national tourism numbers over the past twenty years (including during the pandemic) is its capital, Fortaleza. It offers the advantage of being a major city—one of Brazil's most populated—with attractive beaches accessible from its downtown.

Thanks to this, plus its vibrant nightlife, resorts, and bustling beachfront boardwalk full of shops, restaurants, and small parks, international visitors are starting to take notice of Fortaleza as well.

Hotels in Fortaleza have the highest occupancy rates in Brazil, and its international airport is one of the busiest in the country.

Historically, the coast of Ceará has lacked infrastructure. But Brazil's sandy coasts have experienced an explosion of development. At the same time, this progress is attracting more international tourism.

In 2017, $73.3 million was assigned to revitalize Fortaleza and the northeastern coastline as part of the Fortaleza Sustainable Urban Development Project.

New direct flights from around the world are creating greater access and stronger international tourism.

Traffic from Europe to Fortaleza is expected to increase by forty percent as a result.

I like to think of Brazil as being "one step beyond Latin America," as its culture and language are just a bit more unfamiliar and exotic to North Americans. This country is exciting, romantic, and diverse...

But it's also more accessible than ever before, with new and more user-friendly visa policies for foreign visitors and increased international connections to Fortaleza's airport.

It helps that the Brazilian people are just as warm, friendly, and fun-loving as the stereotypes would have you believe, too.

Brazil is a huge country—it's the world's ninth-largest economy and geographically about the size of the mainland United States. Unlike the States, however, Brazil's middle class is still growing at a rapid clip—about one percent annually, equal to two million people a year.

With its near-perfect climate and spectacular beaches, North Americans and Europeans both want a piece of this paradise.

This is an undervalued market on the rise.

Brazil encourages foreign investment at all levels, but especially in real estate. By law, Brazilians and foreigners are on almost equal ground regarding property ownership and tenant rights.

If the property is in a rural area, some restrictions for foreigners may apply. For rural properties, foreign ownership is limited to twenty-five percent of the total rural municipality area and ten percent of the rural municipality area owned by citizens from a single country. Depending on the size of the land, you may need to request an authorization from the Agriculture Ministry.

The average price per square meter in Ceará is $2,000. Right now, we are on the right side of the window of opportunity to get in early and at a discount, for strong appreciation.

A killer deal on the Ceará coast are beach bungalows going for a cash price of just $77,000. Next to pristine beaches, you will find a thirty-seven-square-meter bungalow with one bedroom and one bathroom. It includes a small but functional and modern kitchen, a personal plunge pool, and a private terrace area for outdoor dining and entertaining. They're also located within a community with shared amenities such as a soccer field, running trails, cabanas, a restaurant, a bar, and a convenience store and bakery... adding more value to your investment. This is the perfect property to rent for profit.

(If you're interested in this opportunity, check out this link: **bit.ly/BrazilBeachBungalows**).

If you are interested in land, you will be able to find beachside lots at premium prices. These lots are vacant, and depending on which one you choose to purchase, they are located either one or two blocks from the white-sand, clear-water beach... just a short walk away.

When buying so close to the shore, rising water levels and climate change are a concern. These lots stand on land that's slightly raised above sea level, eliminating any dread. This is not the case with any other comparable lots in the region.

Prices for these start at $22,900 for a three-hundred-twenty-square-meter lot, making the price per square meter of land $71.56.

(Check out the opportunity here: **bit.ly/BrazilBeachside Lots**).

On the coast of Ceará, it's easy to find incredible property deals that will work in your favor if you wish to use them as short-term rentals. ROIs of more than ten percent are possible here.

Brazil's most notable downsides are its currency controls

and the inability to use dollars or hold dollar-denominated accounts within Brazil. However, transferring money is not a difficult process, and your agent or lawyer will be able to handle the declarations easily for you.

I expect continued strong growth in the value of properties in the state of Ceará and its main city, Fortaleza. They have been dramatically increasing for the past decade all over the city, not just on beachfront properties. You can currently see a capital appreciation of ten to fifteen percent in the state of Ceará.

In Fortaleza's off-beach sector of Aldeota, the cost per square meter (for two-bedroom apartments) grew from 3,700 Brazilian reals to 6,950 Brazilian reals in the five years to 2022. That's an eighty-eight percent increase, or more than seventeen percent annually. And the beachfront areas have grown even faster.

In the long term, this will become a mature and developed market, and the best opportunities to get in on it are happening now.

## #2: Montenegro—Europe's Last Frontier

This tiny Adriatic country of some six hundred thousand people dispersed over thirteen thousand eight hundred square kilometers (five thousand three hundred square miles)—slightly smaller than Connecticut—is located in Southern Europe, nestled between Croatia and Albania.

Overlooking the same stretch of water as eastern Italy and boasting calm inlets and a pristine landscape, this yachting paradise is treated by the ultra-wealthy like their own riviera…

Real estate here is significantly more affordable than neighboring Croatia's—yet equally as spectacular. Both Croatia and Montenegro offer dazzling beaches on the Adriatic Sea, majestic mountains, and a history that goes pre-Roman.

Montenegro, however, is a fraction of the price. On top of all that, Montenegro's tax climate is favorable, with low capital gains tax, property tax rates, income tax rates, and real estate transfer taxes.

Montenegro became independent in 2006 and is expected to join the European Union in the coming decade…

In the last decade, Montenegro has developed considerably. It has opened its economy and became a WTO member; it has no major issues with its neighboring countries; it joined NATO; and it is the only aspiring member country that is showing one hundred percent alignment with EU foreign policy.

A big part of the surge in foreign investment in the last decade is the country's official status as a candidate to join the EU. However, to advance in the accession negotiations, Montenegro still needs to make significant progress in several areas, including the rule of law and the fight against corruption and organized crime.

The government has a vision for the future of Montenegro and the Bay of Kotor in particular, with a focus on massive developments that target the one percent.

Today, luxury penthouses here sell for millions... the shopping center includes high-end brands like Dior, Rolex, Burberry, Balenciaga... and A-listers flock here to berth their super yachts.

This part of Montenegro is quietly transforming itself into a luxury travel destination.

And while you might not be looking for somewhere to park your yacht, surprisingly enough, you can own here for the low six figures... which means we stand to profit as Europe's "Secret Rivera" takes its spot in the limelight.

All we need to do is step back a few minutes from the marina to a hillside location nestled between high-end Porto Montenegro and UNESCO-protected old-town Kotor on the other side... the city of Tivat.

In Tivat, you can find high-quality projects with a myriad of amenities with net yield projections that push into the double digits.

Rental and property management companies are not popular in the country, so if you buy with the intention of renting for profit, this might prove difficult if you are not living in Montenegro. However, some developers (including the ones I recommend) have created projects with a serviced apartment concept, making your investment turn-key and hassle-free.

Montenegro has no short-term rental restrictions, making it an ideal place to buy for profit.

Montenegrin real estate law is based on reciprocity; whatever a Montenegrin can do in your country, you can do in theirs. In the case of the United States, any foreigner can purchase without restriction, meaning a U.S. citizen can also purchase without restriction in Montenegro.

Buying in Montenegro as a foreigner is as easy as it gets. With the introduction of notaries in recent years, the process is safe and transparent for both the buyer and seller.

Montenegro's constitution protects private ownership, and this includes equal treatment of foreigners.

Unfortunately, Montenegro stopped providing loans to foreigners, either residents or non-residents, a couple of years back. However, options for developer financing are available with the contacts I have on the ground. It is most common to pay a thirty percent down payment and pay the rest in installments while the project is under construction.

If you are looking to buy from the secondary market or a ready-to-move home, it is likely you'll need to pay the total purchase price in cash.

Montenegro has become a high-interest place for property investment, more so in the last couple of years. With the recent global crises (a pandemic, war, inflation, and supply chain issues), foreigners are more interested than ever in securing their Plan B, and this Balkan country has caught many eyes around the world.

Because of this surge in demand, property values and prices have gone up. My sources tell me the property market was not hindered by the crises, but more likely they have helped this market's growth.

The vacation rental market for Montenegro has historically come from Serbia and Russia. Big resorts were built for this market farther south in Montenegro in places like Budva.

That has changed since their independence, and as their EU entry date gets closer, more and more tourists are making their way from Central and Western Europe, opening the vacation rental prospects that get you attractive double-digit yields.

Tourism and real estate are among Montenegro's top industries, and together they have brought about 3.5 billion euros to the economy in recent years.

According to the World Travel and Tourism Council long-term forecast, an average annual growth rate in tourism revenues of six percent is expected in the following decade.

By getting into this market with a pre-construction project from a reputable developer, you will have the best chance of getting true bang for your buck.

Ready-to-move units for new buildings in Montenegro go for much higher... reducing your returns. This does not mean they are not up to the mark, as buying in the right location and project keeps those ROIs in the golden five- to eight-percent net return range.

Montenegro's undeniable tourist success and real estate market growth are excellent news for property investors looking to rent for profit.

And there are additional perks to buying property here...

Montenegro is one of the few countries where you can get legal residency by just buying a property—any residential property—at any price (unlike the Golden Visa programs in the EU that have minimum real estate purchases of 250,000 euros and up).

Your spouse and children under eighteen years old will also be entitled to residency.

(Find out more about opportunities in Montenegro here: **bit.ly/MontenegroOpportunities**).

## #3: Northern Cyprus—"The Las Vegas Of The Mediterranean"

Cyprus is an island country in the Eastern Mediterranean Sea with a rich history spanning more than ten thousand years... making it one of the oldest civilizations in the Mediterranean. You can find here a myriad of museums, historical sites, monuments, and galleries.

Because of its unique geographical position—at the crossroads of three continents—the country is a multicultural, multilingual, and multireligious place.

Our area of interest, with low capital entry points and double-digit net rental yield potential, is the northern part of the country...

Here, you get all the perks of a Mediterranean lifestyle, but at a much more attractive price. This country has all the right ingredients for a dream retirement and fantastic investment opportunities.

The northern part of the island is arguably the most beautiful in the country, boasting incredible castles, colonial villages, and miles of untouched sandy beaches.

As well as attracting sun worshippers, it has a strong casino industry (hence its reputation as the "Las Vegas of the Mediterranean") and a burgeoning medical tourism sector. All of this means an increase in demand for tourist accommodation.

This northern area of Cyprus is a strong contender for a retirement destination, a second home, and property investment.

Northern Cyprus is beautiful and underrated, with a favorable climate most of the year, affordable property that gives you high ROIs, a low cost of living, and a standard of living that is up to par with what you would get back home.

What has led to this part of the island in particular offering exception value?

Since 1974, Cyprus has been divided in two—the ethnic Turkish Cypriot side in the north and the ethnic Greek Cypriot side in the south. Its capital, Nicosia, is the last divided capital in the world.

The division happened after troops from Turkey invaded the northern part of Cyprus after a short Greek Cypriot coup caused by enosis (the movement for reunification with the historical Greek homeland). Turkey took over thirty-seven percent of the island.

Eventually, both parties agreed to a ceasefire, and the ceasefire line became a UN buffer zone, known as the "Green Line," still in place today.

This part of the island then became the de facto Turkish Republic of Northern Cyprus in 1983. Please note that this does not mean the northern area of Cyprus is a part of Turkey, nor is the southern area of Cyprus a part of Greece.

Traffic across the green line in Nicosia was limited until 2003, when the Turkish Cypriot Administration eased travel restrictions, allowing Greek Cypriots to cross over. A year later, the Republic of Cyprus joined the European Union, abolishing restrictions for EU citizens. Currently, anyone is allowed to cross over the green line.

The north and the south are at peace.

In April 2021, the United Nations held a meeting in Geneva to resume talks about reunifying the island country after the previous attempt at negotiations fell through back in 2017.

Involved were the two Cypriot parties, along with their guarantor countries: Greece, Turkey, and the United Kingdom. However, despite these efforts, not enough common ground was found among both sides to allow formal negotiations.

Our man on the ground in Northern Cyprus tells us that seventy-four percent of its population supports the reunification of the island. For locals, the reunification will mean wages paid in euros instead of Turkish lira. He tells us that reunification will only mean good things for the country.

For the foreign investor, however, this will mean a significant rise in property prices. Gone will be the days of pocket-money opportunities on this side of the island. This means the window of opportunity is getting smaller, and the time to invest is now.

The Turkish lira is the currency of Northern Cyprus, and developments in the Turkish economy and the Turkish lira are two factors that would affect the Turkish Cypriot economy. The Turkish lira has been devaluating every year since 2012 because of a credit-driven economy dependent on imports, dollar funding, and a loose monetary policy.

The devaluation of the Turkish lira is good for you if you

are earning income in U.S. dollars, making the cost of living in Northern Cyprus extremely affordable.

For the property investor, fluctuations in the local currency do not affect their investment. The value of property is denominated in British pounds, and rental income is earned in British pounds.

In Northern Cyprus, foreign individuals or married couples can purchase one property or up to three properties on a maximum of one thousand three hundred thirty-eight square meters (fourteen thousand four hundred square feet) of land per person. It deems married couples as one person unless they have different last names.

However, by purchasing with a trust company, there are no limitations. If you wish to purchase more than one property, using a trustee or registering the title deeds under a local company name are options that you can discuss with a local lawyer to ensure the safest and most affordable option for you.

Foreign nationals and companies must request permission to acquire property in Northern Cyprus. You will need a valid passport and a clean criminal background record from the local police department. This step can take up to a year to complete, but it is mostly a formality as you can go ahead with the purchase and even live in your new property while the Permission to Purchase is being processed. Your local lawyer can help you with this application and follow it up until completion.

Northern Cyprus has been growing for the past twenty years. It is a developing area with many rising opportunities for growth because of its location, relatively small population, and rich land availability.

All of this makes it great for investment with low prices and high rates of return in the long run.

It has excellent universities, and, as a result, education is one of its most profitable and rapidly growing sectors. More than one hundred thousand foreign students live on the island, providing guaranteed rental income.

Progress is happening right now. Because of the sudden surge of interest, infrastructure has already greatly improved, especially in road and air access.

The property market is booming, which means prices will continue to rise in the near term.

But because this is still a relatively new place of interest, property is still incredibly cheap—a fraction of the price you could get in the U.K. or even in the southern part of Cyprus.

And with the tourism industry attracting more than two million visitors each year, about five times the local population, the short-term rental industry is strong.

Oceanfront and beach properties benefit from capital growth the most, with between ten and twenty percent annual capital appreciation in the last decade. Foreign investment has been the key to this strong and rapid growth.

Within a year, apartments that sold for $50,000 at Iskele Long Beach were worth about $65,000. Prices continue to go up, but they still have a long way to go before they converge with the rest of the Mediterranean.

The best time to get in was yesterday. The next best time is right now.

The Northern Cyprus real estate market is one that I haven't seen in a long time. You can buy almost anything, even a resale unit that's twenty years old, and expect to make money, whether it's through rental yields, appreciation, or both.

In this region, it's still possible to find incredible deals, such as a condo right on the path of progress with eight percent annual net returns.

Purchasing a property in the country with a government-registered Contract of Sale makes you eligible for residency as long as you have a clean background check. The residency process in Northern Cyprus is straightforward and painless.

(If you're interested in this Northern Cyprus opportunity, go here: **bit.ly/NorthCyprusOpportunity**).

## #4: Panama City, Panama—"The Hub Of The Americas"

Panama City offers a different caliber of lifestyle experience—a more comfortable, well-appointed standard of living than anywhere else in Central America.

It's changed drastically as it pushes for growth. This city is constantly under construction as it builds and rebuilds, expands, and develops...

By settling or making an investment in Panama, you can avail of the many benefits that this country has to offer: quick and easy routes to residency, special benefits and discounts for retirement-age expats, life in a U.S.-dollar, low-tax environment...

Nicknamed the Hub of the Americas, the capital is well-connected by Tocumen Airport, which serves the United States and Canada (as well as a host of other countries) with direct flights daily.

Panama City has U.S.-style malls and traditional open-air markets, skyscrapers alongside Spanish-colonial architecture, five-star restaurants and hole-in-the-wall eateries... a mix of old and new, laid-back and chaotic...

It's a heady combo and certainly not for everyone. Ultimately, what it offers is the chance to live in a tropical urban setting, a hub of trade and industry, and the only true cosmopolitan environment in Central America.

When much of the rest of the world was in a severe state of economic shock, Panama pulled through the 2008 crisis more or less unscathed. And with the canal adding to its coffers every year, Panama is insulated from global shocks in ways others are not.

The time to capitalize on outstanding real estate deals has never been better. Seeking foreign investment to work with the U.S. dollar-pegged economy, Panama is offering several quality programs to attract foreign nationals, including tax abatements.

One important factor to consider is that, in Panama City, you cannot rent out your property for less than forty-five days, which creates too much inventory for long-term rentals.

Because of the number of options available, this might lead you to decrease your rental rates to be able to compete with the long-term rentals in your area. You'll need to keep up with the market constantly to determine when demand is changing so you can make shifts in your rates accordingly.

On the other hand, there are a few developments available with permits to lease units as short-term rentals. This creates a unique opportunity for the investor, placing you in a smaller market where you can profit generously compared to the country's long-term rental market.

Foreigners have the same legal rights as Panamanians in property ownership, and the purchase process is straightforward if you are purchasing titled land. Foreigners can easily use a self-directed IRA or an LLC or buy in their own name.

In Panama, untitled land must be owned by a Panamanian

citizen for at least two years before it can be owned by a foreigner. After this period, it can be titled and resold.

Foreigners cannot own land within ten kilometers (six miles) of international borders, ten meters (thirty-three feet) of the Atlantic Ocean, or twenty-two meters (seventy-two feet) of the Pacific Ocean (from the high-tide line). Special permits are needed for some types of waterfront construction.

Additionally, rights-of-possession titles are common in some parts of Panama, especially the Bocas del Toro region, for example, and this is something all buyers should be wary of.

Rights of possession is not the same as a full title, but it can be converted to full title in some cases. To do this, you need the help of a trustworthy attorney who is familiar with the process.

## #5: Las Terrenas, Dominican Republic—Stake Your Claim In Paradise

This Caribbean escape has more than just good-value property...

If you are interested in miles of golden-sand beaches and clear, blue waters, friendly locals, small-town vibes, a wide array of international cuisine, and outdoor and water activities, Las Terrenas could be your Shangri-La.

This country has no restrictions on foreign investment. It has an open-door policy, which is one of the reasons it's so popular with foreigners. The Ministry of Tourism is heavily involved with and encourages practices that will bring people to the DR. Property prices are quoted in U.S. dollars.

In the 1970s and 1980s, the French were the first group of expats that decided to trade their rough winters for Las Terrenas' gold-sand beaches. They started building their own little houses, and throughout the years, they have left their mark and influence.

In 2008, a new highway spanning one hundred six kilometers from Santo Domingo to the Samaná province was inaugurated. This cut the six-hour journey by car down to two-and-a-half hours and opened up the northern coast of the country.

Today, the Las Terrenas community is a mix of locals and expats, the latter historically from France, Italy, Spain, and Germany but recently also Canadians and Americans. It has become one of the main tourist hot spots in the Samaná province.

Las Terrenas has been growing exponentially over the past decades, and the pandemic only seemed to accelerate this. Every year, new businesses and developments establish themselves on this beautiful coast of the Dominican Republic. What was once a hard-to-access area is now a tourism hub, easily accessible by air and land and with all the conveniences to make it a part- or full-time home.

The market is hot, but opportunities to stake a claim in this Caribbean paradise still exist.

On average, the price per square meter in Las Terrenas is about $2,000 for construction and $450 per square meter of land. Most developments at the moment are happening on beachfront property, or if not beachfront, just a couple minutes from the beach. When you go inland, away from the beach, the land becomes hilly in many areas, meaning properties with great views.

Industry professionals tell me that sales are through the roof right now. This market is the hottest it's ever been. They barely had any inventory to show me when I requested to see new developments or get information on pre-construction buildings. Las Terrenas is a thriving safe haven and Plan B destination.

Las Terrenas has been more popular with European expats, but after the pandemic, lawyers and agents have received an influx of Canadians and Americans looking to get residency and buy property along this coast. Puerto Plata, Sosua, Cabarete, and Las Terrenas are hot spots for North Americans right now.

Our trusted lawyer in DR gets requests every day from people seeking legal services to live and invest in the country—and not only from retirees. Her clients include many young families from Canada and the United States.

Historically, yearly capital appreciation in this town has been four to eight percent.

There was a boom during and after the COVID-19 pandemic, with so many eager to stake a claim in paradise—agents have seen appreciation of ten percent, twenty percent, and more.

This is a particular boost thanks to the post-pandemic surge. Appreciation won't continue at these levels but will keep going strong. Las Terrenas is not yet as much of a household name as the DR's Punta Cana, but this shows that the secret is out.

A big potential advantage is the availability of bank financing here, which is rare in many foreign markets (at least for expats).

Formally, banks express that you do not need to be a resident to be able to get a mortgage. However, this depends on your relationship with your bank, the bank branch, and the bank representative.

According to our source, it does not seem to make a difference in the bank's eyes if you are resident or not, as they still see you mostly as a foreigner, as Dominican law does not oblige residents to actually reside in the country for any amount of time.

Overall, as the Dominican Republic is pro-foreign investment, getting financing shouldn't be difficult.

Property owners in Las Terrenas are mostly on the short-term rental market. In a lot of cases, it's because they like to use their property for several months throughout the year. Pure investors will choose this route because this is where you can see big returns in Las Terrenas.

Las Terrenas has no short-term rental restrictions, and it's fairly easy to find property management. Many of these condo residences have management in-house and come furnished, making an investment here as turn-key as they come.

## #6: The Azores, Portugal—The Hawaii Of Europe

The Portuguese Autonomous Region of the Azores is an archipelago in the Atlantic Ocean composed of nine volcanic islands and an islet cluster.

It is the first archipelago in the world to be certified as a sustainable tourist destination because of its natural beauty and strategic location. The islands are popular for their varied gastronomy scene, favorable taxation, security, lower cost of living, and friendly, authentic population.

The property market is booming and will continue to grow. Even during the pandemic, the demand for houses exceeded the existing supply in Ponta Delgada, the regional capital.

Until recently, the Azores were largely ignored as a destination to invest in. Therefore, you will find that this region has incredibly affordable property prices compared to mainland Portugal. But now, all eyes are on the Azores.

The secret is out. This is your chance to invest in this growing market with an enviable lifestyle, low prices, and jaw-dropping natural beauty.

When acquiring property in Portugal, foreign individuals and companies are given the same rights as Portuguese citizens. Buying and selling real estate in Portugal is a simple, transparent process, but it takes time.

The property market in Portugal is well-established. There are no restrictions on foreigners purchasing real estate, and transaction costs are generally low. Most property is sold freehold.

The country's property registry system is centralized and reliable. The law protects property, property rights, and the right to access and use one's own property. Portugal also allows co-deeding of properties, even between unrelated parties.

The average price per square meter for an apartment on San Miguel Island is 1,114 euros, and 1,229 euros in Ponta Delgada. In some municipalities of Ponta Delgada, the average price per square meter ranges from 1,474 euros to 1,553 euros.

On other islands, it is even more affordable, with prices per square meter of 890 euros in Terceira, 864 euros in Pico, and 998 euros in Faial.

If you are looking to buy a bigger property, like a villa, with ocean views and amenities, this could average between 500,000 and 600,000 euros.

Forbes has listed the Azores as one of Europe's best places to live, invest, and do business.

The real estate market in the Azores is expanding in large part due to a high demand by American investors, who are attracted to the region because of its convenient geographical position in the Atlantic Ocean, in the middle of North America and Europe. There's a flight that can take you from Boston to João Paulo II International Airport in Ponta Delgada in under five hours.

The Azores have quality infrastructure—the port, airport, and road networks have made it accessible to travel between the islands, mainland Portugal, and the rest of the world. Plus, a massive submarine fiber-optic cable infrastructure keeps the islands globally connected.

Special tax conditions for the Azores also keep investors coming to this nature haven. The VAT (sales tax) rate in the Azores is sixteen percent, compared to twenty-three percent in mainland Portugal. Certain goods and services are taxed at reduced nine percent and four percent VAT rates.

The Azores have historically come on top for price growth among Portugal's regions. Pre-pandemic, property prices in the Azores increased by over four percent, while in Lisbon they increased by over two percent.

It is possible for foreigners to get mortgages in Portugal, and the terms for non-residents are more generous than in most other EU countries.

You will need to provide the bank with proof of your current income through pension slips, tax returns, and bank statements; proof of address; a copy of your passport; a Portuguese tax number; and the property sales contract, among other documents.

The mortgage requirements and conditions may vary slightly depending on the bank, so compare several to make sure you are getting the best terms.

Portuguese banks have a higher level of scrutiny for buyers with "unusual" income streams such as trusts and LLCs, and you may be refused a loan based on just that.

For them, the best source of income to use as a guarantee is a salary. Passive income such as dividends, rentals, or interest is also not highly regarded as a proper guarantee, regardless of the amount.

For non-residents, the minimum deposit for a mortgage is thirty percent, with a maximum loan-to-value ratio (LTV) of seventy percent.

A solid and well-managed property investment in the Azores usually generates between three and seven percent rental yields.

As more of the world discovers the region, with its low prices, natural beauty, and incredible investment potential, I expect yields in this market to reach the golden five to eight percent ROI range.

Real estate in the Azores is diverse. You could buy a two hundred twenty-seven-square-meter detached house for 290,000 euros and rent it for about 1,050 euros per month. This could earn you a potential four percent ROI per year.

A two-bedroom apartment of seventy-eight square meters of living space on San Miguel Island can set you back about 90,900 euros. You could rent it for 800 euros per month for a potential seven percent yield.

## When You're "In The Market," The Best Deals Find You

Here's one of the most important things I've learned in my three decades of experience investing in real estate around the world…

The best deals find you.

But you've got to be "in the market." By that, I mean you need to have done your market due diligence.

You need to have connected yourself on the ground. You need to put in the time and effort to establish relationships with local attorneys, real estate agents, property developers, resident expats, etc., letting them all know that you're actively shopping and looking to make a purchase.

You need to have established your personal parameters for things like price range, type of property, size, location, intended use, etc.

You need to understand relevant country-specific issues—restrictions on foreign ownership (if any), for example, plus the costs of buying and selling, property taxes, capital gains taxes, etc.

To be "in the market" anywhere in the world, you also need to understand relevant investment-specific issues—for example, which are the most rentable neighborhoods, which kinds of properties rent best (an apartment with one bedroom or two?), what's the rental season, and who might best be targeted as a potential renter (traveling executives or tourists, for example).

Once you've carried out all this background work, you can set off on a property hunt. You can meet with local agents, read local classifieds, call local owners, and pound the pavement in search of "for sale" signs.

You can and should do all those things...

But, in my experience, again, often, the best deals come to you.

This isn't only chance. It's because the best deals don't ever make it to agency windows or classified ad sections. They're sold without any public marketing, under the radar.

This was the case for the first apartment we purchased in Paris.

We were well established in this market and had been nosing around for an apartment to buy for months. Then, finally, one day, one of the agents we'd been working with happened to mention that a friend of a friend was getting divorced and needed to sell her apartment quickly. The place wasn't yet officially for sale, and the agent didn't yet have a signed listing agreement.

We persuaded her, nevertheless, to arrange for us to see the apartment that same day.

That's how we were able to buy in one of Paris' most sought-after neighborhoods for well below market value. We were in the right place at the right time.

Today, that apartment is worth more than three times what we paid for it... and it has thrown off significant cash flow.

If we hadn't jumped on the opportunity when it presented itself, someone else would have. This apartment listing, once it was official, never would have made its way to an agent's window.

In Paris, as in many other markets, the places you see listed in the agents' windows are the leftovers.

So, educate yourself about your favored markets... make contacts on the ground... and the best deals will come to you.

(Looking for a shortcut? Sign up for "insider" services like my *Global Property Advisor* and *Simon Letter* publications—where deals I receive from my on-the-ground connections are published—and you'll be well ahead of the game.)

## CHAPTER V

# Eight Things You Need To Know About "Frontier" Markets

I often tell a story about a guy I met in the Dominican Republic when I traveled there for the first time in 2005.

I was hosting a real estate investment conference, and the guy came up to me during the first coffee break to introduce himself.

He told me he was a real estate investor from the United States who had spent time in Costa Rica researching that property market for four years.

"What have you invested in in Costa Rica so far?" I asked him.

"Nothing," he replied.

I tried to dig a little deeper and asked about where he'd looked and what kind of property, specifically, he was interested in buying.

He told me he had looked all over Costa Rica, at all kinds of properties.

He wasn't just looking for a great deal, he told me. He was looking for the best deal.

Every time he found a good investment, he wondered whether he might find a better opportunity if he kept looking. That line of thinking extended his search into a four-year research project... and still, again, he'd bought nothing.

"In the end," he told me, "the market passed me by."

"Ah," I said.

"How long have you been looking at the Dominican Republic?" I asked, trying to push the conversation in a more positive direction.

"Two years," he said.

"Ah, wow," I said. "You've got great timing. 2003 was the perfect time to get into this market. What have you bought?"

"Nothing," he replied.

He'd yet to pull the trigger on anything because he was still looking for the best deal.

Whether you're shopping for a new car, a new wife, or a piece of real estate, you can't hold out for the "best" deal. While you're being picky on the sidelines, questioning what's in front of you, great opportunities can pass you by.

This guy had a fair amount of experience investing in real estate in the United States. He just couldn't get himself to take the leap overseas.

I understand that. The markets are different overseas...

sometimes there are quirks that might be very different from what you're used to back home.

I'm hoping the insider tips and intelligence in this chapter will help give you the courage to take the leap... because you don't want to end up like this guy and let the market pass you by.

You need to do your research and due diligence and get to know the market—knowing the local quirks can certainly help you...

When you're forewarned, you're forearmed, as they say.

Not everything will be how it is back home... but isn't that the fun part?

When you understand the local markets, you'll know a good deal when you see one. Just don't let a desire for the "best deal" stop you from taking a good deal that meets all your criteria.

If the market is right and the deal is good... if you've done your due diligence and you're happy... get in while you can.

## #1–4: The Basic Differences When Buying Overseas

The fact of the matter is that buying real estate overseas is nothing like buying real estate in North America. So it's best to go into this process with realistic expectations.

Here are some of the major differences that you should expect when buying real estate overseas:

- **Language barriers.** It's likely that you will encounter a language barrier in the country where you are planning to make your purchase.
- **No multiple listing services (MLS).** Unfortunately, there's usually no MLS in overseas markets, which significantly slows down the property search process.
- **Price padding (or gringo pricing).** When there's no MLS system in place, you will experience inflated pricing. However, you can counter this with some in-the-trenches market research.
- **Different buying processes and property laws.** The buying process and property laws will be different in every country, which is why you should familiarize yourself with them before you buy to make sure all bases are covered. I highly recommend that you work with an experienced local attorney.

## #5: Price-Negotiation Secrets

A friend told me over dinner once about a property purchase he tried to make in Mendoza, Argentina.

He likes the city, but he travels a lot and has property investments in many other countries. He didn't really need an apartment in Mendoza, and owning one would further complicate an already complicated life.

On the other hand, my friend thought that having an apartment in Mendoza would give him more reason to return more often to Argentina.

The negotiation for the apartment, my friend told me, went something like this:

He offered eighty-five percent of the asking price. The seller countered with the full asking price.

My friend then offered about ninety-two percent of the asking price. The seller countered with the full asking price.

After some deep soul searching and because he really liked the apartment and really wanted an excuse to spend more time in Argentina, he finally went back to the seller a third time and offered his full asking price. The seller countered with one hundred ten percent of the asking price.

That may seem crazy, but it's not uncommon. It's happened to me several times in different countries.

Once, when looking at some land in Panama, I sat down with the owners and made an offer based on the asking price quoted to me by their real estate agent.

They immediately declined the offer and said the new asking price was forty percent more than the original asking price. We left that meeting further apart than when we started.

After running some numbers, I made another offer that was less than the original asking price but more than my initial offer. They declined. No counter-offer, just a simple "no," and the meeting ended.

A couple of weeks after that meeting, the sellers called my real estate agent, asking when they could expect a new offer from me. I took that as a sign that they were finally interested in negotiating, so I returned to the table with yet another offer... still below the original asking price.

At that meeting, they gave yet another "no" without countering and suggested that they were going to raise the asking price to an amount that was double their original asking price.

I explained that we were never going to pay their original asking price, let alone more, and that that day's offer was my final offer. We walked away again without making a deal.

For weeks and maybe even months later, the sellers called my real estate agent, asking when we were going to make our next offer. The real estate agent tried to explain that we were done. There would be no more offers. Eventually, the sellers stopped calling.

That property remained listed at double the asking price I'd initially responded to for more than a year... without selling.

The sellers eventually increased the price again, this time to triple the original asking price.

The logic these owners applied is one I've encountered

often. It goes like this: "My property hasn't sold since I listed it more than a year ago, but meanwhile, property values in my area continue to increase. My property must be worth more, so I'll increase the price."

Generally, that logic doesn't fly. A property that is overpriced to begin with isn't going to gain more traction if you increase the price.

Still, many people whose only asset is a piece of land can't bear the thought of selling too cheaply, so they end up not selling at all because they don't really understand their own market.

I knew better after the first conversation with this seller than to continue negotiations. When a seller increases his price when you show interest, the best thing to do is walk away.

That negotiation can't end well, and no matter how much you like the property, you'll resent your purchase if you end up paying more than the original asking price.

Of course, real estate prices do go up... just not, normally, during negotiations.

Developers increase prices over time as infrastructure is installed and progress is made. You can't expect to inquire about a project today and pay today's prices when you come back to the developer in a year or two.

One prospective buyer at a project in Nicaragua that I

managed years ago had received the original email detailing launch pricing, which included beachfront lots for $25,000.

He didn't act, but he followed the project over the next several years, eventually writing in again to ask about current prices.

When he saw that all the beachfront lots were gone and ocean view lots were selling for $75,000, his response was, "Well, it's too late for me with this project." He couldn't bear the thought of paying more when he knew what the original price had been. That perspective kept that investor from making money a second time.

Just as with any investment, you can't judge the upside potential of a piece of real estate based on what that property sold for a couple of years earlier. You have to analyze current prices in the current market and project appreciation from the current point, not from some past point.

If the investment makes sense at current prices, then make it. The investment's history isn't relevant.

In the case of the Nicaragua beachfront lot, the investor didn't buy when he first heard about the project because he determined there was too much risk. The project had just gotten underway, and no infrastructure had yet been installed.

By the time the guy made his second inquiry, infrastructure was in place, and the project risk had been reduced significantly. Now, though, all the investor could think about was the profits he missed out on. He seemed to have forgotten all about the early risk he had avoided.

Had he invested the second time he inquired about prices, he still would have made money, as prices continued to go up for the next couple of years as the developer made further progress.

The potential rate of annualized appreciation was lower, but so was the level of risk. Bottom line, though, the project still had upside potential that this investor missed out on a second time.

## #6: Market Fundamentals Matter More Than The Exchange Rate

Remember our guy from the DR investment conference I talked about at the start of this chapter?

Had he bought any property—and I mean anything; any piece of real estate anywhere—in the Dominican Republic as soon as he got off the plane in 2003, it would have been worth at least twenty-five percent more when I spoke with him in 2005. Had he bought any piece of property on the beach, it would likely be worth fifty percent more.

Prices for property along the Dominican Republic's coast were low in 2003 and saw huge appreciation in the following two years... yet, still, prices for DR beachfront property were a good deal in 2005 relative to other coastal markets. I know people who bought in 2005 who have enjoyed good appreciation since then, even with the intervening global real estate downturn of 2008/2009.

Another property investor wrote to me in 2010 after I published an article on my property purchase in Medellín, Colombia. This reader called me a "moron" (it's OK... I don't pull punches, and I don't expect my readers to either), for buying in Colombia at the time... not because of any safety or political worries he had, but because he thought the currency was too strong. At the time, the Colombian peso was trading in the range of 1,750 to 1,800 to $1.

This investor believed that it "should" be closer to 3,000 to $1, and, he explained, he was going to wait to buy property in Medellín until the currency hit that target. Only then would he pull the trigger, thereby, he implied, showing me how stupid I was for buying when I did.

I don't try to time my property purchases according to exchange rates. I focus on market fundamentals. You want to buy when a property market makes sense. Wait for a better exchange rate, and you can lose the good deal in front of you.

It was five years from the time of my conversation with the would-be Medellín property investor before the Colombian peso hit his 3,000 peso per $1 target. I wonder if he finally bought at that point. I'm guessing he didn't.

I say that because Medellín property prices in U.S. dollar terms were about the same or higher at that point as they were in 2010, when I bought. How did that happen? Appreciation.

The Medellín property market has appreciated nicely since I bought my apartment there.

Five years later, my apartment was worth about eighty percent more in pesos than it was when I purchased it. The peso was down about forty percent against the dollar in that time.

You can do the rest of the math.

The smart guy waiting, who called me a moron for buying when I did, didn't buy because he didn't like the exchange rate in 2010. However, he probably still didn't buy a few years later because of the higher peso values of the real estate... which would have been his second mistake.

The fundamentals of Colombia and specifically of the Medellín real estate market still make sense—namely, a strong economy and a growing middle class. Today, in addition, U.S. dollar buyers can take advantage of a weak currency. As I write this, $1 has topped 4,000 Colombian pesos.

But again, currency rates shouldn't be the primary factor when sizing up a real estate market. The primary factor is the market itself. Do you have reason to believe it will expand and appreciate?

Property markets, like exchange rates, go up and down. You have to work with the information in front of you to decide whether and when to pull the trigger.

Waiting for a better or the best deal might, in theory, make you more money in the long run... but it'll cost you opportunities all along the way.

## #7: This One Thing Can Make Or Break Your Rental Yield

My first rental property was a three-flat apartment building I managed myself in the United States. I lived in one of the apartments and rented out the other two long-term and unfurnished. I might have had an empty apartment for a few days between tenants during the two-and-a-half years I owned the building... but my occupancy rates were very high. Better than ninety-five percent.

All in all, it was a positive experience despite a few tenant issues, like a broken window when the second floor had a party and they tried to blame the window... or the time the hot water heater for the building decided to die on New Year's Eve (thankfully, Sears was open on New Year's Day).

That personal rental-management experience didn't prepare me for the short-term furnished rentals I would own overseas.

Not living where the properties are located requires hiring a local rental and property manager. Rental management is a low-margin, high-volume business where service can be atrocious if the management company doesn't have serious systems in place.

My first experience with this was in Buenos Aires, Argentina, where the real estate company that I bought the apartments from ended up setting up their own rental management company to service their international clients.

In fact, this is what most real estate companies that have mostly foreign buyers end up doing. It helps them make sales.

However, while they may understand the sales market for real estate in their country, running a rental management company is a different animal.

The company in Buenos Aires put one of their top administrators on the job to get the rental management up and running. The year and a half she was running things, the reports were timely, and the rental yields were good.

At that point, the owners thought the business and systems were established enough that the lady who started things could move on. She did, but the rental business went downhill rapidly. Reporting was no longer timely, and rental yields fell as the company didn't keep up with the marketing.

I switched to a long-term furnished rental for a while and then sold the apartments for a nice profit. Overall, the rental yields for the time we owned were good despite the hiccups, but it was my first lesson in how different your yields can be depending on the rental management company.

The next lesson came in Paris, where the first apartments we bought there were placed with a rental company recommended by the real estate sales agent. The properties were set up for short-term rentals, and they started renting... but no reports were coming.

We were seeing deposits into the bank account. The apartment was renting, and the yields were good. We just weren't getting reports.

The lack of reporting was frustrating, as it was impossible to tell what rental rates were being charged or what occupancy rate we were getting. All I could calculate were the rental yields, which, again, were good. Nevertheless, we needed better... or any... reporting.

So we switched rental managers to someone a friend was working with.

We started getting regular reports showing the rental rates and occupancy.

Unfortunately, the numbers were low, and the yields went down.

The first company was great at filling the apartment... and probably too busy marketing and managing renters to get to reports. The second company was great at reporting but fell short on filling the apartment.

From a pure investment perspective, the first company

was better for returns.

However, without any reports, it was impossible to say if they couldn't have been doing better.

Eventually, we moved on to a third company, where reporting and returns were fine.

Similar stories can be told for most rental properties I've owned overseas.

A new company set up to help buyers in a specific location can do well until it's turned over to a new manager. Besides Buenos Aires, this has happened to me in Panama City, where the first year of a short-term rental property had huge returns... then the manager left and returns dropped.

In that case, the market had changed a bit as well, so it was a double whammy. The new manager simply didn't do anything, and the demand in the market was down.

In that case, I simply switched from a short-term furnished rental to a long-term furnished rental... and took over management myself because I had moved to Panama by that time.

The only lesson to take from my experience is that there are good rental managers out there and there are bad rental managers... and a good rental management company can go bad with a change of staff.

So how do you choose a rental manager for your property overseas?

Referrals are the best option. If a company has happy clients, then that's hard to argue with. However, just because they have an unhappy client doesn't necessarily mean they are not good at their job. The property does play a role.

One reader bought an apartment in Medellín back when the rental yields were well into the double-digit range for short-term rentals in certain neighborhoods. However, she bought outside of the area the rental manager recommended—an apartment that wasn't really suited to short-term rental. Her yields didn't match what others were achieving at the time because of the property... not the rental manager.

A friend of mine starts his search for an investment rental by finding a rental manager first and asking them what and where to buy. Rental managers know what they are renting, so they should be the best source for what to buy as a rental.

This has worked for me in the past... and, of course, finding a rental manager before you buy a property helps take some of the uncertainty out of the equation.

## #8: No If's Or But's... You Need A Good Attorney

Whenever I'm asked to offer advice to someone considering the idea of buying a piece of property in another country... there's one piece of advice I offer that's maybe more important than all the rest. It's this:

Use an attorney.

It's not a given for Americans, who don't typically engage an attorney to help with the purchase of real estate unless they're buying commercial property.

In the United States, the process for the purchase of residential property is usually managed completely by the real estate agent. Contracts are standardized with sections that can be easily modified for contingencies. A title company handles the review of the history of ownership (that is, title), and title insurance is usually standard, especially if a bank is giving a mortgage.

However, the real estate purchase process is different in the rest of the world. In fact, it's different from country to country. It's not that you must use an attorney when buying property anywhere in the world outside the United States; it's that it's a really good idea, precisely because the process, the culture, the local norms, and the idiosyncrasies (every place has them) vary, sometimes in dramatically unexpected ways.

Your most important ally throughout the process is your attorney. He or she should be your attorney, not that of the seller or the property developer you're buying from, for reasons that should be obvious.

This, too, is not a given overseas. Especially in civil law (as opposed to common law) countries, it can be the norm for one attorney to represent both the buyer and seller in a transaction.

**COWBOY MILLIONAIRE—THE NEW AMERICAN PIONEER**
*Chapter V: Eight Things You Need To Know About Frontier Markets*

Since civil law depends much more on statute and much less on interpretation by the courts, it's assumed that the attorney is simply there to help both buyer and seller follow the legal process correctly.

I'll use two examples from my own property purchase history to reinforce just how important it is to use an independent attorney you trust when making any property purchase anywhere.

For a purchase in Panama years ago, I had an attorney represent me as the buyer. The seller did not have an attorney to represent his interests. As we worked through the purchase process—which stretched over three months—I came to understand why my seller hadn't engaged an attorney. He didn't want to make the investment. That's usually the reason people forgo legal counsel: They don't want to pay for it.

Often, buyers will try to save money by piggybacking on the available counsel of the seller, allowing him to write the purchase contract and trusting him to carry out the title check.

That's just a bad idea.

The seller's attorney works for the seller. Let the seller's attorney write it, and the purchase contract will favor his client.

In the case of my purchase in Panama, because the seller didn't have an attorney, my attorney wrote the contract... and, surprise, surprise... it favored me. The seller made comments and changes, but, even after all the back and forth, the contract leaned my way.

If I hadn't had an attorney, I'm not sure how we would have completed the sale.

My other example is an apartment I bought in Portugal. The attorney I engaged carried out a search on the property title before even entertaining discussion about the purchase contract. The title came back clear with the exception of a current mortgage, which the seller had disclosed.

What hadn't been explained was the balance or the type of mortgage. It seemed the mortgage amount was at least as much as the sales price, maybe more. It also seemed that the loan may be a line of credit rather than a straight mortgage, suggesting the possibility of further drawdowns.

Had I not hired an attorney, this information probably would have been overlooked... and it revealed a risk that I needed to mitigate.

The property was a rental apartment, occupied by a tenant whose lease allowed him to remain through the end of November (I was purchasing in July).

The seller had asked that we not close on the property until the renter's lease was up in four months. I was OK with that. However, before I understood the particulars of the financing, I agreed to pay a deposit immediately to hold the purchase and the price.

After learning the particulars via my attorney, I was no longer interested in running the risk that the seller might spend the deposit before closing.

This seller was in a tight financial position. She needed every dollar of the purchase price to cancel her mortgage. And she couldn't close before the end of November, when her tenant's lease was due to expire, because she'd already spent the prepaid rent, so she couldn't refund it.

What if she spent my deposit, too, and then didn't have enough to pay back the bank?

Speaking with my Portugal attorney, I considered walking away from the deal. It had suddenly become a lot more hassle. Then I reminded myself of the fundamentals of the property and of the market.

Still, I might have opted out had my attorney not suggested a couple of reasonable options. The best one was that we close right away, leave the tenant in place, and discount the sales price for the four months' rent the seller already pocketed (and spent).

Meantime, my attorney and I thought through the best way to hold the property to mitigate tax issues. Without the attorney's feedback, I likely would have arranged for the apartment to be held by an entity I already use for holding real estate.

Had I done that, I would have created a big tax mess in Portugal. The entity I would have used was from a country

(Nevis) on Portugal's tax haven black list. That list, as my attorney pointed out, is long and includes several U.S. territories: Puerto Rico, Guam, and the U.S. Virgin Islands.

All in all, this attorney proved himself well worth the expense.

So, again, my best advice for anyone considering buying property overseas is this:

Don't try to save money by not using an attorney. In many cases, your attorney will save you more than you're paying him.

## All The Right Questions To Ask When Buying Property Overseas

Once you've identified a property that you're interested in... there are many questions that you should ask before actually making a deal.

Again, in the case of overseas property purchases, the due diligence process is considerably different, and there are specific questions that need to be asked... and, more importantly, specific things that you should know before making any final purchase decisions.

I've compiled a list of what I think are the most import

ant things that you should inquire about before considering any overseas property investment...

## Permits, Licenses, And Other Legal Issues

When it comes to new projects and developments, having the necessary approvals, permits, and licenses is critical, as their absence can lead to huge issues later on down the line.

As a buyer, it's important that you ask the developer about the status of development permits, construction permits, applicable licensing, and approvals.

It is also important to note that the necessary approvals, permits, and licensing generally come in stages. That is, there will be cases where the developer is in the process of getting the necessary permits, licensing, and approvals.

Unfortunately, this process can take time. Nevertheless, the developer should be able to provide you with some type of evidence that they are in the process of getting all of the required permissions and documentation.

Some questions that you should ask include:

- What is the overall status of all required per

mits, licenses, and approvals? If in progress, when do you expect to have them all in place?
- Is the development zoned for residential development?
- Has the development master plan been approved by the appropriate authorities?
- Has the development's infrastructure plans and design been approved by the appropriate government authorities?
- What individual building permits and licenses will I need to build my home?
- Can the lots be titled at this point? If so, can they be titled in my name?
- If the developer is unable to secure all of the necessary permits, licenses, and approvals, will the buyer be able to cancel the purchase contract and be refunded all monies paid?

## Project Funding And Developer's Financial Health

It is also important to learn about how the developer is funding the project and their current financial situation. Both of these factors will affect whether a project will be completed or not.

A few questions that you should ask regarding project funding and the developer's current financial situation include:

- Where is the money coming from to develop the project? Is it from investors or sales?
- How much more money will it take to complete the project?
- How much cash have you invested in the land, design, permits, infrastructure implementation to date, and any construction? In other words, does the developer have any skin in the game?
- Are there any liens on the property or land (taxes, government, or debt)?
- What other projects does the developer have in progress that could require additional capital?

## The Developer's Level Of Experience

The developer's level of experience is something that I definitely take into account when deciding whether or not to invest in a development or project overseas.

Essentially, I want to know if the developer has some type of track record.

There will be some cases where you will find that a project or development is being done by first-time developers. And while this is certainly a concern, it's not a deal-breaker.

In instances like this, I would delve deeper into the backgrounds of the principals involved in the development.

Some specific questions that you should ask developers regarding their level of experience include:

- What are the names of some of the other projects or developments that your development company is part of? Are these other projects similar to the current project in question?
- What is the current status of these projects? Are residents living there? If so, what is the current feedback from the residents?
- If this is your first development, are you working with an experienced partner(s)?
- If you are a first-time developer (or principal), what developments or projects have you personally been involved in and at what capacity? What is the current status of these projects?

## The Location Of The Property

One of the key factors to consider before investing in property overseas is the location of the property. For one, the location of the property will have a huge influence on potential rental yields and, ultimately, capital appreciation.

Some of the things that you should look at with regard to location are:

- Accessibility to an airport, including drive time from the airport to the property. Also, are there direct flights from major international cities?
- Is there access to major medical care? If so, how far is it from the property?
- Is there access to major shopping centers, pharmacies, banking, and entertainment?
- How is the city's infrastructure, including reliable internet and telecommunications access, electricity access, roads, and public transportation?
- Is the property situated in the path of progress? Are there any infrastructure improvements planned, such as a new airport, a new hospital, new highway, or a new train station? Or has the government targeted the area for

economic development?
- Is the area safe and secure? Does the property have twenty-four-hour security?
- Is the property located near the beach, in the mountains, or in the city?
- What is the weather like? How long is the dry season (and the rainy season)?
- How suitable is the location for the target market (vacationers, retirees, second home owners, or primary residence seekers)?

## The Market

In terms of the market, you are referring to the type of residents that the development or project is geared to. For example, a development can be geared toward active retirees who enjoy golf. Or the development could be targeting only expats from North America. On the other hand, the developer could be seeking out local residents looking for second homes in addition to foreign buyers.

Essentially, you need to find out what the developer's ultimate vision is for the project or development. That is, who is the ideal resident, and what type of community are they aiming for? In addition to the location of the property, understanding the market will help you optimize rental yields and develop an exit strategy.

Some questions that you could ask the developer to understand the market include:

- Who is the market for this development or product?
- How do you market the development to potential buyers?
- What is the overall demographic of your current buyers or residents (retirees, expats, professionals, mid-level executives, etc.)?
- Are there similar developments in the area? Who is the competition? In other words, is this development unique to the market in this area?

## Construction, Design, And Infrastructure

Other critical details to pay attention to when purchasing property overseas, specifically, lots in a new development, are building standards and guidelines, architectural design, and the level of infrastructure.

These details will not only give you better insight into

the overall development but also a better understanding of any additional building costs you may have to incur.

Some specific questions that you should ask the developer with regard to construction, design, and infrastructure are:

- Are there any building requirements (specifically for lots)? Is there a deadline to begin construction on my home?
- What architectural and building guidelines are in place and enforceable?
- Are there any turn-key home options available? If so, what is included? If not, who can oversee the construction of my home? Do you have a list of recommended builders?
- What type of infrastructure is in place? Does the current infrastructure include high-speed internet, a fiber-optic network, underground electricity, paved streets, sidewalks, and storm drainage systems? Is there a central sewage system?
- Is there enough fresh water and water pressure? Is the house plumbed with hot water?
- Are there any planned amenities for use by owners and visitors?

## Extra Costs With A Property Purchase

Another key component that you should look at is the additional costs associated with the property purchase. Firstly, you need to understand the purchase process and general transactional costs.

Furthermore, I recommend that you familiarize yourself with local standards when buying property. For example, in some places, when you buy new or resale properties, they do not come with lighting fixtures.

Depending on the market, some of the extra costs associated with an overseas property purchase could include:

- Legal fees
- Transfer taxes
- Notary fees
- Stamp duty
- Power of Attorney costs
- Title insurance (not always common or available overseas)
- Registration fees
- Title deed

Again, it's highly recommended that you familiarize yourself with the local market to get a general idea of the costs that you will incur with your property purchase. As well as that, you should work closely with a local attorney who is experienced with the purchase process.

## The Rental Income Potential

If you are purchasing a property for rental purposes, then it's a good idea to understand the rental income potential. Generally, a developer will be able to give you a baseline of what to expect as far as rental yields are concerned, but I suggest that you do some independent market research using rental sites like Airbnb and Vrbo, along with getting intel from local real estate agencies.

Your rental income potential will be impacted by the location of your property and the market. It is also important that you gauge the local competition in your area, like hotels, B&Bs, and other rental properties on the market. On top of that, you will need to get an idea of your monthly expenses associated with renting the property.

Here are some specific questions to ask the developer regarding rental income potential:

- Is there a turn-key rental program in place? What is the rental management fee associated with the program?
- If there is no turn-key rental program in place, can you recommend any reputable property managers? If so, what are their typical property and rental management fees?
- What is the expected occupancy rate?
- What are the expected average rental rates for this property (nightly or monthly)?
- Is the property best suited for long-term or short-term rental?
- How much should I expect to pay in utilities (electricity, gas, cable, phone, etc.) monthly?
- What are the expected HOA fees?
- Is there income tax on rental income?
- What are the expected property taxes?

## Exit Strategy And Resale Market

If your plan is to invest in a property overseas with the intention of flipping for a profit in the future, then you need to understand the resale market in order to properly plan your exit strategy.

First and foremost, the appreciation in the value of your property will depend primarily on its location, market, and the overall progress of the development in which it is situated.

All things considered, if you've done your due diligence with regard to the location of your property, the market, and the overall project, then you can reasonably expect your property to increase in value over time.

In addition to normal appreciation, your property could increase in value due to a change in the currency.

With regard to the exit strategy and resale market, some questions that you should ask the developer include:

- Should I decide to sell my property, does the developer have a resale program in place? If so, what sales commissions should I expect?
- Is there a local residential market for my property?
- Are there any capital gains taxes due on the resale? If so, is there any way to alleviate capital gains tax?
- Are there any restrictions on transferring funds out of the country after you have received the proceeds from the sale of your property?

## Don't Ignore The Red Flags

Remember that if you ask a question and the answer isn't what you want to hear, then you have only yourself to blame if you move ahead with the purchase.

I've known many examples of this over the years in Mexico, for example, where people fall in love with a piece of oceanfront property only to find out that it is *ejido* land—community land that can't legally be held in private ownership.

They knew enough to ask the question, but when faced with a response they didn't want to hear, they chose to ignore it. This happens with *ejido* land in Mexico, *cooperativa* land in Nicaragua, and rights of possession property in Panama. People buy knowing they can't get title because prices for this kind of "unownable" land can be a fraction of the cost of comparable titled land.

The price is so low, people sometimes think it might be worth taking the risk that the property could be taken from them at some point.

On the other hand, developers buy *ejido* and rights of possession land, too, in these markets and then offer it for sale at titled land prices. Sometimes they even represent *ejido* or rights of possession property as titled property. You're counting on your attorney to help you identify when this is the case.

If a title search shows that the property in question is some form of *cooperativa* land, move on.

## See It For Yourself

Lastly, I'll add that while you can gather most of this information over the phone, via email, and from the internet, the best way to perform due diligence on an overseas property purchase is to be there on the ground.

Of course, you can get the ball rolling by asking questions over the phone and through email, but in order to get the best intel you need to be on the ground. Unless you are entirely happy and satisfied with a virtual tour, which is more and more common these days...

Most developers offer some type of on-the-ground property tour, during which potential buyers can see the property for themselves. In some cases, the developer will credit the cost of the tour to your property purchase. I encourage you to take advantage of property tours in order to learn more about the property that you are interested in.

CHAPTER VI

# Three Hard Assets That Preserve Your Wealth

I used to think I was "diversified enough" because I owned property in many different countries.

A stockbroker colleague approached me at a conference a few years ago and said, "Lief, you're not diversified, because ninety-five percent of your wealth is in real estate."

I was well diversified beyond my home market, the United States, because I owned real estate overseas in numerous jurisdictions.

But I wasn't well diversified when it came to asset classes...

## Why I'm Looking Beyond Real Estate

Yeah... that stockbroker was right.

I've taken his comment to heart.

More than that: As I get older, I want more options. And I want some assets that are easier to liquidate, should I need to do so.

I've started to grow my stock portfolio. My stockbroker friend would be proud.

But I still have the same basic personal problem with stocks and even mutual funds: You have to pay a lot of attention to them. The market is more volatile.

I now recognize that a fully diversified portfolio would not only include real estate and stocks but also a variety of alternative assets…

It might even include crypto, if you want to go that route.

But personally, just like with real estate, I prefer assets that I can touch and feel.

It makes them real—and have real value—to me.

A few years ago, I started a coin collection with the help of a group that speaks at conferences for my Live And Invest Overseas business, International Coin Alliance (ICA; website: **internationalcoinalliance.com**).

Another alternative investment I've dabbled in over the years is wine. I first bought some primeurs while living in France twenty years ago.

Some wines I bought are worth well more than double what I paid for them.

Average annual appreciation probably didn't hit double digits, but I have a full cellar of wine worth much more than I paid…

More recently, I've turned to art—because art continues to be one of the best-appreciating asset classes if you buy well.

In this chapter, I thought I would share with you—since we're on this diversification journey together—exactly what I've learned about my favorite "alternative assets" to invest in: How to get started and what you can expect if you invest in numismatics, wine, and art.

These hard assets are a solid way to diversify and see strong profit potential. Plus, they're all linked to the internationalized lifestyle I love to live.

The thing about all these investments... unlike stocks, at least for me... is that, in addition to being potentially profitable, they're also fun.

So, you're buying yourself "lifestyle insurance" with alternative assets, but you can also enjoy collecting coins and learning their history. Wine—it's obvious how that can be enjoyed (but just be sure to only drink the bottles from "bad" years)...

Art, well, that's also an asset that comes with a mix of personal appreciation and taste—and, if you buy right, price appreciation.

## Own (And Profit From) Pieces Of History

Do you like shiny baubles?
I ask this question at conferences, and the women's hands

shoot up... but the men are interested in these shiny objects too.

That's how I like to introduce Al Mignone, our speaker from International Coin Alliance.

Like I mentioned, we've been working with them now for years, and I personally have been collecting numismatics through them, as a client, for a number of years.

Most every time they're at a conference where I'm emceeing, I'll buy something.

Like everything else in the offshore world, finding trusted partners to work with is key to growing your portfolio in a way that's right for you.

Collecting is different for everybody...

Personally, I like old coins. Old coins have stories, which is nice... and I go for new coins with stories or something related to my lifestyle.

For example, I've bought a bunch of Chinese coins, mostly because my son Jackson went to NYU Shanghai.

My favorite coins that I've bought from ICA are a series of spheres from Djibouti.

The first one came out right before the first time ICA presented at one of our conferences, so they had a sample at the event. It's a one-kilo silver sphere with a relief scene of the Big Five game animals from Africa.

The country then decided to do a series with each animal

individually, so I bought the next one in the series each year.

These sell for a hefty premium over spot rates... but they are also artwork that I put out for display.

This is the enjoyable part of collecting. You can complement or document your lifestyle and have fun doing it.

At the same time, you're investing in an asset with (if you pick the right coins) strong appreciation potential.

Gold and silver coins are also, as Al points out at conferences, the ultimate portfolio insurance, in a sense.

If monetary systems collapse and paper money becomes worthless (as has frequently happened in Argentina, for example... or the hyperinflation that occurred in Germany before the Nazis rose to power, due to government printing and printing paper money without tying the value to any solid assets—a case with strong parallels to the developed world today)...

If this happens, precious metals will remain viable tools of exchange, even when fiat currency is not—because precious metals have fulfilled this function for thousands of years, long before the existence of central banks.

So, with numismatics, you have a portable monetary insurance policy.

But, of course, we hope that the doomsday scenario doesn't happen. In which case, numismatics carries strong appreciation potential over the medium to long term.

**COWBOY MILLIONAIRE—THE NEW AMERICAN PIONEER**
*Chapter VI: Three Hard Assets That Preserve Your Wealth*

Al cites a study by the Knight Frank consultancy, "an index of tangible alternative asset classes," which showed that returns in rare coins over ten years were one hundred ninety-five percent, beating out art (one hundred thirty-nine percent), stamps (one hundred thirty-three percent), furniture (thirty-one percent), and the S&P 500 index (fifty-eight percent).

As Al points out, coins are more portable than paintings or furniture and boast a higher value-to-volume ratio. Stamps may be lighter, but, come doomsday, you can't melt them down.

The right coins can be worth a fortune down the line. A rare 1958 penny sold at auction in 2023 for $1.136 million.

Generally, you want to look for coins with limited mintages, which soon become rare.

You want to look for "firsts" or "lasts" in a series. For example, many coins minted in British Commonwealth countries in 2022 and 2023 may be the last to feature Queen Elizabeth, since King Charles III took over as the new monarch on the obverse.

Anniversaries are also big for collectors... 2026, for example, will be huge for numismatics. It's the two hundred fiftieth birthday of the United States, and Al assures me that mints around the world are preparing special commemorative editions.

Legal-tender coins—these limited editions issued by worldwide mints—are no longer always just flat round discs. I mentioned the coins from Djibouti I bought that were spherical, making them an even more interesting conversation piece…

You'll find pyramids and other-shaped coins on the market these days. Many mints are going for unique shapes with higher precious metal content to attract collectors.

What other factors should you look for if you want the best appreciation?

Al points out that you want to own coins that will have broad appeal to many people. For example, at one conference, Al spoke about a James Bond five-ounce silver coin issued during the pandemic. Two hundred fifty of them were minted. One sold at issue for $1,195… and seven months later, the coins were selling on the internet for up to $3,000.

That kind of rapid appreciation is unusual—and in this case, due to the popularity of 007 and the timing of the release of the last Daniel Craig movie… but it does happen.

In general, ICA recommends holding your coins for three to five years so they can appreciate.

You also want to buy coins of the highest quality you can afford—coins are graded from one to seventy; the higher the number, the better the quality. (Six factors affect the grade: strike, preservation, luster, color, attractiveness, and sometimes the country or state where it was minted.)

When you do want to sell, ICA recommends you bring your

coins to auction, where collectors can bid, and you're sure to get the best price possible. Don't take them to a coin dealer who will lowball you to get the best deal for himself.

Here are some other advantages of numismatics that Al and ICA like to point out:

- Numismatics aren't reportable to the IRS or on any tax forms (unlike certain kinds of bullion).
- Daily metals markets don't determine the value (again, unlike bullion).
- Coins are portable and easily divisible (unlike gold bars, say).
- You can get started at any price… ICA might be selling coins starting at $250 up to $15,000 at a LIOS conference, for example.

One of the most fun aspects of collecting numismatics is getting to own a piece of history.

At one of our conferences in Panama, for instance, ICA was selling two-thousand-five-hundred-year-old Athenian "owls," with Athena, the Greek goddess of wisdom, on one side and an image of an owl on the other.

As the myth goes, every night, the owl would fly off and search the world for knowledge and information to bring back to Athena…

**COWBOY MILLIONAIRE—THE NEW AMERICAN PIONEER**
*Chapter VI: Three Hard Assets That Preserve Your Wealth*

This is the coin from which the phrase "heads or tails" originates—since it has Athena's head on one side and a "tail," a bird, on the other.

Ancient Athens minted untold numbers of these coins in its glory days using silver from a mine near the city, which became the source of much of its wealth.

These hand-hammered "owls" were one of the most common mediums of trade in the ancient world...

Holding something like this in your hand is a reminder that great civilizations rise and fall... but you can protect yourself by investing in those very reminders.

## The Secret World Of Wine Trading

Wine is another subject (like shiny objects) that's easy to get passionate about....

But what the casual wine-drinker may not realize is that they're consuming what could be a very profitable asset...

For several years, I invested in French wine primeurs. These are vintage pre-sales. You receive your wine when it's eventually bottled. Depending on the vintage, the appreciation can be very good indeed.

I like making money... and I like drinking wine. This allowed me to do both of those things.

I still own most of those primeurs. They're too expensive

to drink, and I really don't need to sell them (not yet anyway).

My kids will probably break some of them out for my funeral. This is another great aspect of all these alternative hard assets: You leave a fun and different kind of legacy for your kids, if that's what you want to do.

I add to my wine cave here and there from time to time… and I'm interested in delving deeper into the topic of wine trading.

The French wine sites I've bought from in the past include Les Echos Wine Club (**wineclub.lesechos.fr**) and Vignerons Indépendants, a trade association of independent winemakers in France (**vigneron-independant.com**).

For wines that should appreciate in value over time, I go with the big names of Bordeaux for the most part, like Lynch-Bages and Pomerol.

You have to pay attention to the harvest quality each year by reading the wine news. The year 2005, for example, was an excellent year and happens to be when I started buying wines. So I have a bunch of 2005's from a handful of big names that have gone up in value more than the same chateaux from 2006.

The thing to watch out for at this point is that many of the big-name chateaux have secondary and tertiary levels of wines they bottle. So the names are similar, but the wine quality and, more importantly, the demand for them aren't the same.

Like many investing opportunities that are off the mainstream radar, getting "in" on wine trading—in the way that's most profitable and best suited to your circumstances—can depend on who you know and getting the best advice.

There is a right way to go about it. In fact, wine trading is like this whole secret economy: You need to already be in the know to get the best opportunities.

That's why I want to share what I know with you...

A contact of mine in Ireland is an acquaintance of wine expert and enthusiast Michelle Lawlor, who traded fine wines in Hong Kong for years.

Michelle gave us the inside scoop on how the world of wine investing really works...

For serious investors, there are really just two regions in France to consider: Bordeaux and Burgundy.

Michelle compares this market to real estate. They're not making any more land... so land values and real estate values tend to go up and up over time. In the same way, all the land for wine production in Bordeaux and Burgandy is already taken. No new land will ever be discovered in these top-tier wine regions. So, the existing growers and operators have the high-end wine market sown up. And demand and prices tend to go up over time...

The business model is called *en primeur*, "and it's genius," as Michelle says.

She explains how it works: "So, for example, your grapes are grown in the year 2022. So the fruit appears on the vine at, say, Easter 2022. You pick the grapes in September or October 2022.

"And then the next year, in 2023, the winegrowers of Bordeaux and the Burgundians invite over all the main buyers in the world.

"Hundreds and hundreds of people come to Bordeaux and get to taste the wine, but it's en primeur. It's gone through the fermentation process, but it's when the wine is still really young. What you're trying are wines that aren't ready yet. So you need a really specific skill to be able to try a wine that's not ready and judge—will this be nice in three, four, five, ten, fifteen, or twenty years' time?

"When I was working in Hong Kong, here's how it would go: The prices of the wines get released. If my buyers wanted to commit to, say, a box of Château Lynch-Bages, they'd get their price. The wine gets sold. It arrives a couple of years later...

"So, the growers get their cash flow in, and they now have the money to keep the operation going.

"It's a really clever business model."

Critics rate the *en primeur* wines every year, and that feeds into the price...

But here's the catch for primeur buyers: If you, as a

buyer, want to keep your annual allocation, you have to buy every year—in other words, you have to purchase the "bad" vintages as well as the good. Another clever trick of the business model.

If you love wine, this isn't necessarily a downside, as Michelle points out. While the good vintages will see nice appreciation... "The beauty of a bad vintage wine," Michelle says, "is that they drink really well in youth, and they tend to be very good value for money.

"And when I say 'drink well in youth,' if you've got a big fancy Bordeaux, youth isn't, say, three years old. Youth is ten years old. So you're able to get a flavor of the chateau or the wine without having to spend a fortune on it."

What sort of annual appreciation could you see on the good vintages?

It totally depends on the wine, the vintage, and the condition it's been kept in. But, Michelle says, twenty-five percent is not untypical.

"Better than the banks will give you," she remarks.

How long should you hold your wine for?

Again, it all depends on the wine, the year, and the condition...

"With a bad vintage, you could sell that on and make money after five years. A really good vintage—if you held onto a box of wine, say, the 2010 or 2015 of a wine that got a really high score, the longer you hold on to it, the more return you'll get."

Bottles of Bordeaux from the 80s, which would have been bought for hundreds, could sell for $10,000 today.

## How To Store Your Wine For The Best Return

If you're serious about making money from wine, it's important to know how to store your bottles properly.

Here's Michelle's advice:

"The first thing is keeping it in its original wooden box. If you ever have a look at a list of wines in an auction, you might see "OWC" or "OC" after the listing. They're telling you it's in its original wooden case.

"As soon as you open the box, even if you don't take any of the bottles out, you lose value. So you really want to sell it in its original wooden box.

"The boxes—sometimes people will use them as bookshelves or decorations, or if you're in a nice restaurant, they might have some of them on the walls, basically like ornaments.

"If you're looking at doing it really seriously, you want

> to store your bottles, in the original case, in a bonded warehouse—because the bonded warehouse also acts as a passport or a guarantee of provenance and where the wine has been.
>
> "If you just keep the wine in one of the rooms in your house, that room might be really cold in winter or really warm in summer, and that temperature fluctuation will have a big impact on the quality of the wine, particularly over a long period of time. Over one year, you might not see a huge impact on it. But if you're going to hold it for five or ten years, it's definitely going to be bad for the wine to be under that pressure.
>
> "With a bonded warehouse, they're normally temperature controlled, so it guarantees to the person who's buying it that it's been in a place where it's been stored correctly.
>
> "They're probably the two really important things—original packaging and temperature-controlled storage."

What's the best way to get started in the world of wine trading?

Well, you can get started with a simple Google search, but it gets more complicated from there...

"Google fine wine merchants in whatever your local area

is. And then look at the big ones globally. Berry Bros. & Rudd is huge. Get onto their website, become a subscriber to their email flyer, contact them, and let them know you want to purchase *en primeur*."

You can chart fine wine prices on the website Liv-ex (**liv-ex.com**). You can also use Wine-Searcher (**wine-searcher.com**).

Michelle highlights a few other useful resources…

"I would definitely suggest getting subscriptions and reading a lot of the wine journals. *The Wine Advocate* is very good." That's Robert Parker's publication—one of the industry's most influential wine critics. "*Decanter* is very good. *Wine & Spirits Magazine* is very good.

"You want to keep on top of the wine releases from Bordeaux and Burgundy, and these publications will help with that."

You might have to start with some of the less-fancy wines and work your way up to the fancier ones, because the best stuff may already be allocated well in advance. In a sense, you have to prove your value and staying power as an investor.

"Definitely, the best way to get started is to purchase en primeur; start when you're buying the wine at its lowest possible value. You don't want to buy it when it's already gone into the market. If you do that, you're already buying it with margin on it. You're already on the back foot."

## Three Ways To Invest In Art

Something that's common to all three assets I'm writing about is that selling them at auction is often your best route.

You could also use respected wine dealers for wine and art dealers for art.

Recently, I decided to start adding some artwork to my investment portfolio because art remains one of the best-appreciating assets.

Like with numismatics and wine, if you're serious about art as an investment, you'll need to separate out what might have a strong appeal to you personally from what might be a great investment.

My wife, Kathleen, and I own some nice art pieces that are on the walls. Most of them are likely worth more than we paid, but we didn't pay much, and the artists aren't known… and those pieces weren't meant for investment. They were meant for lifestyle, i.e., looking good on the wall next to our furniture.

The art I'm interested in buying now that the walls are all full is investment art.

According to Deloitte, eighty-five percent of wealth managers suggest a well-diversified portfolio would include art.

And according to a U.K. gallery I've started working with: "One of the key benefits of art investment is that the art market is both resilient against financial crises and quick to recover in the event of an economic recession. Following the 2007–2009 recession, global auction sales were only slightly below the 2008 figures. By 2011, the figures were almost on par with the 2007 figures.

"This recovery demonstrates the resilience of the art market when other financial markets have been hugely impacted. For example, the S&P 500 figures didn't match pre-recession figures until 2013, which was two years more than the art market took to recover."

The name of this gallery is Grove Gallery (**grovegallery.com**); it's based in London and offers turn-key art investment services.

Grove has a deal with an art storage place, so you don't have to take delivery of your art. And there's no storage fee because they do so much business with the place (although I'm sure the storage costs go to the investors on one end or the other of the buy/sell transactions).

They have art experts on staff that research artists to work with... and they have retail galleries where they can place the art when it's time to sell to the non-investor world.

So, this is a full service: Grove Gallery sources the artists and artwork, stores the art, and suggests when to sell. The minimum hold time they recommend is two years.

They have no upfront fees (although I'm sure a commission for the sales guy is already in the price I'm paying) and no storage fees... just a backend upside fee of twenty percent of the profit at the time of sale.

That's just like a hedge fund, which I presume is how they came up with the model.

I bought my first piece in early 2023. It cost 3,000 British pounds.

I planned to hold it for at least two years and see what happens...

For comparison, this price is about the same as a quality gold coin from ICA.

The difference is that the upside potential of these particular artworks is probably bigger over the long term, but it's also not as liquid an investment... (And if civilization ends, your art probably won't have much tradable value. The metal in your coins will still be worth something.)

I'll keep looking at new pieces Grove Gallery sends me and will likely buy a couple a year...

The entry point is less than what I know some people pay for cheap designer watches, so it's not big money... yet.

If the gallery can prove itself, maybe at some point in the future I'll buy more expensive pieces.

The turn-key investment option is one way to go about art investing and probably the simplest for most people... and most affordable from an entry-level perspective.

Then there's finding a gallery that you like and building a relationship with the salespeople there. That's where the other art investing resource I'm currently using comes in. I was referred by my daughter, who has a friend who works there: Kasmin Gallery (**kasmingallery.com**) in New York...

The art Kasmin Gallery deals in isn't specifically for turn-key investment like what Grove Gallery does. They deal with real art collectors with serious money... and the artists the gallery deals with have low-end pieces starting at $15k to $20k—so it's more of a financial commitment.

So, they sell art "retail," but, again, mostly to collectors. Of course, collector doesn't necessarily mean investor. Some people just like to buy art as a place to store their wealth, and while the value may go up, they probably don't ever intend on selling it.

As I've said, one key to art investing is that it doesn't matter if you like the art. It only matters if enough other people like it to bid up the prices for works by a particular artist.

There are tons of artists out there who sell their stuff well. How do you find an artist that will really take off in the art world? That's why you need expert contacts by your side...

I haven't bought anything from Kasmin yet, but I'm looking...

Who knows? Maybe in five years I'll have an art collection that could be put up for auction, and I could make a killing. That would be nice.

**COWBOY MILLIONAIRE—THE NEW AMERICAN PIONEER**
*Chapter VI: Three Hard Assets That Preserve Your Wealth*

A third way to invest in art is what Masterworks does. Masterworks (masterworks.com) allows you to buy and sell shares in multimillion-dollar blue-chip artworks by big names like Banksy or Andy Warhol.

Masterworks buys the art and sells shares in it to investors...

Masterworks recommends a three- to ten-year hold period, and then you sell your shares...

I suppose, on one level, it's fun to own a piece of something that might otherwise be outside your price range, like a Warhol. But this is obviously very different from owning physical artworks yourself (even if storage, etc., is managed by the likes of Grove Gallery)...

Live And Invest Overseas Publisher Harry Kalashian had a call with a Masterworks agent. He was given the hard sell but came away unimpressed...

I'm not sure that I personally would recommend a service like this. The fees are comparable to investment services in other areas (one-and-a-half percent of your investment annually plus twenty percent of sale profits—similar to the hedge fund "two and twenty" model), but the platform is so new, the returns over time are unproven...

For me, knowing who you're working with and knowing you can trust them and their advice are important parts of how I like to invest.

It makes the opportunity real to me... just like assets I

can see and touch are more tangible (obviously) than stocks or crypto.

## The Sum-Up

It goes without saying that you should speak to a trusted investment advisor and do your own due diligence before you invest in any asset.

My goal with this book is to present you with all kinds of options to boost your portfolio and protect your lifestyle.

You make the final decision on what's right for you.

---

### Why An "International Lifestyle" Is The Ultimate Inflation Hedge

Inflation erodes buying power over time. That's why inflation-resistant investments like real estate and precious metals should be a part of everyone's investment portfolio.

However, I see spreading your life across different countries, currencies, and economies as an inflation hedge as well.

If you were worth $1 million in 1986, you'd have to have $2.3 million today in the United States just to have kept up with U.S. inflation. A million dollars just ain't what it used to be... in the States.

Even with globalization and the same Samsung TV being available for basically the same price in the United States, France, and Panama, you can still find certain things cheaper in different places... especially depending on currency exchange rates compared to your operational currency.

My operational currency is the U.S. dollar, but when I'm in Europe, of course, I shop locally in euros. Good French wines, cheeses, and baguettes are all cheaper in France than in Panama.

Even though Panama is nominally the country with the lower cost of living, it all depends on what you buy. In Panama City, a baguette is about fifteen percent more expensive and about forty percent less good than the real thing in Paris. So I take advantage of that pricing arbitrage when I'm in Paris.

A Venezuelan rum that I like is expensive in Paris, but I saw a bottle in Portugal for thirty percent less (not in duty-free but in a shop in Lagos). I brought it back to Paris with me.

I shop for clothes and shoes in the States for the most part, where, even if I end up buying something not on sale, it's generally cheaper than in Paris or Panama... and they have my sizes. Of course, half of everything in most clothing stores in the States is on sale on any given day.

I bring A.1. Sauce to Paris with me from Panama or the States because it's about twice as expensive in France.

Of course, the travel expense offsets some of my savings, but I'm traveling anyway for work or to check on my investments. That's part of the lifestyle as well.

While shopping for certain things only when I'm someplace where that product's cheaper is not always the most convenient, it does allow me to live a slightly better lifestyle.

Inflation will keep eating away at our purchasing power... but arbitraging your international lifestyle can help improve your quality of life while you pay less for it. You just have to look for the possibilities.

## PART II

# How To Protect What's Yours (When Everyone Wants A Piece)

## CHAPTER VII

# Five Keys That Secure What You've Built

The Five Flags theory of diversification was put forward decades ago by a guy whose name I don't remember.

Guy's name doesn't matter anyway, as it's a pseudonym. He has written to me a few times over the years to complain about me using his "Five Flags" term. He signs off as Grandpa.

I'm not the only one to have borrowed the phrase. It's used commonly in the offshore world.

For reference, the Five Flags are residency, citizenship, asset protection, banking, and business.

The idea is that you want to "plant a flag" in different countries beyond your home country—stake a claim and store some of your wealth in those countries, so all of your net worth is not tied to one country should things go bad in that country.

Pioneers plant flags...

It's a simple enough idea. But it doesn't capture the whole story.

*Chapter VII: Five Keys That Secure What You've Built*

## The Wrong Way To Diversify

At my annual Offshore Wealth Summit one year, one attendee proudly commented that he was well into his flag-planting and had already taken several important steps toward internationalizing his life.

He had a bank account in Panama... had made real estate investments in Panama... had actually moved to Panama... and was on his way to a Panamanian passport.

Four flags down.

On one hand, great. Congratulations.

On the other... not so fast. While this conference attendee had indeed planted three flags—banking, residency, and assets—with a fourth under way—citizenship—every one of the flags is in the same country.

He hadn't diversified his life or his finances. He'd simply moved them both from his home country to Panama.

Now, instead of being completely at the mercy of the goings-on in the United States—from its economy and currency to its political situation—he's in the same vulnerable position in Panama.

Years ago, a real estate investor came up to me at an investment conference to boast that he had diversified his real estate portfolio overseas. He told me that he had sold all of his U.S. real estate, which had been a sizable portfolio, and bought a bunch of properties in Nicaragua.

This guy hadn't diversified either. Again, he'd simply moved all of his real estate risk from one country to another. Now he was completely exposed to whatever might come to pass in Nicaragua that could affect his wealth.

## Don't Put All Your Eggs In One Basket

In this case, something big happened.

Daniel Ortega was reelected president in 2007. The old communist's continued presence at the helm of government scared off both investors and tourists.

Property values and rental returns suffered. Of course, if the guy in our story had kept all of his holdings in the United States, he would have been hit hard a year or two after Ortega took office in Nicaragua, so maybe his portfolio was doomed either way.

And that's precisely my point. Had the guy kept a property or two in the States, bought a property or two in Nicaragua, and bought properties in two or three other countries (he had the budget to accommodate it), then he would have been diversified.

He would have been insulated against the fallout of the 2008 global financial crisis in the United States... as well as from the return of Ortega in Nicaragua.

His real estate assets in those countries would have seen losses, but some of his holdings in other markets could have sailed through unaffected, continuing to generate rental income and perhaps—because every market has its own cycle—enjoying value appreciation way ahead of the U.S. and Nicaraguan markets.

## Beyond The Five Flags

You have good options for diversification beyond the five flags.

And, of course, not all of the original five flags are relevant to everyone. Not everyone has a business offshore, for example... or needs to.

Another important piece of your flag-planting puzzle has to do with taxes.

The tax implications of any move—any investment, business, asset protection strategy, and residency or citizenship choice—should be considered from the start of the planning process.

On the other end of the spectrum, over-diversification is a trap that's easy to fall into. You have to plant your flags in a way that is manageable and makes sense for your level of income and net worth.

Don't open ten bank accounts in ten countries with

$5,000 in each one. The administration and bank fees outweigh any possible benefit of swinging that far in the other direction.

If you find yourself getting to that point—as I have when it comes to my real estate investments—work to bring yourself and your plan back to an equilibrium that makes sense for you.

What all this is really about, as I say, is a strategy that works for your own situation.

## The Five Keys To Securing Your Wealth And Future

Just like on the old frontier of the Wild West... you need ways to protect yourself on the new frontier... protect what you're building and what you've built.

The reality is that all kinds of folks want a piece of what's yours. Uncle Sam. Foreign taxmen. Creditors or ambulance chasers... even old-fashioned con men and scoundrels...

You need to fashion the right keys to lock up and protect what's yours.

All these things... banking, taxes, asset protection (including estate planning), and overseas residency and citizenship... they are keys that you can use to safely and legally protect what's yours.

Keys that you can use to unlock and maximize your wealth when the time comes...

You see, keys not only lock things up... they also open doors and unlock opportunities...

Beyond the Five Flags, I give you... the Five Keys.

The Five Keys I'll write about in the remainder of this book are related to:

- Banking (protect yourself from banking troubles... open up banking opportunities offshore)
- Taxes (protect yourself from paying too much... open up tax savings only available to expats)
- Assets (protect your assets from lawsuits and more... open up overseas business and IP opportunities)
- Legacy and estate planning (protect your heirs... open up their future in unimaginable ways)
- Residency and citizenship (the ultimate protection for your lifestyle... opens up the right to live and work in another country, if things turn bad at home)

## Key #1: The Bank Key

This is the key to banking security and peace of mind... protecting yourself from bank failures, wherever they

**COWBOY MILLIONAIRE—THE NEW AMERICAN PIONEER**
*Chapter VII: Five Keys That Secure What You've Built*

> happen...
> The key to international banking—which might be important for your life overseas, real estate holdings, and more...

The first step for many people who realize the benefits of going offshore is opening a bank account.

One reason that opening a bank account can be a good way to get started at this is because you can do it without moving to another country (although, sadly, options are more limited these days—thanks largely to U.S. government overreach when it comes to Americans holding accounts abroad).

Of course, if you do move to another country, opening a local bank account is typically a necessity. I opened my first "offshore" bank account in Ireland, but it wasn't offshore for me at the time because I was living in Ireland.

With bank accounts in different countries, you are diversifying your risk at several levels. The first is economic. You remember the U.S. banking crisis of 2008... and you probably have heard about the Iceland banking crisis, also in 2008... and the one in Cyprus in 2012... to give a few examples of why having all your money in one banking destination carries risk.

This is true no matter what country you're talking about. I knew Americans who had moved all their liquid cash from a U.S. bank to one in Cyprus. They wanted to take advantage of the very high interest rates being paid on Cypriot accounts at the time... and they thought that because the account was in Cyprus, rather than the United States, they were diversified... and safer.

Moving all your money from your home country to another country isn't diversification. It's just shifting all your risk from one jurisdiction to another. People with all their cash in accounts in Cyprus in 2012 learned that lesson the hard way when deposits over 100,000 euros were simply seized by the government.

In addition to diversification of economies, holding funds in bank accounts in more than one country can also allow for diversification of currency.

Many banks around the world (and today, various online banking apps, too) let you hold different currencies in your accounts with them. However, even if they only allow you to hold the local currency, you're enjoying diversification from your home currency.

Another benefit of having liquid assets in different banks in different countries is access. If you're unable for some reason to obtain cash or to make a transfer from an account in one country, you have other options for getting the money you need where you need it... and, remember, options are what going offshore is all about.

Chapter VIII deals with all this in much more detail.

## Key #2: The Taxpayer's Key

> This is the key to lower taxes... protect yourself from paying a cent more than you have to...
> The key to opening up expat tax advantages...

There are plenty of advantages to living (and investing) overseas when it comes to your U.S. taxes. But not having to file every year is not one of them.

Simply moving outside the United States does not remove your obligation to pay U.S. taxes. U.S. citizens must file a return with the IRS every year, regardless of where in the world they reside.

However, living overseas can substantially reduce your U.S. tax bill...

There are three main tax advantages available to Americans overseas.

We'll cover those advantages, plus some of the essentials to know about taxation abroad, in Chapter IX.

## Key #3: The Asset Key

> The key to keeping your assets safe...

You need a strategy for keeping your assets safe—out of the hands of anyone who might get it into his head to try to take them from you (think frivolous litigant)... and going offshore opens up a whole world of options.

Many Americans set up U.S. trusts to protect their assets. That's a misguided approach. U.S. trusts can help with estate planning, but they do not protect your assets against U.S. threats.

For that, you have to move the assets offshore... with the help of a foreign corporation, for example, or a foreign trust.

By its very nature, moving capital outside of the States may also mean finding business opportunities offshore...

We cover this in Chapter X.

## Key #4: The Legacy Key

> The key that secures your legacy... they key to passing on what you've built to your heirs...

## Chapter VII: Five Keys That Secure What You've Built

Generational wealth bothers some people, from politicians who want to seize and redistribute it to the super wealthy who don't see the point of leaving everything to their kids.

Warren Buffett and Bill Gates are on record stating their kids aren't going to inherit the majority of their respective accumulated wealth. They plan to give most of what they've amassed to charity.

Still, Buffett's children will receive $2 billion apiece... or about two percent of his current net worth per child.

Many superrich and famous people decide not to risk spoiling their kids with mega-inheritances. I understand. Why would a parent want to contribute to making it easy for his children to be useless members of society?

There's a balance to be struck between training the next generation to live responsible lives of their own... and giving them the keys to the kingdom.

But I think most of us are happy to know that what we've built, or owned, during our lifetimes... can continue to be of benefit, or enjoyed, by others after we're gone.

Whether it's a business... a fortune... or even a single property... proper estate planning is the key to ensuring your "kingdom" remains intact for those who come after you... and that your legacy continues.

Estate planning gets more complicated when you own assets overseas... Chapter XI is your guide.

## Key #5: The Master Key

> The key to living long-term overseas... and to escaping home at a moment's notice if you need to... is residency and/or citizenship overseas...

You can obtain residency or citizenship in more than one country. However, most expats obtain residency or a second citizenship in just one country outside their home country. Which country depends on your personal goals.

Maybe you simply want to know you have a place to retreat to if things get too bad in your home country...

Or perhaps you want to be able to spend more time each year in a country than that country's tourist visa allows...

Or maybe you're looking to move to another country full-time...

While most countries offer viable options for taking up full-time residency, some countries make more sense than others as backup residency options (i.e., for your emergency "get out of dodge" plan).

Acquiring a second citizenship is typically a later step in any go-offshore plan. Most people don't start here.

And not everyone is interested in the idea of obtaining a

**COWBOY MILLIONAIRE—THE NEW AMERICAN PIONEER**
*Chapter VII: Five Keys That Secure What You've Built*

second passport at any stage.

Understand, though, that this can be the single most powerful option for creating options... not only for you but also for your children (because you can pass on your citizenship rights).

The world is an ever-changing place. A U.S. passport is still one of the best in the world today, but what value will that passport have in ten or twenty years... or a generation after that? Impossible to say.

In the late 1800s, the U.K. was recognized as the major world power... and many probably expected that to continue indefinitely. But Britain's global reign ended after World War II and the breakup of its empire.

Today, the country is still economically, politically, and militarily strong, but it's not a superpower.

The United States could still be the major power in the world in another one hundred years... but it probably won't be.

Will it still be someplace your great-grandchildren will be able to find economic and personal security? I hope so.

But why not give them options and hedge their bets by obtaining a second citizenship that can be passed down to them?

A second citizenship also gives you immediate residency and the right to work in the country.

Maybe those things are important to you now... maybe they're not. But maybe they could be important to your future generations.

We'll cover residency and citizenship fully in Part III of the book.

It requires its own full part because there are so many options open to you, as you'll see when we get there…

## The Goal: Live Free Of Bad Politics

A reader of my *Simon Letter* publication (see more at this URL **bit.ly/TheSimonLetter** or by scanning the QR code below) once wrote this to me…

"Lief,

"You probably won't read this, but you are now suggesting very socialistic countries and are not always sure of their particular politics.

"Ecuador is in this camp as well as Nicaragua. Things will change for your beloved expats there as the noose gets tighter. The United States is not a favored nation in many of the countries you recommend. I'm not a pessimist just a realist. Cuba is coming around, they would have you believe, but there is not much chance of change as we would have it... one person, one vote.

"You have the right idea but be careful of the countries you get too high on.

"Please review politics before raving on about how great country X is."

– R.G.

I think R.G. misses one key benefit of being an expat: You can move when you don't like the politics of the country you're living in, just as many are leaving the United States right now because they don't like the politics.

More to the point, politics play a limited role in your life as an expat...

France could be described as a socialist country flirting with communism.

Yet, living in France as I have done, the politics don't have to matter to me at all. Occasionally, the French would riot or strike, but my day-to-day life wasn't affected...

Your goal as an expat is to be in a place where the local politics don't affect you too much either way. This is true freedom.

Even countries where the politics make it tough on the locals can be pretty neutral or beneficial for expats because of special visas and tax arrangements for foreigners and new residents (especially those more likely to have and spend more money than the locals)... or because you're not there long enough or often enough to be subject to the same rules as everyday residents.

Yes, politics can affect the long-term investment climate of a country.

However, bottom line for us is that it's personal property rights that matter. As long as they're respected, we can size up the market as we would any market otherwise, based on market fundamentals...

Economies matter to expat retirees and investors. Politics, not so much.

That's the beauty of expat life. You really can have your cake and eat it too.

There will always be countries around the world that have special incentives for foreign investors and expats... countries on the "new frontier" are, quite frankly, competing to attract us relatively wealthy westerners...

And if the politics get truly troublesome in any one place, you can take out your trusty bunch of keys (which you hopefully have fashioned well in advance)... and unlock another door.

## CHAPTER VIII

# Never Worry About A Bank Collapse Again

It looked like 2023 was about to become another 2008. History repeating itself, fifteen years later...

You probably watched the news at the time...

After three banks collapsed in one week in America—including the second and third-largest banking failures in U.S. history (Silicon Valley Bank and Signature)—the FDIC and the Biden administration stepped in, guaranteeing deposits even above the FDIC limit of $250k...

The move was designed to prevent a further run on banks and stop the bleeding...

But the chaos continued: The stock prices of regional U.S. banks took huge hits, and the "contagion" spread as far as Europe, with the stock of Swiss lender Credit Suisse dropping to a record low, and the Swiss government stepping in to arrange a "shotgun marriage" with UBS, a former rival bank, which bought Credit Suisse for just over $3 billion.

Meanwhile, back in the States, eleven major banks grouped together to provide a $30 billion bailout to embattled First Republic Bank, which still did not halt its troubles. It soon went out of business, too.

The whole episode—the "bank crisis of 2023"—was a wake-up call for Americans…

Few people in the States—at least in normal times—think their bank will fail.

But this story just proves, yet again, that it can happen—even in supposedly the most developed economy in the world, even with a bank serving what many believed to be a gold mine that would never run dry (the Silicon Valley start-up sector)…

I can personally empathize with the depositors…

## Banks Fail… And Accounts Get Shut— Here's Three Times It Happened To Me

I've had three banks close on me overseas. Two in Panama and one in Andorra.

In each case, the bank was bought by another bank and reopened. But it took around eighteen months each time for us to get access to our funds again…

The first time was in Panama, and the bank was a subsidiary of a bank in Aruba that was owned by an American

# COWBOY MILLIONAIRE—THE NEW AMERICAN PIONEER
*Chapter VIII: Never Worry About A Bank Collapse Again*

from Texas (I think). He had some issues with the U.S. government (the SEC, if I remember correctly), and the bank in Aruba and a sister bank in the United States were taken over by U.S. authorities.

They tried to seize the assets of the Panama subsidiary, but the Panama Superintendent of Banks didn't let them. The Panama bank had nothing to do with the allegations against the guy or the bank in Aruba.

Eventually, that bank was bought by someone, and we got one hundred percent of our money back.

The third time was in Panama as well… and was the new bank that bought the bank above. I didn't move the bank account when the bank reopened the first time because I thought lightning wasn't likely to strike again… but it did.

This time it was because the bank was accused of being complicit in a money laundering operation by the family that owned the biggest duty-free shops at Panama City's international airport.

The U.S. government (concerned about money laundering) was the triggering factor in this case as well.

In fact, this case caused upheaval in Panama as the businesses involved were shut down for a while, and when the duty-free shops reopened at Tocumen International Airport, they couldn't accept credit cards. They were blocked from having a merchant account for credit card processing. They were only accepting cash.

That bank was bought by a bank from Costa Rica, but they didn't want to take on the risk from the loan portfolio, so anyone who had more than a certain amount on deposit took a twenty or twenty-five percent haircut (I was one of those).

The haircut was converted to preferred shares in the bank, and shareholders would be paid back their percentage of the loan portfolio as it was collected. So far, almost nothing of the loan portfolio has been recovered. Many of the properties are just sitting there with a trustee trying to sell them.

Of course, the trustee gets paid, so there will never be anything substantial for the account holders. The preferred shares pay out a dividend each month or quarter that will never repay the money either, based on current numbers. Still, we got eighty percent of our money back.

The second time was an Andorran bank that was, yes, you guessed it, shut down by the U.S. government after accusations of money laundering.

That bank was also eventually bought by another bank and reopened. We got one hundred percent of our money back, but they had to redo the Know Your Customer (KYC) process with every account holder, which meant Kathleen and I had to go to Andorra to meet with a banker.

We had originally opened the account with an interview at their Panama branch, which was obviously easier for us. The

**COWBOY MILLIONAIRE—THE NEW AMERICAN PIONEER**
*Chapter VIII: Never Worry About A Bank Collapse Again*

Panama branch wasn't directly affected by the accusations, like in scenario one, but was no longer part of the parent bank in Andorra.

So, we drove from Paris to Andorra. That's a beautiful drive... but ridiculously long. It took about ten hours. We did eventually move all our money out of that bank, as it just wasn't convenient or useful by that point.

What's the lesson from all that?

Bank closures happen in the States as well as overseas.

More than likely, unless you have huge sums on deposit, you'll get all or most of your money back at some point.

But it's just another reason to hedge your bets and spread your wealth around...

## Change How You Bank

At the root of the bank contagion of 2023 was a lack of diversification...

Silicon Valley Bank marketed itself as the bank of Silicon Valley. Its client base was the Silicon Valley start-up sector. It did not have a diverse client base...

When the tech sector slumped and the economic conditions changed because the Fed started to raise rates, Silicon Valley Bank was completely unprepared... (SVB was heavily invested in government bonds, which went down in value after the rate rises)...

Silvergate and Signature—the other two banks to fail—also both relied heavily on one sector: crypto in the case of Silvergate and real estate in the case of Signature...

The speed of the failures led to jitters everywhere about the state of the banking sector overall...

My message to depositors—to bank customers, like you—is the same as my message to bankers themselves...

Just as banks need a diverse range of clients, you, as a customer, need more than one bank.

It probably never occurred to many depositors who had all their money in Silicon Valley Bank that their bank could fail.

But this is why you want your money in more than one bank... preferably in more than one country.

In a crisis like this, some places and some people suffer while some places and some people gain.

In the 2008 crisis, for example, while U.S. and European banks were hit hard, the banking sector in Panama was unscathed.

Crises like this do not hit every part of the world equally...

This is why you want to be diversified.

The more accounts and jurisdictions you have your money in (within reason; whatever's convenient and doable for your lifestyle), the more likely it is that most or all of your cash will be accessible to you at any given time. No matter what happens.

**Chapter VIII: Never Worry About A Bank Collapse Again**

# Overseas Banks 101

Unfortunately, while diversification is important and necessary, it won't help you with the major problem with banks today... banks suck.

You'll hear me say this at every Live And Invest Overseas conference.

At any given time, some countries have better banking sectors than others—and some banks suck more than others.

But banks generally suck. Things have only gotten worse since the financial crisis of 2008: Banking customer service got worse and worse, and it hasn't improved. The consolidation of the banking sector globally left fewer options available in many locations...

But here's the thing: The world needs banks. Banks will always exist.

Some may be worse, some may be better... individual banks may come and go (with hell for the depositors involved). But the world's workers, employers, pensioners—all of us—can't do without banks.

Because banks suck, you may be surprised to hear me say that you should deal with more than one bank.

In fact, it's essential that you do—this is the only way to spread your risk in a sector that, as we've seen, is prone to risk.

## Offshore Banking—How To Get Started

If you haven't attempted opening an overseas bank account before, the idea can be intimidating. How? Where? Why?

And, the reality is that, simple idea as this is, opening a bank account in another country is sometimes easier said than done. Especially if you're an American, thanks to the U.S. government's requirement that foreign banks report on accounts held by U.S. persons (thanks to the 2010 FATCA law).

Jurisdiction options are many. The traditional "banking havens" are well-known: Switzerland, Austria, the Channel Islands, and the Caymans. These choices are for high-rollers with lots of cash.

A bank account in one of these places would generally be what is considered a "private" account—that is, an investment account—and would generally come with a minimum deposit requirement of as much as $1 million.

I work with a wealth management firm in Switzerland that has options from $250,000. (You can contact them here: **bit.ly/SwissWealthManagement**)

However, there are other options for where you could open your bank account...

Belize, Panama, and Uruguay are three good locations for establishing an offshore bank account that also qualifies as a private (or investment) account but for which the account minimums are much lower.

Another option would be a "local" account in a place such as the U.K. These accounts aren't typically investment accounts but operating accounts. Still, they provide a place to park cash outside your home country and (verify that this is a possibility in advance of opening the account) in different currencies. Look for banks that allow currency accounts in the major hard currencies (U.S. dollars, euros, and pound sterling) at a minimum.

For this kind of account, there is no minimum opening balance required, but I'd suggest that you'd want to keep at least $25,000 on deposit considering the ongoing fees and the time and trouble involved with opening the account in the first place.

Other jurisdictions I'd suggest today include Singapore and the Cook Islands. However, opening an account in these countries can be difficult without an introduction. Banks in these jurisdictions require personal interviews (which means long plane rides) and can come with high fees, including fees to get the account opened in the first place.

It's the fees that get most Americans riled up when considering offshore banking options. We Americans are used to free checking accounts in the United States, where the banks all clamor for business. However, those banks typically make their money on your money as well as by selling you other products... like credit cards.

Offshore banks are more conservative in their lending habits, and, unless you're using them for investment, they make their money by charging fees.

If you are moving to a particular country, you may simply open a local account and keep a minimum amount there for paying local bills.

A local account is typically attached to some local agenda, either living in the country full- or part-time, or managing a rental or business investment there... rather than purely a diversification play.

When shopping offshore banks, start by checking minimum balance requirements and fees, both ongoing and one-off fees, such as the fee charged for sending a wire. These things vary considerably.

For opening any account, you'll need documents such as an ID and residency information...

Being an American not living in the United States seems to confound many offshore banks. At a minimum, it increases the chances that the bank won't deal with you.

This is just the reality of the post-FATCA world. And it increases the importance of other aspects of your diversification strategy—like overseas residency and citizenship...

Wherever you decide to open an offshore bank account, keep it active. You might not have the possibility of opening the same account at the same bank in the future.

In the current climate, my mantra is: once you get an account open, keep it open.

Offshore banks are available in dozens of jurisdictions. Most people take the approach of trying to choose the best offshore banking jurisdiction, but the reality is that the best depends on the person and their goals. More important, you shouldn't just find one bank in one jurisdiction and call it a day.

## Forget Customer Service—Here's The Number-One Thing Your Offshore Bank Needs To Offer

The sad truth is that finding a financial institution with consistently good customer service is virtually impossible anywhere in the world.

What should you be looking for in a bank, including an offshore bank where you're considering opening an account?

First and foremost... automation.

You want a bank that lets you do as much as possible yourself.

Specifically, you want a bank that allows you to initiate wire transfers online. You also want to be able to check account balances and transfer funds among accounts (if you have more than one at the bank) online.

### COWBOY MILLIONAIRE—THE NEW AMERICAN PIONEER
*Chapter VIII: Never Worry About A Bank Collapse Again*

If you're going to have multiple accounts, entity or personal, confirm that you can have them all under the same login so you don't have to remember multiple user IDs and passwords (and so you can transfer funds directly among the accounts).

The less you have to interact with bank personnel, the better. Human beings slow things down and make mistakes.

In the good ol' days, when you opened an account with a bank, you were assigned a banker who knew you and who knew your accounts. You could contact your banker directly and get things done with some level of reliability.

Today, unless you have a big balance or are banking at a small local bank, you aren't going to have a dedicated banker. You'll have to speak with whoever answers the phone. Better to use the internet.

Another thing you should at least be aware of is correspondent banks. This is something that I admit did not occur to me at first, and I paid the price for my own ignorance. A correspondent bank is a money-center bank that smaller banks use (and need) to conduct international transactions, such as wiring money to other countries.

In small countries, Belize for example, the banks are relatively small, as well. They all have correspondent banks that make it possible for them to conduct business around the world.

It's a big deal for a bank to lose its correspondent bank. Thousands if not tens of thousands of individuals are affected. Not having a correspondent bank means, in effect, that a bank is out of business.

It's easy enough to find out which correspondent banks any offshore bank you're considering working with is depending on. Simply ask for copies of incoming wire instructions; these will list a correspondent bank if one exists.

If the bank is working with more than one correspondent bank, it should have more than one set of wire instructions… so ask to see all versions. Or, simpler, just ask your banker which correspondent banks his bank works with.

## My Basic Three-Point Advice For Banking Overseas

1. Create redundancies. For every person or entity for which you have a foreign bank account, you need a second, backup account at a different bank. Maybe that bank is in a different jurisdiction, but it doesn't have to be.
2. When you have the opportunity to open an offshore account, open it. You generally need to be

in a country to open a local account, so if or when you visit any place where you can open a foreign account, do so. At least begin the process, which may end up taking many months. Before you travel, though, make sure you know what paperwork you'll need, as you'll likely need to get it before leaving your home country.

3. Don't close any foreign account you have if you don't have to—even if you have no immediate need for it. You never know when or if you'll be able to replace it in the future.

## The Six Top Banking Havens

I still say the best first step you can take to internationalizing your life—one that I strongly recommend you make a plan to take as soon as possible, if you haven't done so already—is to open a bank account in another country.

If you've come this far in the chapter, this is probably obvious... but I'll say it anyway: Despite everything that is going on right now, it is not illegal for an American to have a bank account offshore.

It's a simple, straightforward recommendation.

If you're an American, don't let the growing compliance concerns and expanding restrictions scare you away from opening the offshore bank account you probably should have.

The downside risk is too great and growing. Whether it's the U.S. economy, the collapse of the dollar, another U.S. banking crisis, a pandemic, or some other right-now-may-be-unnamable calamity, you need to diversify. It is the only way to take control of your future and to protect yourself and your family long term.

Global banking is easier than it's ever been. It's getting the bank account open in the first place that continues to grow more difficult, but it is doable.

Let's explore the best jurisdictions where you can open a bank account right now.

## Show And Tell, Not Hide And Seek

Americans with bank accounts offshore end up with reporting requirements. At a minimum, you have to indicate on Schedule B of your Form 1040 that you have an account offshore.

If you have more than $10,000 in aggregate in financial accounts offshore, you'll also have to complete the For-

> eign Bank Account Report (FBAR).
>
> If you live in the United States and have more than $50,000 ($100,000 if you file a joint return) in foreign financial assets (which includes bank accounts), then you'll also have to complete Form 8938.
>
> See the next chapter for more details.

## Panama

Banking options are great in Panama, with more than fifty banks operating here.

Panama has three types of banking licenses: general, international, and representative office. Simply put, a general banking license allows the bank to operate locally; an international license is for banks that offer private banking options for investment accounts; and a representative office license allows a bank not in Panama to solicit business from inside Panama.

Most Panama banks won't open a consumer account for you unless you have a connection to Panama, either through residency or because you own real estate in the country.

However, if what you're looking for is an operating account for your offshore financial activities, Proven Bank, based in St. Lucia has a representative office where you can open an account in St. Lucia from Panama. They offer day-to-day consumer banking options.

Private banking accounts are easier to open but require high minimum balances, ranging from $25,000 to $1 million at the high end.

You can also open a corporate account if you open a Panamanian corporation. Investment opportunities in Panama are mostly related to real estate—rental investments, timber, land banking, and development.

To open a bank account in Panama, you've historically been required to show up at the bank for an in-person interview. It's a key part of their know-your-client and anti-money laundering processes.

Panama banks have become more stringent about who they do business with since the U.S. FACTA laws came into place, and the U.S. Treasury has turned its attention to money laundering.

Using Panama as a base for incorporating your business can make sense, as the country doesn't tax entities that aren't operating in Panama. You can set up a business in Panama and have an office in the country and still pay no Panama taxes if all your income is derived from outside Panama or if your business qualifies under the rules of one of the incentive areas of Panama Pacífico or the City of Knowledge.

Panama is Central America's preeminent banking desti-

## COWBOY MILLIONAIRE—THE NEW AMERICAN PIONEER
*Chapter VIII: Never Worry About A Bank Collapse Again*

nation. Its thriving banking sector has fueled the growth of the country's economy and attracted dozens of international banks from around the globe.

Why Panama, you ask?

For starters, the country boasts strong regulatory oversight that maintains the stability of the banking system, and banks tend to stay afloat during periods of economic turmoil.

Favorable tax incentives and high certificate of deposit (CD) rates draw in a constant flow of cash from foreign individuals and entities. On top of that, there are several laws in place that help ensure the privacy of clients.

Together, these factors contribute to Panama's appeal as an offshore banking haven.

While Panama has many banks, on any given day, some are better than others for customer service. I've had bank accounts with at least six banks in Panama over the years, and the customer service levels vary by bank, branch, and day of the week. When you want something from them, the process can be maddening. When they have a product they really want you to use, somehow things are much easier.

All that said, here are some options to try for what I would call a 'local' bank account in Panama...one for paying local bills and holding small amounts of cash.

Citi bank, a subset of Citigroup Inc., is one of the largest banks in the world, with more than two thousand five hundred branches across ninety-eight different countries, spanning Africa, Asia, Europe, and the Americas—including a few branches in Panama City. Citi is listed as a general license bank on Panama's bank superintendent website.

There are a couple different ways to open an offshore Citi account in Panama. If you're a legal resident of Panama, you can open an account by showing up to a branch in person and presenting your residency certificate, evidence of income (e.g., a pay stub or bank statement), and a banking reference letter from another local or foreign bank.

If you are not a resident of Panama, you can open a Citi account there by linking a preexisting account from your country of origin—which must be active for at least twelve months prior. Then you can show up at a Panamanian branch with your passport, a bank reference letter from the Citi branch that you have an account with, and evidence of income.

Regardless of whether or not you are a legal resident, the minimum balance for a savings account is $500, and the minimum amount for a CD is $10,000.

## General Bank Requirements

Speak with a representative prior to making any appointments to open accounts in order to confirm which documents you must bring.

It's also a good idea (and sometimes required) to notarize all copies of your official documents.

Typically, the following documents will be required at any bank:

- **Proof of address.** A valid driver's license, a property tax receipt, posted mail with your legal name, a lease agreement, an insurance card, and/or a utility bill.
- **Bank reference letter.** A letter written and signed by a representative of a bank with which you have an account. This letter confirms that you are a client, how long you have been a client, and that the banking relationship has been satisfactory (i.e., no defaults). Note that the letter must be addressed to the bank you're trying to open an account with. Most banks won't accept a 'to whom it may concern' salutation.
- **Proof of income or earnings.** A pay stub, bank statements (personal and business), a copy of last year's federal tax return, and/or wages and tax statements (W-2 and/or 1099).

> - **Character reference letter.** A recommendation provided by someone who knows you on a personal basis and can attest to your character and abilities. A local attorney is the best option and should be simple if you're buying property or setting up a company.

Banistmo is a Colombian bank with a general license. It's the third-largest bank operating in Panama.

You can open an account remotely by filling out an application and sending it via mail, by visiting a branch, or by contacting them to schedule a meeting via Zoom.

I recommend that you visit a branch in person to open an account, as this reduces the likelihood that documents get lost and may expedite the process of approval. Fortunately, there are many branches across the country.

You must present several documents to open an account—a valid passport, a second valid original identity document with a photo (e.g., work permit or driver's license), and proof of income (e.g., bank statement, commercial reference, letter from employer).

You must also satisfy one of the following extra conditions in order to qualify:

- Provide a bank reference letter from a bank in the Bancolombia Group;
- Provide a reference letter from a local Panamanian bank (with six months or more as a client);
- Have a blood-related family member in Panama who is a client of Banistmo;
- Have ties to the country of Panama (Panamanian spouse, commercial activity in Panama, own real estate in Panama);
- Have a loan processing with Banistmo;
- Provide a certification from a lawyer confirming your immigration to Panama;
- And/or provide a valid Panamanian work permit.

The required minimum balance for both savings accounts and CDs is $5,000.

Banistmo has branches in many of the main cities in Panama.

Scotiabank in Panama only has branches in Panama City and David, but tends to have more English-speaking staff than other banks in Panama. Although their parent company is the Canadian bank, having an account in Canada or another country with Scotiabank doesn't carry any weight when opening an account in Panama.

However, having the parent company that it does, offers

a comfort level to what is otherwise a relatively small bank by assets.

In fact, many of the general license banks in Panama are small compared to U.S. banks. The biggest banks in Panama don't compare in size to most regional banks in the U.S.

If you're planning on living in Panama outside the capital, then you'll want a bank that has branches in the town you're living in, so your choices will be more limited.

The bank with the most branches across Panama is Banco Nacional, one of the two national banks in Panama (the other being Caja de Ahorros).

The issue with Banco Nacional has been that it is one of the most difficult banks for North Americans to open a bank account with according to years of anecdotal stories by expats.

Europeans seemingly have an easier time, which may indicate that Banco Nacional wants to avoid any money laundering concerns from the U.S. Treasury Department.

Global Bank has branches across the country and is considered one of the better options in Panama by many. They also have many ATMs throughout the country, which is another consideration to help you avoid bank fees if you're going to be withdrawing cash from your Panama bank account.

Unfortunately, the vetting process for U.S. citizens is rigorous at Global Bank. First, you need to have ties to Panama—you must be applying for a residency visa, working, or have investments in Panama (e.g., real estate) to even be considered for a bank account.

In addition, besides all of the standard documentation required by all banks, you may be asked for your professional history and documentation about your source of income.

You will also need two personal reference letters—one from someone in your country of origin and one from a person known in Panama.

Furthermore, you will need one letter from an attorney in Panama attesting that due diligence has been made in accordance with the law, and one letter from a certified public accountant who verifies your sources of income.

UniBank is a small Panamanian general license bank with only two branches located in Panama City. However, UniBank does not have particularly strict requirements for opening an account as a U.S. citizen. They do have higher minimum balance requirements, though.

## Uruguay

Uruguay's banking system is sound. It offers attractive interest rates, and it's not hard to open an account here.

This South American country is a good offshore destination for many reasons, but banking is probably the number-one diversification opportunity here for foreigners.

Uruguay is also a good destination for currency diversification, especially because you can hold different currencies in its banking system and even move freely among accounts.

Although Uruguay has an open financial system, you have to find the right fit… especially if you're an American.

Uruguay has signed tax information exchange agreements with several countries, including Canada, Denmark, Ecuador, Faroe Islands, Finland, France, Germany, Greenland, Hungary, Iceland, Liechtenstein, Malta, Mexico, Norway, Portugal, Republic of Korea, Spain, Sweden, Switzerland, and, as of 2023, the United States.

Thanks to the long arm of the U.S. Treasury service, some Uruguayan banks are not interested in dealing with Americans. They don't want attention from the U.S. government or the potential associated liability.

Ironically, over a third of all bank deposits in Uruguay are held by non-residents. Traditionally, many of these deposits come from Argentina and Brazil, but, more and more, in the current climate, people from many other countries are also looking to Uruguay as a good alternative to more traditionally recognized international banking jurisdictions.

The country is quiet, peaceful, and, very important in this context, off the radar of most of the world.

If your goal is banking diversification, Uruguay is an excellent option. It's far more straightforward to open a bank account, even as an American, than it is in many places in the world in the current climate today, and the accounts offered are flexible and useful.

Deposits in Uruguay can be held in the local currency or in a number of foreign currencies, including the U.S. dollar, the euro, and the Brazilian real, for example.

Check with the bank before you open an account to make sure you can hold the currency(ies) you'd like there. What's even better, you can move money among those accounts by virtue of a simple, free transfer.

Despite what many are saying, banks in Uruguay do currently open accounts for non-residents. The caveat, as noted above, is that some banks won't open accounts for U.S. citizens. But some will. You have to find the right bank, given your circumstances.

Your choices aren't as wide as in Panama or Singapore, as Uruguay grants banking licenses rarely and has chosen to focus on a limited number of solid, well-established banks. Nevertheless, you do have choices.

Banks operating today in Uruguay include:

- Banco de la República Oriental del Uruguay (BROU, or Banco República), the largest bank in the country (government-owned)

**COWBOY MILLIONAIRE—THE NEW AMERICAN PIONEER**
*Chapter VIII: Never Worry About A Bank Collapse Again*

- Banco Itaú (Brazil's largest bank)
- Scotiabank
- Santander (Spanish)
- BBVA (Spanish)
- HSBC (British)
- Banque Heritage (Swiss)
- Citibank (American)
- Banco de la Nación Argentina (Argentinian)
- Bandes (local)
- Banco Hipotecario del Uruguay

Banco de la República Oriental del Uruguay (BROU) and Itaú will currently open accounts for non-residents of any nationality easily (including U.S. citizens).

At BROU, you can open an account with as little as $500 and pay no fees if the balance is maintained at that amount or more. Itaú requires a deposit of $750 to open a savings account and $2,500 to open a checking account.

For more personalized services, investments, and English-speaking staff, the foreign banks are recommended. BROU is recommended for more basic functions (savings accounts).

If you only need an account to receive your income in Uruguay for legal residency application purposes, BROU is a practical choice, as it has the lowest minimum deposit requirement.

**COWBOY MILLIONAIRE—THE NEW AMERICAN PIONEER**
*Chapter VIII: Never Worry About A Bank Collapse Again*

The required documents to open an account in Uruguay are:

- Your passport;
- A second ID (a driver's license, for example);
- Proof of address: any utility bill from your home country (or country of residency), not more than thirty days old;
- A bank reference letter;
- Proof of income. This can be a Social Security document, a CPA letter stating your monthly income, proof of rental income, tax returns, etc.

In addition, a Uruguay bank will require a brief personal visit, during which you will sign the relevant forms. It will also ask for an estimate of the funds that will be coming into the account, along with an explanation of their origin.

If you choose to open an account at BROU, bear in mind that the "proof of income" document has to be previously "legalized" (stamped) at the Uruguayan consulate in your home country. Then it must be translated into Spanish by a certified translator in Uruguay.

If you have applied or will be applying for residency in Uruguay, then the "proof of income" documents that you use for the residency application will work for the BROU bank account application process as well, as they will have been legalized and translated for the residency filing.

**COWBOY MILLIONAIRE—THE NEW AMERICAN PIONEER**
*Chapter VIII: Never Worry About A Bank Collapse Again*

# Liechtenstein

The German-speaking Principality of Liechtenstein is considered one of the biggest banking hubs in the world. It's located in the heart of Europe, between Switzerland and Austria.

It was born in a time when Central Europe was one big mix of small states ruled by the Holy Roman Empire. (The large countries of today didn't exist yet.) In reality, it was run by local wealthy families.

The Counts of Hohenems were one of those families. They found themselves in a less than desirable financial situation at the end of the eighteenth century, leading to them selling the Lordship of Schellenberg and the Country of Vaduz to the House of Liechtenstein (the name of their home castle just outside Vienna). They brought the two pieces of land together and created the Principality of Liechtenstein.

The Principality of Liechtenstein today is a sovereign and politically stable country. The state's capital is Vaduz, and the population of the whole country is less than thirty-seven thousand.

Liechtenstein is one of the few countries in the world with more registered companies and jobs than citizens. The country has been internationally recognized as a financial center for decades, especially with regard to the formation of foundations. Additionally, Liechtenstein has diversified as a financial center by offering alternative investment funds.

The United States established diplomatic relations with Liechtenstein in 1997. Both have signed a mutual legal assistance treaty, focused largely on jointly combating money laundering and other illegal banking activities, a tax information exchange agreement, and an agreement to implement the provisions of FATCA.

There are twelve licensed banks currently operating in Liechtenstein. The banks primarily focus on private banking and wealth management. To give you an idea of how well-oiled the banking system is in Liechtenstein, the assets under the management of Liechtenstein banks amount to over $395 billion.

Liechtenstein would not exactly be the place to go to open a personal bank account to pay your day-to-day expenses. The reasons that non-residents and foreign companies come here are wealth management and private banking.

Liechtenstein-based entities are great for wealth structuring or tax purposes. It makes sense to consider Liechtenstein if you're after wealth management, asset protection, or multi-generational wealth planning. Banks here are familiar with all types of international structures, and foreign companies can open accounts here too.

What makes banking in Liechtenstein so attractive? Banks are considered safe and super conservative. The government of Liechtenstein is fiscally responsible, like many other small principalities.

During the financial crisis, Liechtenstein's banks did just fine. One of the reasons for that is the way that banks in Liechtenstein make money; they generate revenue by charging fees, not by making risky investments.

Paying one percent of your total deposit is not uncommon, even if fees here are on par with those of other wealth management hubs. Clients include royal families, large holding companies, and the crème de la crème of the world, so quality and service here are unmatched. Liechtenstein bankers are a different breed.

Minimums at Liechtenstein banks are higher than in other places. They'd not normally accept a client who deposits less than 100,000 Swiss francs, and you have to keep that amount in your account to keep it open.

Liechtenstein banks will accept non-resident clients when they have enough money to deposit. Many banks will also expect you to invest a certain amount of money in the bank's investment products, depending on the amount that was initially deposited and which other bank services you use.

Before applying for an account in Liechtenstein, think carefully about which bank is best for you. Not all of them provide services to non-residents. Also bear in mind that deposit requirements, fees, and perks can vary drastically from bank to bank.

# COWBOY MILLIONAIRE—THE NEW AMERICAN PIONEER
*Chapter VIII: Never Worry About A Bank Collapse Again*

To choose the best bank in Liechtenstein for you, ask yourself first: What are you looking to do, and how much money do you have?

If you're a non-resident with 100,000 Swiss francs to deposit, you're going to look for banks that have a history of accepting clients with lower deposits. If you're able to deposit 1 million francs, you'll have a wider range of options to choose from.

LGT Bank, originally known as the Liechtenstein Global Trust Bank, is the largest of the banks in Liechtenstein, holding a market share of around forty-six percent.

It was founded in 1920 and currently operates in over twenty countries. The bank is owned and operated by the Princely House of Liechtenstein and is known for providing highly specialized private banking and asset management services. It is headquartered in Vaduz.

Liechtensteinische Landesbank AG (LLB) was founded in 1861 and is one of the oldest and largest financial institutions in the Principality of Liechtenstein. Although LLB was privatized in 1993, the state of Liechtenstein remains its largest shareholder.

LLB is the second-largest bank in Liechtenstein and offers a wide range of services to its customers. These include retail banking, corporate banking, investment management, and private banking. Headquartered in Vaduz, LLB holds a market share of around twenty-two percent.

## COWBOY MILLIONAIRE—THE NEW AMERICAN PIONEER
*Chapter VIII: Never Worry About A Bank Collapse Again*

VP Bank is the third largest of the banks in Liechtenstein by assets. Founded in 1956, VP Bank provides private banking services, specialized asset management, and specialized investment advisory services.

The bank owns and operates a subsidiary known as Centrum Bank, which provides a wide range of standard commercial banking services. VP Bank holds a market share of around seventeen percent and is one of the fastest growing banks in Liechtenstein. It is headquartered in Vaduz.

Valartis Bank was set up in 1998 and is the fourth-largest bank by assets in Liechtenstein. Valartis Bank offers specialized private banking services, which include asset management services, to its wealthy customers.

The bank also operates as a standard investment bank, and its investment advisory team is one of the best in Liechtenstein, offering investment in financial instruments across the world. Valartis Bank Liechtenstein is headquartered in Gamprin-Bendern and holds a market share of around two-and-a-half percent.

Banque Havilland Liechtenstein was created in 2014 when Banque Havilland acquired Banque Pasche Liechtenstein.

It is the fifth-largest bank in Liechtenstein by assets and holds a market share of around two-and-a-half percent. Banque Havilland Liechtenstein specializes in providing private banking services to its customers. The bank is headquartered in Vaduz.

Bank Frick Liechtenstein was founded in 1998 and is a family-run private bank. Bank Frick offers private banking services such as specialized asset management, investment advisory services, and estate management.

In addition, the bank develops and manages real estate investments in Germany, Switzerland, the U.K., and Liechtenstein. It is the sixth largest bank in Liechtenstein by assets and holds a market share of just under two-and-a-half percent. The bank is headquartered in Balzers.

NEUE Bank is a private bank founded in 1992. The bank offers private banking services such as asset management, investment advisory services, and estate management services to its wealthy clients.

Unlike the majority of private banks in Liechtenstein, NEUE Bank operates like a classic private bank—it does not offer any investment products. It is the seventh-largest bank by assets in Liechtenstein and holds a market share of under two percent. The bank is headquartered in Vaduz.

Volksbank is an Austrian bank that set up operations as one of the banks in Liechtenstein in 1997. Volksbank Liechtenstein started as a private bank but has since grown into a fully fledged commercial bank offering services such as retail banking, mortgages, and business financing.

However, it still offers a wide range of private banking services to its wealthy customers. Volksbank Liechtenstein is the eighth largest bank in Liechtenstein by assets and holds a market share of around one percent. Volksbank Liechtenstein is headquartered in Schaan.

Kaiser Partner is a private bank that was originally set up in 1931. Kaiser Partner offers a wide range of private banking and asset management related services.

As an investment bank, Kaiser Partner has earned a reputation for its responsible and sustainable investment practices over the years. It is the ninth largest bank in Liechtenstein by assets and holds a market share of under one percent. The bank is headquartered in Vaduz.

Raiffeisen Privatbank offers private banking related services to its customers, providing them with highly personalized services. These services include traditional asset management, investment advisory services, and estate management.

Along with its partnerships with other investment banks around the world, Raiffeisen Privatbank is the tenth largest bank in Liechtenstein by assets and holds a market share of around half a percent. It's part of the Austrian Raiffeisen Banking Group and is headquartered in Vaduz.

## Singapore

Singapore has close to two hundred banks, including representative offices. The overall banking sector's assets were recently valued at more than $2 trillion. I suggest your focus should be on the three largest locally incorporated "full banks," as they are able to offer the widest range of services allowed under Singapore's Banking Act.

United Overseas Bank (UOB) was founded in Singapore in 1935 as the United Chinese Bank. The bank grew steadily through a series of acquisitions, and, in 1965, it changed its name to UOB. It owns the Far Eastern Bank in Singapore, along with other major banking subsidiaries in Malaysia, Thailand, Indonesia, and China.

The UOB group has more than five hundred offices in nineteen countries, including branch offices in New York, Los Angeles, Vancouver, London, and Paris. UOB offers a wide range of services, including private and investment banking, futures brokering, asset management, and brokerage services. In Singapore, UOB is a market leader in credit card products and residential home loans.

UOB offers online banking and various personal banking and wealth banking instruments. It also offers private banking services if you invest at least S$5 million.

It also offers several options for investors. In addition to basic checking and savings accounts, you can invest in a range of foreign currencies, bonds, and funds. Singapore Government Securities (SGS) is an example of one type of government-issued bond brokered through UOB.

If you are comfortable with FOREX trading, you may want to look at MaxiYield accounts. These accounts are dual-currency-linked investments that can earn high yields by capitalizing on potential gains from foreign exchange movements. You can invest in a range of currencies and receive your money back in that same currency.

MaxiYield accounts work like this:

1. Choose your base currency;
2. Choose a second currency as your alternate currency;
3. Decide the tenure of your investment;
4. Agree on the preferred exchange rate—the rate with which you are comfortable exchanging your base currency for the alternate currency;
5. Accept the enhanced (or effective) yield.

A MaxiYield account is not considered a fixed deposit and is not insured. UOB requires a minimum investment of S$50,000 to open a MaxiYield account.

Fixed deposit accounts, similar to Certificates of Deposit, are available in single or multiple currencies. A minimum investment of S$20,000 is required to open a fixed deposit account.

Yields on Singapore dollar accounts are relatively low. Although high rates can be quoted, those rates require you to direct deposit your salary, buy insurance products from the bank, and make investments through the bank. Take a close look at the fine print before deciding to open an account with any bank just for the advertised interest rates on a savings account.

Foreign currency fixed deposit accounts are available in nine global currencies: the U.S. dollar, Australian dollar, Canadian dollar, British pound, euro, New Zealand dollar, Swiss franc, Japanese yen, and Hong Kong dollar. A minimum deposit of S$50,000 is required to open a foreign currency fixed deposit account.

UOB's Wealth Premium Account is an interest-bearing combined checking and savings account that requires a minimum investment of S$100,000.

Benefits include an ATM card, online banking, free checks, and overdraft protection. It is possible to open an account remotely with UOB by applying in person at one of their global branches.

You'll need to bring a letter of reference from your current financial institution or a letter of introduction from an individual who is currently a UOB banking client.

You will also need to bring your passport and proof of residence. The final approval of the account will be at the discretion of UOB. Also note that you can hold gold at UOB. They sell physical gold as well as gold and silver accounts.

Oversea-Chinese Banking Corporation, or OCBC, is another of Singapore's "local" mega-banks. It's been around since 1932, making it Singapore's longest established bank. Assets today exceed S$521 billion.

OCBC has more than five hundred branches worldwide, including in Brunei, Indonesia, Malaysia, Philippines, China, Vietnam, Thailand, Hong Kong, Taiwan, Japan, South Korea, Australia, Dubai, the U.K., and the United States.

OCBC offers consumer, corporate, investment, and private banking, asset management, brokerage services, and insurance. You can open a Premium Banking account with OCBC with a minimum deposit of S$200,000.

Premium Banking benefits include preferential interest rates on a variety of interest-bearing accounts.

Foreign-currency fixed deposit accounts are available with a minimum initial investment of S$30,000. Foreign currencies available for fixed deposits include the U.S. dollar, Australian dollar, Canadian dollar, Chinese yuan (offshore), euro, New Zealand dollar, Hong Kong dollar, British pound, Japanese yen, and the Swiss franc.

As with the other major banks in Singapore, OCBC has dual currency accounts that offer potentially higher yields in exchange for assuming the higher risks of currency fluctuation.

OCBC has an investment called a structured deposit

(SD), which you can access with a minimum investment of S$5,000. The SD is a combination of a traditional deposit and an investment product, with a higher rate of return than normal deposits.

The return is dependent on the performance of the underlying financial instrument (an equity or foreign exchange, usually) and the length of time that you hold the investment. If you hold your investment to maturity, the full principal amount of your investment is guaranteed.

OCBC does not sell or hold physical gold. OCBC Premier clients have their choice of several investment instruments, including equity-linked convertible investments, reverse equity-linked convertible investments, unit trusts, and brokerage services, as well as traditional savings accounts.

There is no need to travel to Singapore to open an account with OCBC. Just go to any of their global offices with your valid passport and current bank statements.

The Development Bank of Singapore Limited (DBS) is headquartered and listed in Singapore. It is one of Asia's leading banks, with over two hundred branches in fifty cities.

Established in 1968, DBS commands a large presence in Singapore. It is a major financial institution that offers a full range of investment products.

Its primary operations are in Singapore and Hong Kong, with branches in China, Taiwan, India, Vietnam, Japan, Korea,

Indonesia, Dubai, Bahrain, and elsewhere in Asia and the Middle East. There are DBS branches in Los Angeles and London, as well.

Like UOB, DBS offers specialized services for foreign investors. Some investment plans, such as their foreign currency fixed deposit accounts, have initial minimum deposit requirements of only S$5,000.

Those with investable assets of at least S$200,000 can participate in the DBS Treasures program. There are no fees associated with this account as long as you maintain a total balance, including deposits and investments, of at least this amount; otherwise, a monthly charge of S$50 will apply.

Other services, like the DBS Private Client investment products, are tailored for those with S$1.5 million of investable assets. Access to the entire range of DBS products comes to those with investable assets of at least S$5 million through DBS Private Bank.

Foreign currency fixed deposit accounts are available in ten currencies: the U.S. dollar, Canadian dollar, New Zealand dollar, Singapore dollar, euro, Swiss franc, British pound, Hong Kong dollar, Japanese yen, and Chinese renminbi.

DBS's Currency-Linked Investment (CLI) is very similar to UOB's MaxiYield account. It's a way to earn potentially higher yields through your choice of a base currency and a secondary currency, based on the fluctuations of the currency market.

## COWBOY MILLIONAIRE—THE NEW AMERICAN PIONEER
*Chapter VIII: Never Worry About A Bank Collapse Again*

DBS requires a minimum investment of S$50,000 for a CLI. DBS recommends this type of investment for those who are familiar with currency trading, prefer short-term investments, and are willing to take higher risks for potentially higher rates of return.

You can purchase bonds and funds through DBS that offer potentially higher rates of return than basic interest-bearing accounts or foreign currency accounts.

Singapore Government Securities (SGS) are also brokered through DBS. DBS's Private Client and Private Bank have similar product offerings but may offer slightly higher yields.

Private Client customers are eligible for a wider range of investment products, such as the opportunity to purchase hedge funds and systematic macro funds, which have less exposure to market fluctuations than many traditional mutual funds. Private Client customers are also eligible for credit cards, debit cards, checking accounts, and mortgage financing.

DBS offers checking and savings accounts, safety deposit boxes, loans, and wire transfers. They have a user-friendly online banking website called iBanking.

You can open an account with DBS from overseas by going to one of their global branches, bringing your passport and completed application with you. DBS does not sell or hold physical gold for its clients.

## The Next Evolution Of Banking

Online banks have gone mainstream.

As the name suggests, they operate fully online, meaning that they do not have any physical branches. They offer many of the same services as traditional banks, and in some cases, a few services that the traditional ones don't.

Some people are uncomfortable with online banks because they view them as unsafe or too complicated, or they just simply find comfort in their bank's physical presence.

But change is sure to come.

They can be a big asset to an international lifestyle. For example, the Revolut banking app lets you hold multiple currencies in different digital "pockets" in the same account.

And when you use your card, it automatically uses the currency of the country you're in (assuming you have that currency in your account).

You can also track FX rates and automatically buy and sell different currencies when the rate is favorable, right from your phone. The exchange rates are excellent, too.

## Shopping For The Best Online Bank

Top so-called "neobanks" (where banking services are provided only through an app) and online bank offerings in different jurisdictions include:

- Ally Bank
- Axos Bank
- CapitalOne 360
- Chime
- Discover Bank
- EverBank
- N26
- Quontic
- Revolut
- Vio Bank

Not all services, of course, are available in all jurisdictions, so check your jurisdiction and the available services and make your decision from there...

## What To Look For In Your Online Bank

The best online bank will depend on your financial

needs and banking goals.

Do you want to earn more interest on your savings? Look for an online bank that pays higher annual percentage yields (APYs).

Do you want to replace your current bank? Consider the overall package—fees and minimum requirements, low, high-yield savings accounts, ATM accessibility, multiple banking products, a great mobile app experience, and excellent customer service.

Here is a list of things to look for when shopping for an online bank:

- **Fees.** Look for an online bank that keeps fees to a minimum, including monthly, overdraft, and ATM fees.
- **APYs.** I love an online bank with a high APY. As a result of not having to deal with infrastructure and overhead costs, online banks tend to offer higher yields on savings accounts.
- **ATM network.** Many online banks offer access to extensive networks of ATMs.
- **Multiple banking products.** Online banks are offering a wide variety of options for banking products and services and are not limit-

ed to just savings accounts. Some are even expanding their offerings to include checking and money market accounts, CDs, credit cards, currency transactions, loans, and other types of financial services, such as investments (including crypto).

- **Digital user experience.** Your main interaction with online banks will be via the bank's website or mobile app. Check out the reviews on the App Store and Google Play to help you determine which one's the best for your banking needs.
- **Customer service.** As online banks generally don't have a physical location, their customer service support is essential to keeping their clientele happy. Look for those who offer easy access to customer service representatives or great online chat alternatives.
- **Safety first.** Look for online banks that are backed by the Federal Deposit Insurance Corporation (FDIC), or the equivalent in other countries.

### CHAPTER IX

# Beat The Bureaucrats... Wipe Out Your Tax Bill

What do the world's only superpower, the United States, and a tiny African backwater, Eritrea, have in common?

America and Eritrea are the only two countries in the world that tax citizens on their worldwide income, no matter where they live. Other countries tax their citizens only if they live or earn money in the country.

Americans living abroad have no congressmen or senators representing their interests. Back in 1764, I think we referred to this as taxation without representation...

There are plenty of advantages to living (and investing) overseas when it comes to your U.S. taxes.

But not having to file every year is not one of them...

Simply moving outside the United States does not remove your obligation to pay U.S. taxes.

U.S. citizens must file a return with the IRS every year, regardless of where in the world they reside.

**COWBOY MILLIONAIRE—THE NEW AMERICAN PIONEER**
*Chapter IX: Beat The Bureaucrats... Wipe Out Your Tax Bill*

# Three Ways To Cut Your U.S. Tax Bill Overseas

However, living overseas can substantially reduce or even eliminate your U.S. tax bill.

There are three main tax advantages available to Americans overseas...

## 1. Foreign Earned Income Exclusion (FEIE)

This is one of the most well-known and most commonly used expat tax advantages.

With the FEIE, you can exclude up to $126,500 of your income from U.S. taxation (the amount increases every year... thank you, inflation).

The income must be earned outside the United States (from employment or self-employment—passive income doesn't count), and your tax home must be outside the States too.

What does it mean that your "tax home" is outside the States?

You need to meet either the "physical presence test" or the "bona fide residence test."

To meet the "physical presence test," you must be physically outside the States for at least three hundred thirty days in a twelve-month period.

To satisfy the "bona fide residence test," you must reside in a foreign country for an entire tax year—January 1 to December 31. This does not mean you can't visit the States, however.

In addition to the FEIE, there's a related exclusion...

## 2. Foreign Housing Exclusion (FHE)

If you're a U.S. expat earning overseas, the Foreign Housing Exclusion (FHE) allows you to exclude thousands in foreign housing expenses from your U.S. taxes.

For the 2024 tax year, the standard housing exclusion is $17,710. However, you could exclude a much larger amount, depending on where you live.

The IRS issues an annual notice identifying countries and locations within those countries where housing costs are high relative to those in the States, allowing for a larger exclusion.

The FHE can include rent, housing provided in kind by an employer, utilities, insurance, occupancy taxes, household repairs, residential parking, and more.

## 3. Foreign Tax Credit (FTC)

This third common expat tax advantage could be the most powerful.

With the Foreign Tax Credit, you receive a U.S. tax credit

for every dollar you pay in tax to a foreign government.

The Foreign Tax Credit may suit people who don't qualify for the FEIE, or Americans who are tax resident in countries with a higher tax rate than the States.

If you pay more abroad than you would have in the States, you can carry the excess taxes paid as a credit for ten years.

One big advantage of the FTC is that it can apply to so-called unearned income, such as dividends, interest, and royalties.

Exactly how you employ the strategies I've mentioned will depend on your particular circumstances. The best use of the rules for one person may not be the best use for another.

But here's the key point: The amount of tax you owe often depends entirely on your knowledge of IRS rules and how to use them to your advantage.

Depending on which strategy you employ, you could fill out your tax return in completely different ways—each entirely legal, but each resulting in a different amount owed to the taxman.

This is why I always recommend you employ a professional when filing your annual return, unless you are one yourself.

And keep in mind that as an American abroad, you need someone well-versed and experienced in expat tax affairs, not just any CPA.

Find yourself an expat tax expert—and take their advice.

**COWBOY MILLIONAIRE—THE NEW AMERICAN PIONEER**
*Chapter IX: Beat The Bureaucrats... Wipe Out Your Tax Bill*

The tax guy I work with is Vincenzo Villamena. You can contact him here: **bit.ly/VincenzoVillamena.**

## How I Doubled My Tax Refund

This won't come as news to you...

The IRS tax code is one of the densest, most complex, most labyrinthine, most incomprehensible sets of rules known to man.

And you have to make sure that every one and zero is in the right place, or the IRS could come down on you like a ton of bricks.

You do not want to be audited... and be found wanting.

And it is a simple fact that the more money you make, the more likely you are to face an audit.

As you get richer, the IRS becomes more and more likely to train its eyes on you.

Net worth is a much better indicator of whether you'll face an audit than living overseas or doing business offshore.

If you are an American, there is simply no way to escape the IRS. No matter where you live in the world, U.S. citizens are required to file U.S. tax returns every year.

But here's the thing: The IRS is big, bad, and scary... but you don't have to be afraid of the IRS.

I don't mind telling you: My tax affairs are complex. I've obtained multiple overseas residencies, I own property in several different countries, and I run a successful business incorporated outside the United States.

I could be an IRS target...

I may get audited, but I'm not scared of it.

I know how to speak to the IRS. In fact, I was an Enrolled Agent for a brief period.

An Enrolled Agent isn't an IRS auditor, but someone who passes a test given by the IRS that allows them to represent taxpayers in Tax Court. CPAs and attorneys are allowed as well.

So, I know how to talk to the IRS... especially about my personal taxes.

Here's a story I like to tell. One year, I knew I was due a substantial refund. But the IRS assessed that I in fact owed a substantial bill. My accountant at the time (an idiot) suggested that I should just pay the bill to make the dispute go away.

That's not my style. I relish this stuff.

I filed my return, which showed that a substantial refund was due. The IRS sent me a check for half of what I'd calculated...

> What?
>
> When I phoned and eventually got a hold of the agent who'd dealt with my return, she admitted to me that she simply did not understand my calculations.
>
> So, she had cut my refund in half in the hope that I would just accept the lower amount and walk away. To avoid further conflict.
>
> But when I talked the IRS agent through my return and how I had arrived at the original amount... she had to admit that I was right.
>
> I got my full refund.
>
> My message every tax-filing season is simple: You have to know how to beat the IRS at its own game.
>
> That labyrinthine set of rules... all those different deductions and credits... and form after form after form... if you know how to play the game, it's a set of instructions for never paying a cent more than you have to.

## Comply And Conquer: Expat Taxes Made Simple

Having looked at the big benefits, let's now go through the reporting requirements for Americans offshore...

It's a level of administration that keeps some Americans

from diversifying offshore... and pushes others living overseas to give up their U.S. citizenship simply because they don't want to deal with the paperwork of being an American any more.

The only way to escape the requirement to at least file with Uncle Sam is to relinquish U.S. citizenship... which you can only do once you've become a citizen somewhere else.

Here's what Americans living abroad or who have investments outside the United States need to pay attention to when filing their tax return.

## Foreign Bank Accounts

If you have one or more bank accounts outside the United States, the threshold for filing the Foreign Bank Account Report (FBAR) hasn't changed since it was first introduced decades ago, although the form name as well as how and when you file it have.

Officially FinCEN Form 114, the FBAR is where you list all of your offshore financial accounts and how much money you have in each. The form must be filed electronically.

Foreign Financial Accounts include bank accounts, brokerage accounts, and securities accounts. Basically, any account held with a financial institution.

If you have $10,000 or more (or the foreign currency equivalents) in one or more financial account(s) at any time during the calendar year, you have to file the form.

The "at any time" part can catch some people unawares. For example, if you open a bank account in Portugal to buy a piece of property and send $100,000 to the account for the purchase, you meet the requirements for filing the FBAR even if that money is in the account for a single day.

The threshold is an annual test. Using the same example, if you open an account in Portugal to buy a piece of property in 2024 and transfer $100,000 for the purchase, you must file the FBAR. However, if in 2025 you use the account only for paying local bills and the account never contains $10,000, you don't have to file for 2025.

The $10,000 threshold is for aggregate balances at any time during the year. One account with $10,000 in it meets the requirement, as do ten accounts containing $1,000 apiece on a single day.

The number of accounts isn't the trigger, and neither is the amount in any one account. It's the highest aggregate value on any given day.

Note that the FBAR isn't an IRS form; it's a Treasury Department form (the IRS' boss). However, the filing date for the FBAR is the same as your tax return. That means April 15, unless you file for an extension.

Those living outside the United States get an automatic

extension to file until June 15 for their tax return. However, you need to file extension form 4868 by April 15 to get a full extension to October 15.

All that said, the Treasury Department is still giving an automatic extension until October 15 to file the form for anyone who misses the April 15 deadline.

No specific request for extension is required... for the FBAR. While this could change at some point, it's been in effect since they changed the filing deadline from June 30 to April 15 for the 2016 tax filing year.

Still, file the FBAR as soon as you can just to get it done. You don't want to run the risk of forgetting about it. The penalties for not filing are draconian.

The information required for the FBAR includes the financial institution's name, address, account number, and the highest balance in the account during the year.

That information is required for all accounts that you have a financial interest in. You also have to report accounts you have signing authority for but no financial interest in, unless that account is reported by someone else on your behalf.

The signatory thing can cause problems since most people aren't aware of it. It means that, if you're an expat working for a company in another country and you have signatory authority over the company's local bank account, you have to report the account if the company isn't reporting it... which is likely the case if the company isn't a U.S. company or subsidiary.

You can save time if you have twenty-five or more offshore accounts to report. In that case, you don't have to complete the account details on the form. You just check the box indicating that you have more than twenty-five accounts.

You're still required to maintain the information that would have been included on the form had you filled it out in full, but, for some reason that no one seems to understand, if you exceed the magic number twenty-five, you don't have to provide individual account data on the FBAR.

Note that, even if you don't meet the requirements for filing the FBAR, you still have a filing requirement if you hold any bank account offshore. In that case, you must tick a box in Part III on the 1040 Schedule B Form and list the countries where you have an account. Many people don't realize this, and it is one easy way for the IRS to get you for noncompliance.

## Foreign Financial Assets

Foreign financial accounts reported on the FBAR are a subsection of total foreign financial assets.

Foreign financial assets are "any financial account maintained by a foreign financial institution" and "to the extent held for investment and not held in a financial account, any stock or securities issued by someone that is not a U.S. person, any interest in a foreign entity, and any financial instrument or contract with an issuer or counterparty that is not a U.S. person."

Form 8938 is used if you have foreign financial assets that meet the threshold. It's possible to meet the requirements for Form 8938 without meeting the requirements for the FBAR, and vice versa. You have to look at each reporting threshold individually.

If you're living in the United States, you are required to complete Form 8938 if you have foreign financial assets of more than $50,000 on the last day of the year or of more than $75,000 at any point during the year. These are the amounts for single filers. The amounts double for married couples filing joint returns.

If you live outside the United States, the threshold amounts move to $200,000 on the last day and to $300,000 during the year for singles and double that for married couples filing jointly.

(Check the limits each year before you file your return, as they may change.)

While foreign financial accounts get reported on Form 8938 even if they are reported on the FBAR, certain other assets don't have to be reported on this form if they are reported elsewhere... specifically on Form 3520 for foreign trusts, Form 5471 for foreign corporations, and a few other more obscure forms.

One thing to understand is that, even if you're not required to complete a Form 5471 for shares you hold of a U.S.-controlled foreign corporation, you still have to report the existence of those shares if you meet the overall value threshold for Form 8938.

Invest $50,001 as a minority shareholder in some private company in Canada, and you have to report it. Invest $10,001 in five different private companies outside the United States, and you have to report all five investments... and any offshore bank accounts, even if the bank account balances fall below the FBAR threshold of $10,000.

## The Three Assets You Never Have To Report

Two foreign assets specifically exempt from Form 8938 are real estate held in your own name (if the property is held in an entity, ownership of that entity must be reported on Form 8938) and precious metals.

Offshore attorneys and tax experts still debate what "held directly" means. However, besides the bullion you keep under your mattress, it's generally accepted that metals in allocated accounts (that is, metals you own,

> identified in a vault as yours) aren't reportable.
>
> Foreign currency isn't reportable either so if you have 100,000 euros stuffed in your mattress, whether that mattress is in Iowa or Portugal, you don't have to report the cash (as long as you're not traveling with it).

## Foreign Rental Property

While real estate held in your own name doesn't need to be reported on Form 8938, any income generated from property you own overseas does get reported on your tax return.

Rental income for non-U.S. real estate gets reported the same way as rental property in the United States. You put the income and expenses for the property on Schedule E on the 1040. You are able to take deductions against the income just as you would for U.S. rental property.

In addition to depreciation and other normal deductions, such as mortgage interest (note that you won't receive a 1099-B from the foreign bank for this; you'll have to ask the bank to send you a letter detailing the exact amount of interest you paid for the calendar year), utilities, and property and rental management expenses, you will also be able to deduct the cost of checking up on your rental property, i.e., the plane fare to get to the country, etc.

Depreciation, however, is amortized over forty years for foreign property rather than the twenty-seven-and-a-half years for domestic property.

Deducting the cost of checking up on your rental property can also apply to other real estate investments, including agricultural investments. If you fly down once a year to Uruguay to check on the farm you own there, that's an expense against the income from that property.

Years ago, one reader bought two lots on the coast of County Kerry in Ireland and built a house on each. She furnished both... one for herself and one to be a rental.

She hired a local rental management company to take care of the rental property. However, she visited once or twice a year to check up on her rental, staying in the other house.

She'd inspect the rental, make any repairs, and then spend a few days or weeks in her house. The cost of the flights and other direct travel expenses were deductible on her U.S. Schedule E... and on her Irish tax return for her rental income.

Yes, along with reporting your rental income on your U.S. tax return, you may likely have a tax filing obligation in the country where the rental property is located, as well.

You should seek help from a local tax expert on this, keeping in mind that the tax accounting requirements in the foreign country will probably be different than those in the United States.

For example, you probably won't be able to deduct property depreciation. Many countries don't depreciate built property for tax purposes, and no place I know of, including the United States, allows depreciation of the land value.

If no depreciation is allowed in the country where the property sits, you could end up with a tax liability and tax owed in that country on your net rental income. Meantime, on the U.S. side, you could have a tax loss thanks to the depreciation.

Depending on the net income from your rental(s), you may not have to file a local tax return (or may be required to file, but not owe any taxes).

Many countries, including the United States, have minimum thresholds for the amount of taxable income that must be earned before any tax is due. That threshold may be higher than your net rental income if you have only one rental in the country, depending on the size of the property.

For example, the tax threshold in Panama is $11,000. Net rental income below that amount isn't taxed in Panama, but you are still meant to file a tax return.

Other countries tax rental income at the gross level and sometimes as it is earned. This means that in Portugal and Colombia, for example, you pay the tax (well, your rental management company is meant to withhold the tax from the rent they collect on your behalf and pay the tax for you) when the rental income is received.

## Why You Won't Pay Tax Twice If You Live Overseas

If you're earning money in a foreign country where you're investing or doing business, taxes paid in that country on income that is also taxable in the United States are generally recoverable as a Foreign Tax Credit or a tax deduction. Taking the tax credit is almost always better. To use the tax as a deduction, you have to itemize your deductions.

So, for example, taxes paid on rental income in France can be taken as a credit on your U.S. tax return against taxes due on that same rental income.

If your France rental income ends up being a loss on your U.S. return thanks to the property depreciation, then you have two choices. You can carry the credit forward or take the deduction if you have enough total deductions to make itemizing worthwhile.

The Foreign Tax Credit also applies to taxes paid on other income. If you have interest income on your foreign savings account, any taxes (typically withholding taxes taken by the bank) can be applied to your U.S. tax return through the Foreign Tax Credit form.

The same goes for taxes on earned income… but those credits will get complicated if you're eligible for the FEIE.

The bottom line is that you aren't going to be double-taxed

on income earned in a foreign country, even if your foreign income has been earned in a country with no double-taxation treaty with the United States.

Double taxation treaties can make things simpler by determining which country gets to tax what income, but, even when one doesn't exist, you're going to be able to offset the foreign tax paid against any U.S. tax owed.

---

## Tax Treaties Versus Tax Credits

Many people believe that if the United States has no income tax treaty in place with a country, they'll pay taxes in both countries if they earn income in that country.

However, that's not the case.

A tax treaty defines which country gets to tax which income an individual or company earns that could otherwise be taxed by both countries.

A good example for individuals is pension income. Most U.S. tax treaties allow for the United States to tax Social Security payments made to recipients living in the tax treaty country.

If that person is collecting a pension from a company, then the country where the individual is residing collects tax due on the pension income.

So if Joe retires to France and is collecting both Social Security from the United States and a pension from IBM, Uncle Sam will tax the Social Security, and France will tax the pension from IBM.

Absent a tax treaty, when income is taxed in the source country and is also taxable in the States (for U.S. citizens, income is almost always taxable in the States), then any tax paid to the country of the source of the income can be taken as a tax credit on Form 1116 (or deduction on Schedule A).

Generally speaking, you should never pay more in total taxes on any income than the highest tax rate of either the source country or the United States.

## Working Tax-Free Overseas

The Foreign Earned Income Exclusion (FEIE) is meant to mitigate how the United States taxes its citizens on their worldwide income. However, sometimes you might be better off not taking the FEIE if you're earning a high salary (above the FEIE limit) in a high-tax country. You could owe less U.S. taxes if you take the Foreign Tax Credit.

You cannot claim the FEIE and the Foreign Tax Credit for

the same income. You must choose one or the other.

I was once preparing tax returns for an overseas client. He had always claimed the Foreign Earned Income Exclusion and expected to do so again...

However, when I was computing his tax return, I tried running the numbers in a few different (perfectly legal) ways.

According to my calculations, this client would pay less in taxes if he availed of the Foreign Tax Credit that year rather than the FEIE.

So, I completed the return this way and sent it on to the client for approval.

I was not prepared for the response I got...

This guy sent me a nasty email demanding I use the FEIE because that's what he'd always done...

I was committed to saving this guy money. Even if he wasn't committed to it himself.

So, I sent him different versions of his return—one using the FEIE and one using the Foreign Tax Credit—so he could see for himself what he would be saving by using the latter...

To me, it's just a reminder that even those who have been abroad for a long time and consider themselves savvy can still miss a trick.

Before not taking the FEIE, however, consider your long-term plans. Once you start taking the FEIE, you have to continue to take it unless you revoke your usage.

The problem with revoking your usage is that you won't be able to take the FEIE again for five years. So you want to evaluate your potential long-term situation before deciding how to handle the FEIE...

For most people, it's a straightforward decision, as the FEIE is the biggest tax benefit you have as an American working and earning income overseas... if you qualify.

To qualify for the Foreign Earned Income Exclusion, you must pass one of two tests: the physical presence test or the bona fide resident test.

In some cases, such as a temporary (one-year) assignment overseas, you will have to qualify under the physical presence test even if you can prove compliance with the bona fide resident test.

The physical presence test is fairly black-and-white. To qualify for the FEIE this way, you have to be in a foreign country for three hundred thirty days in a twelve-month period.

The wording of the rule is such that it's not days outside the United States but days in a foreign country. This seemingly small twist can create a problem for people working in maritime industries (days in international waters aren't days in a foreign country), and for all those people living on the lifestyle cruise ships that travel the world from port to port (although those people probably aren't working).

For ordinary people, it means a day traveling through the

States to go from Latin America to Europe can be two days not in a foreign country, as a day is counted from midnight to midnight.

Nevertheless, even given the tight definition of days in a foreign country, it should be fairly straightforward to determine whether you pass this test or not. If you do, then you qualify for the FEIE.

The second test, the bona fide residency, isn't as black and white. Holding a residency permit for another country is only the starting point for qualifying for the FEIE under this test. You must meet other criteria.

One that helps a lot is being liable for taxes in your country of residency. Most everyone who is living full-time in another country should fall into that category.

Your housing situation can also help solidify your bona fide residency status, i.e., by not maintaining a residence in the United States, and/or by investing in a home in the foreign country, it will help show you are truly a resident overseas.

It's not that keeping a house in the United States will disqualify you from the FEIE, but if other factors don't clearly show where you are living, then you might be disqualified.

Having kids who go to school in the country, owning a car, having a local driver's license, being a member of local organizations... all these kinds of things help toward creating a bona fide residency.

If you pass the bona fide residency test, then you don't have to worry about how many days you're in a foreign country (or how many days you're in the United States).

You qualify for the FEIE regardless of your comings and goings day-to-day... except in the case of a temporary assignment overseas, in which case, as I've mentioned, you'll have to meet the physical presence test.

While you won't have to worry about how many days you are in the States for your bona fide residency test, you won't be able to spend more than six months Stateside in a calendar year, as tax residency rules apply to anyone who spends one hundred eighty-three days or more in most countries, including the United States.

Also, the United States has what is called the Substantial Presence Test. This test considers the number of days you were in the United States for the current year and the previous two years.

Essentially, you can spend up to four months a year in the United States and remain below the threshold for being considered a tax resident... and not lose your FEIE. This would only apply to those qualifying under the bona fide residency test.

Additionally, even if you're a bona fide resident of another country, any work you do in the United States is not eligible for the FEIE.

An example would be a vice president of Latin American

operations for a U.S. company going to the States for a two-week training. The salary that relates to those two weeks isn't eligible for the FEIE.

Probably that person has earned income above the annual limit, so this point likely wouldn't affect his tax situation. Nevertheless, it's worth noting.

The FEIE is calculated on Form 2555. You'll have to include information about your earnings, decide which test you want (or need) to qualify under, and your employer's information. It's a fairly straightforward form.

Your earned income is indicated on your 1040 Form under wages (or, if you are self-employed—which, as I'll explain shortly, is generally a bad idea from a tax perspective—on your Schedule C), but you'll enter a negative amount on line twenty-one of Schedule 1 for Form 1040 for the amount calculated on Form 2555 as your FEIE.

In other words, it's an above-the-line exclusion that reduces your adjusted gross income, phasing out many credits and deductions. Some credits and deductions add back in the amount of your FEIE in the worksheets to calculate them, but not all.

In addition to the Foreign Earned Income Exclusion, if you're working and receiving earned income in another country, you may also qualify for the Foreign Housing Exclusion (FHE). You calculate this on Form 2555.

The FHE applies if you are renting your residence while earning income in a foreign country. A base amount of sixteen percent of the FEIE is used to reduce your actual rental expense; this amounts to $22,240 for 2024.

The IRS limits your qualifiable rental expense to thirty percent of the FEIE, or $37,950, unless you live in a high-cost destination. This means up to an additional $15,800 that can be excluded from your income for U.S. tax purposes for tax year 2024 (assuming you spend at least $37,950 on rental expenses and don't live in a high-cost location).

Why is being self-employed a bad idea? If you're self-employed as the sole proprietor of a business and working and living overseas, you'll not only pay Social Security and Medicare taxes as you would if you were in the United States (both the employer and employee parts), but you'll also have your FEIE reduced by your business expenses.

Overall, from a tax point of view, you're much better off setting up a foreign corporation for your non-U.S. business.

The cost of setting up an offshore corporation can run as little as $1,200. The annual cost to maintain the corporation will run around $650.

Even assuming you use a service to set up the corporation that charges you an excessive fee of $5,000 to establish a simple offshore entity, you'll save money in the short- and long-run if you have only $35,000 of foreign-earned income that can flow through your offshore corporation.

Which leads to the next set of tax filings the American abroad may be required to do…

## If You Own An Offshore Entity

Again, setting up an offshore corporation is typically the most tax-efficient approach for an American operating a business outside the United States. LLCs are generally the better choice for holding assets that produce passive income.

While the tax deferral for U.S.-controlled foreign corporations was eliminated with the December 2017 tax law changes, an offshore corporation for a U.S. person operating a business outside the United States still offers key benefits from a U.S. tax perspective.

Being paid by a non-U.S. company, you and your company don't pay Social Security and Medicare taxes. Use a U.S. corporation to run your business, and you'll pay the employee percentage to Social Security and Medicare, and your company will pay the employer portion.

And while the U.S. tax deferral on profits is gone for a U.S.-controlled foreign corporation, in fact, your offshore corporation might be better off owned by a U.S. holding corporation thanks to the changes to section 965 of the IRS tax code.

For small operations, the U.S. parent company may not be

worth the expense and administrative hassle, but if you're running more than a hobby business offshore, seek advice from a U.S. tax professional who understands the rules for Form 5471.

Shareholders of foreign corporations are required to file an information form (Form 5471) each year. Generally speaking, you are required to file the form if you acquire ten percent or more of any foreign corporation, or if you acquire additional shares of a corporation in which you already own shares that put you over the ten percent threshold. In either case, you have to file Form 5471 only for the year in which the event occurs.

In other words, if you acquired ten percent of a foreign corporation in 2024, then you file the 5471 with your 2024 tax form, but you don't have to keep filing the 5471 if the corporation isn't what is called a U.S.-controlled foreign corporation (CFC).

If the corporation is a CFC, then any U.S. person owning ten percent or more of the voting power must file Form 5471 every year in which they retain that level of ownership or more.

## If You Hold Other Entities

The other entity most commonly used for offshore structures and asset protection is an LLC.

An offshore LLC is similar to a U.S. LLC in that it limits the liability of the owners... and both are pass-through entities. This is the structure best suited for holding passive investment portfolios.

You can choose to have a foreign corporation or a foreign LLC treated as though it doesn't exist for U.S. tax purposes, i.e., a pass-through entity. You do this with Form 8832, and, typically, you'd want to do it for an LLC holding an investment portfolio.

A foreign LLC with a single owner can be treated as if it doesn't exist for U.S. tax purposes... and the "single" owner can be a married couple. (In fact, domestic entities can be elected to be treated this way as well, using the same form.)

This means that, for tax purposes, you can reduce your filing requirement by electing to have your LLC treated as though it didn't exist. You simply report the interest, dividends, and capital gains on your 1040 form.

One thing to remember is that you can't elect for certain foreign corporations to be disregarded. The instruction section of Form 8832 has the full list.

For disregarded foreign entities, you'll then have to complete Form 8858 each year. It's a simple, two-page information form.

While a foreign LLC puts a layer of protection between your

assets and some litigant looking for a payout, if asset protection is your main goal, a foreign LLC isn't the best choice, though it can be the simplest.

For stronger asset protection, an offshore trust may be more appropriate for you. (We'll get into that more in the next chapter.) However, it requires a different level of tax reporting for U.S. persons...

## If You Have An Offshore Trust

Two IRS forms are required for reporting associated with a foreign trust: 3520 and 3520-A.

Form 3520 reports the transactions that the trust makes... such as when a U.S. person creates a foreign trust or when a U.S. person receives a distribution from a foreign trust. Form 3520-A addresses the informational reporting requirements when a foreign trust has a U.S. beneficiary.

The filing requirements for foreign trusts are complicated, to say the least, but, generally speaking, you'll need to file one or both of these forms if you are a U.S. person who has created a foreign trust and/or if you are a U.S. person who is a beneficiary of a foreign trust.

I've prepared these forms for others, and I'd say even if you do your own taxes, they are something you want to pay a professional to deal with... at least the first year, so you can better understand what gets reported and how. The required information flow can get complicated.

## Miscellaneous

The other forms required of the American abroad, depending on what he's doing and how he's earning his income—the FINCen 114 (FBAR), the 1116, and the 2555 (there's an EZ version)—aren't too much to deal with for anyone who has done his own taxes in the past.

In fact, TurboTax takes care of everything until you get to forms 5471 and 8858. Those you'll have to complete by hand, as you would the 3520 and 3520-A, if you were to decide to take those on.

The good news is that none of this applies to you if all you have is retirement income. Your tax return won't be any different whether you live in the United States or outside of it.

The safest thing (the thing I strongly recommend) is to engage professional help from the beginning and, meantime, over time, to train yourself on which forms you need and what information they require.

Even if you never plan to prepare your own taxes as an American living, working, or doing business overseas, you should educate yourself to help ensure that your tax return is prepared correctly and compliantly every year. Ultimately, as far as the IRS is concerned, your tax returns are your responsibility.

## The Only Way To Wave Goodbye To The IRS Forever

A lot of people still seem to think that the main reason to "go offshore" is to avoid taxes.

There are legitimate ways to minimize your U.S. tax bill as an American overseas... and we've talked about those methods.

But I've always recommended against Americans using taxes as a reason to go offshore... because, while Americans have been able to (and still can) enjoy some tax breaks by becoming residents of other countries, the reality is that the tax benefits for Americans overseas have always been limited.

An American living and earning an income overseas can take advantage of the Foreign Earned Income Exclusion to exclude his first $126,500 of earned income from U.S. tax (that's the figure for 2024)...

Up until a few years ago, Americans were able to get a tax deferral on retained profits for any U.S.-controlled foreign corporations.

Now, the deferred income of big U.S. companies—think Apple and Amazon—with billions of retained earnings offshore from the United States is taxable in the United States.

**COWBOY MILLIONAIRE—THE NEW AMERICAN PIONEER**
*Chapter IX: Beat The Bureaucrats... Wipe Out Your Tax Bill*

Those rules hit the little guy, as well.

This change came with the Trump tax reforms of 2017, and we were all given eight years to pay up.

As I said, I've never seen taxes as a reason for an American to go offshore (though the tax advantages can be a big benefit for a non-American taking his life across borders). It's even less so today.

I always tell people that taxes should just be one element of what you consider when you look at your offshore strategy... the main purpose is to provide yourself with a great lifestyle overall.

Part of this is personal preference. For example, Americans can already get an exemption from paying Federal taxes and drastically reduce their overall tax bill by moving to the U.S. territory of Puerto Rico.

But I would not want to live in a gated community amid the squalor of Puerto Rico just to save on taxes... I want to spend my time in a place where I feel comfortable and have a great lifestyle overall.

The ultimate strategy for eliminating your U.S. tax bill is to renounce your U.S. citizenship. This is more costly today than ever, thanks to a four hundred percent increase in the associated fees.

Renouncing your citizenship and walking away from being an American for good is also not for everyone, and not only because of the expense.

This is a complicated and potentially emotionally charged decision.

Most people who renounce their citizenship have lived overseas for a long time, obtained citizenship of the country they are living in, and have no expectation of ever traveling to—let alone moving back to—the States.

You cannot renounce your U.S. citizenship without first obtaining another citizenship. You can't be a stateless individual.

One pro of giving up your U.S. citizenship is that you would no longer have to file an annual tax return with the IRS.

One con is that the U.S. government makes it uncomfortable, if nothing else, if you decide to travel back to the U.S. after renouncing. The fact is, they don't have to let you back in, even if you have a solid new nationality and passport, like one from an EU country...

The biggest question you have to ask yourself is whether or not you will want to return to the U.S. for travel or any other reason.

One guy I know gave up his U.S. citizenship only to find himself applying for a Green Card a few years later because his wife, who hadn't given up her citizenship, decided she wanted the kids to finish high school in the States... and he wanted to be with his kids.

When people ask me if I'm ever going to give up my U.S. citizenship, my answer is simple... not likely. I like options, and being a U.S. citizen gives me options to return to the States for travel or to live and work should the need arise.

## "Tax Havens" Can Help You Pay Less... But Not In The Ways You Might Think

Now, all that said, you can certainly end up paying more or less tax overseas, depending on where you choose to base yourself... for your personal income or your business... based on local rates of taxation.

You may not save on what you owe Uncle Sam... but if local rates of taxation are low, you will save overall because you can avail of the FEIE and you won't be taxed in two countries, thanks to tax credits.

Your business can benefit too, thanks to local tax incentives...

On the other hand, choose a jurisdiction with higher overall taxes than the United States, and you could end up paying more taxes than you would back home...

So, location, location, location does matter for taxes...

What you want, ideally, is a country that only taxes income made in that country—your worldwide income from foreign dividends, pensions, Social Security, or even online work, is therefore not taxed locally.

Countries that practice this "jurisdictional" or "territorial" taxation policy are sometimes referred to as tax havens. Most of these countries are in Latin America and the Caribbean.

## Top Five Tax Havens For Americans Overseas

Before choosing where to live, invest, or do business, analyze all aspects of the "where" you're considering. A country's approach to taxation is an important consideration, but only one of many you should undertake.

As I've said, don't choose a place to live or retire based solely on the jurisdiction's approach to taxation. Living somewhere you're not happy just to save on your tax bill isn't worth it in the long run.

That said, the places on this tax haven list all offer interesting lifestyle options as well...

## Panama

Panama continues to be one of the best options for going offshore. As a resident of Panama, you pay no tax on foreign-earned income, nor on bank interest, certificates of deposit, wealth, inheritance, or U.S. Social Security. Property taxes are reasonable, with new properties exempt for up to twenty years, depending on their value.

Panama's *pensionado* program grants retirees a one-time exemption on the importation of household goods and a $20,000 exemption from import duty for a new car. Income earned in Panama is taxed in Panama (at a progressive rate from fifteen percent to twenty-five percent).

## Belize

Like Panama, Belize imposes no tax on a resident's foreign-earned income. In addition, Belize has no capital gains tax and no inheritance tax. Property taxes are low, and the Belizean population is determined to keep it that way.

Belize's Qualified Retirement Program (QRP) isn't just for retired people. So long as you're forty-five years of age or older, you can apply for this type of residency and enjoy incentives such as permanent exemption from Belize taxes, including income, sales, and estate taxes, as well as import taxes on household goods and an automobile, boat, airplane, or golf cart. Local income is generally taxed at a flat rate of twenty-five percent on income over $10,000.

With a Belize International Business Company (IBC), you are not subject to any taxes in Belize, nor are you required to file a return, because you can't do business in Belize with a Belizean IBC. If you do wish to do business in Belize, you would need a Belizean local corporation.

Some tax incentives for local businesses exist and can lead to a five- or ten-year tax holiday. The standard local business tax rate is twenty-five percent.

## Nicaragua

Nicaragua does not tax foreign-earned income. Locally sourced income is taxed at progressive rates up to thirty percent.

Property is taxed up to one percent of the property's registered value, depending on the region.

If you are setting up tax residence in Nicaragua, you should note that Nicaragua has an inheritance tax of one percent to four percent of a property's registered value.

The corporate tax rate in Nicaragua is thirty percent or one percent on income over 40 million Nicaraguan Córdobas ($1.09 million) for small- to medium-sized businesses.

ProNicaragua is a tax incentive program for investors. Under it, you can set up your own free trade zone and enjoy a ten-year tax exemption.

Industries targeted by the program include tourism, food processing, outsourcing services, footwear manufacturing, auto-part manufacturing, and forestry.

## Uruguay

Unlike other tax havens featured here, Uruguay's tax code doesn't fully exempt foreign-earned income.

Tax-resident foreigners in Uruguay enjoy tax exemption on foreign-earned income only during their first eleven years in the country. After that, certain types of income, specifically dividends and interest, are taxed at twelve percent.

Uruguay residents pay a twelve percent tax on local-source income. Property tax in the country is up to one-point-two percent of the property value, and movable property located overseas is also taxed, as well as subject to the country's twelve percent rental income tax.

While Uruguay has no inheritance tax, the country does impose a wealth tax on assets in Uruguay.

## Singapore

Singapore does not tax residents on foreign-earned income, though foreign-sourced dividends can be taxable if received in Singapore under certain conditions.

Local-source dividends are exempt from taxes as long as the company has already paid the reducible seventeen percent corporate tax.

Property tax in Singapore ranges from two percent to twenty percent. Singapore does not tax corporations or individuals on capital gains, unless they are in the business of trading shares. The country imposes neither wealth nor inheritance taxes.

Stamp duties on real estate can be expensive. Property taxes are assessed on a property's gross annual rental value according to a progressive scale of zero to sixteen percent for owner-occupied dwellings, ten to twenty percent for non-owner-occupied dwellings, and ten percent for nonresidential properties.

Singapore's free-port status means that few items are assessed customs duty.

## Special Tax Incentive Schemes... Move To Europe And Pay Low (Or Zero) Tax In These Three Countries

Europe has a reputation for high taxes... but this isn't always fair. In fact, there are many low-tax and even no-tax schemes in place in various countries, which investors, businesses, retirees, and even remote workers can take advantage of.

These schemes are always subject to change or even cancelation... so I always advise people to move quickly if they want in on a particular program.

**COWBOY MILLIONAIRE—THE NEW AMERICAN PIONEER**
*Chapter IX: Beat The Bureaucrats... Wipe Out Your Tax Bill*

## Italy's Seven Percent Tax For Expats

Italy introduced a highly enticing tax incentive for foreigners in 2020...

If you've lived outside of Italy for the previous five years and hail from a country with a tax treaty with Italy (such as the United States or Canada), you can move to Italy and pay a seven percent flat tax on foreign-source income.

So, if you receive a foreign pension, you can avail of this rate—but you have to move to a town with a population of less than twenty thousand in the south of Italy, in a region such as Abruzzo, Basilicata, Calabria, Campania, or Puglia, or the islands of Sicily or Sardinia.

These are some of the most laidback, beautiful, and culture-rich parts of the country... so relocating there is hardly a chore...

You can avail of the seven percent tax rate for up to ten years. When your time is up, your income will be taxed at standard Italian rates, between twenty-three percent and forty-three percent.

Italy has another scheme for businesses, which means you can establish a business presence in Italy while owing no tax there...

Called the "Representative Office Visa," this scheme allows you to open a business office in Italy and pay no tax on that operation—and you don't have to invest any money in Italy either. Just open an office.

With this visa, you can stay in Italy, and you can even bring your family… but you don't have to stay. There are no "minimum presence requirements" in order to keep the visa.

However, the criteria are very specific. You are not doing business in Italy, but rather promoting your business within Italy… make sure you have a good local lawyer on your side to structure the operation properly.

## Two Options In Greece

Like Italy, Greece boasts an enviable lifestyle… sumptuous food and stunning beaches… and one of the lowest costs of living in Europe…

And, like Italy, Greece introduced a seven percent flat tax for certain eligible expats.

The scheme is aimed at retirees, but the seven percent flat rate applies to whatever income a person might have, be that rents or dividends, as well as pensions.

Again, like Italy's program, however, it only applies to those from countries with which Greece has a double taxation treaty (that includes the United States and Canada).

You must have been a non-tax resident in Greece for five of the previous six years.

Athina Kalyva, head of Tax Policy at the Greek Finance Ministry, said the following when introducing the seven percent rate in 2020: "The logic is very simple: we want pensioners to relocate here, we have a beautiful country, a very good climate, so why not? We hope that pensioners benefiting from this attractive rate will spend most of their time in Greece."

You can avail of the seven percent rate for up to fifteen years.

The above scheme is called the Greek Non-Dom Regime for Retirees. Greece also has a Non-Dom Regime for Investors, where if you invest 500,000 euros, you pay a lump sum tax of 100,000 euros per year, regardless of how high your income goes or your level of wealth. Best of all, foreign-source income is not taxed at all under this regime.

## Spain's Lower Tax For Remote Workers

Spain is one of many countries to introduce a digital nomad visa in the wake of the recent boom in remote working (Greece and Portugal have nomad visas too). The aim is to attract mobile workers from around the world.

And the visa also comes with special tax incentives. You'll pay a flat tax rate of twenty-four percent on income up to 600,000 euros, and forty-seven percent above that.

Under Spain's regular tax regime, by contrast, you hit

thirty percent on income over 22,000 euros... forty-five percent above 60,000 euros... and forty-seven percent above 300,000 euros...

So, nomad workers in Spain can save big...

You'll also save on other taxes. For example, Spain's standard freelancer visa—but not the nomad visa—obliges the holder to pay up to nearly 300 euros a month toward public health cover and a pension.

Under the digital nomad visa, you must have a contract with a company that has been operating for at least a year and have been continuously employed by them for at least three months.

You must be a graduate of a university or business school or have three years of previous work experience.

After five years on the digital nomad visa, you can apply for long-term residency.

## CHAPTER X

# Do This Before You Get Sued (And You'll Be Safe)

I read once about a California couple who found one thousand four hundred $20 gold coins from the mid-1800s buried on their property. The store was estimated to be worth as much as $10 million due to the rarity and quality of some of the coins. The value of the gold alone was about $2 million.

What was the guy who buried those coins back in the 1800s thinking? He was thinking he was protecting his assets in a world where banks were robbed, and anyone with a six-shooter could decide to grab whatever he could get his hands on.

Or maybe the guy who buried the coins stole them but got nabbed by the marshal before he was able to retrieve his loot.

Either way, neither the guy nor whatever heirs he may have had were able to enjoy the value of what he had.

## COWBOY MILLIONAIRE—THE NEW AMERICAN PIONEER
*Chapter X: Do This Before You Get Sued (And You'll Be Safe)*

More recently, a guy in Nevada died with more than $7 million worth of gold stored in boxes in the garage of his simple house. He had some stocks as well, but he lived as a recluse. Again, the guy died with his gold "safe"... but useless.

Digging a hole and keeping the bulk of your wealth in boxes in your garage are, indeed, simple, low-tech asset protection strategies. But both approaches come with risk—namely that you aren't able to enjoy the fruits of your labor.

Hiding your money somewhere no one will ever find it, even after you're gone, seems to miss the forest for the trees.

The point of working hard and making some money during your life is for someone to enjoy it—you, your kids, your favorite charity, your cat... someone. What a waste for a lifetime of accumulated wealth to go to no productive use.

An offshore trust is a much more effective way to protect your assets... at least from lawsuits and false creditor claims.

You'll still have to keep your physical assets hidden from the burglars, but, with an offshore trust, you can protect what you've got in a way that allows you to use it and pass it along to your heirs.

The structure of an offshore trust doesn't have to be complicated, though the documentation you put together to create the trust can be, depending on how much direction and flexibility you want.

I recommend engaging an experienced attorney to help you think through the trust in the context of your situation overall and your immediate- and long-term needs and objectives.

This is where the cost can jump. Some attorneys charge as much as $100,000 for a trust document. Most of us don't need that level of documentation. But you have many good options between the attorney who'll charge you $100,000 and an off-the-shelf trust from some structures group you find on the internet.

Of course, midnight gardeners with millions of dollars' worth of gold buried in their backyards won't have much use for an offshore trust; it can't help you protect physical gold sitting in the United States.

To take full advantage of the asset protection benefits an offshore trust can provide, the assets have to be outside your home jurisdiction. Assets owned by the trust but physically present and therefore still subject to the local law where you are residing can be exposed simply by virtue of geography.

You have to weigh the options. You could put all your net worth into gold and bury it in the backyard or store it in your garage beneath the Christmas decorations. Or you could use an offshore trust to protect your assets, thereby diversifying your net worth.

## It Is Not Illegal To Move Assets Offshore

Some reader emails for my Simon Letter service have me scratching my head.

Some dear readers are railing against me for writing about ways to protect assets by moving them offshore.

These readers seem to fully believe that these activities are illegal... but they are conflating agendas.

Hiding assets offshore to avoid taxes—yes, that's illegal. Do that, and, with the IRS on a mission to uncover every U.S. asset held offshore, you're going to get caught. The cost of getting caught is likely to be multiples of whatever you might expect to save in taxes.

As a U.S. person, these days, you can't hide anything from the taxman. I always recommend disclosing everything you're meant to disclose to whatever government or tax authority it's meant to be disclosed to.

## This Is What Moving Assets Really Means

Hiding assets from the taxman is illegal. Moving assets offshore is not.

Don't believe anyone (any media, any accountant, any

attorney) who tries to tell you that moving assets to another country (by placing them in a bank account there, for example, or in a foreign trust) is illegal or a tax dodge. Again, it isn't.

Moving assets offshore is a protection strategy, not a tax strategy. At best, putting your assets in another jurisdiction outside the United States is tax-neutral. You'll continue to be liable for taxes in the United States at normal tax rates for any income and profits you earn from any investment you make offshore.

Offshore trusts come with their own reporting requirements if they have U.S. beneficiaries, as well as their own tax liabilities (see Chapter IX).

Again, a trust isn't about tax savings. It's about improved asset protection. Most attorneys won't attempt a frivolous lawsuit when the assets of the prospective plaintiff are in another jurisdiction.

One more time: Protecting your assets isn't illegal. As a man with a family, I'd say it's an obligation. Using offshore entities is one way to accomplish the objective.

My *Simon Letter* and *Global Property Advisor* colleague, Con Murphy, has also done extensive research on the topic of moving assets offshore. This chapter contains his work.

## Protect Yourself From Frivolous Lawsuits… The Best Countries (And Methods) For Privacy And Asset Protection Right Now

Americans defend themselves against forty million lawsuits every year.

Not surprising—in a country with over one million lawyers. That's more than three times the whole population of one of the best offshore jurisdictions, Belize…

No doubt, many of these lawsuits are frivolous… and even a frivolous lawsuit can wipe out your lifetime's work and leave you destitute.

It's only prudent to protect yourself.

But how do you do that?

You need to have the right structures in place… in the right places… and you need to set these up before you get sued.

Once court papers are served, it's too late to prepare.

Being in the right, or having a good lawyer, doesn't necessarily give you any protection.

Even if you win the legal battle, the costs of defending yourself could bankrupt you anyway.

But there are three basic steps you can take now to discourage unscrupulous legal claims…

1. Move to a country where litigation isn't a national pastime;
2. Increase the privacy of your assets so that no one knows whether you have anything worth suing for or where it is;
3. Protect your assets—prevent third-party access to them—using offshore banks, offshore corporations, and offshore trusts.

Let's review how each of these steps works...

## 1. Move To A Less Litigious Country

Pick any country in the world except Germany, Sweden, Israel, and Australia, and you reduce your chances of getting sued just by moving there.

These are the only five countries in the world that have more lawsuits per person than the United States...

Even if you do move to one of the five countries that are more litigious per capita than America... if you get sued and you lose your case in any of these jurisdictions, the payouts awarded are likely to be far lower than you would face in the States.

The "moving your life and business" option will generally lower your litigation risk, but it might not deter someone who has already decided to come after you, like a bankruptcy court or ex-spouse.

## 2. Increase Your Privacy

Here's the bare-naked truth...

Complete financial privacy no longer exists.

We live in a "show and tell" world, not a "hide and seek" world.

According to a 2022 report by the Tax Justice Network, the "world is galloping towards beneficial ownership transparency."

There are no more numbered (unnamed) Swiss bank accounts, and offshore bearer bonds and shares (where ownership isn't recorded) are almost a thing of the past too.

Panama does still allow bearer shares but taxes dividends at twenty percent. The Marshall Islands is the only legitimate place where bearer shares are still regularly used.

There are countries like Angola or Iran that won't report your assets to the IRS... but I'm assuming you don't want to bank in those countries.

However, there are still very legitimate ways to increase your personal financial privacy... even if, as I say, total (legal) financial secrecy is a thing of the past.

Why would you want to increase the layers of privacy surrounding your assets?

Well, it's very simple: If somebody knows you own XX assets, they may be more likely to sue. If they don't know the extent of your assets... litigation may be a less appealing prospect.

This type of privacy is far from a perfect security mechanism, but it can be a good first step to keep the vultures off your trail.

Offshore jurisdictions can help to increase your layers of privacy through methods like anonymous companies, trusts, offshore banks, unchecked mutual and hedge funds, and unregulated private investment industries.

However, to curtail money laundering, most countries have brought in beneficial ownership registries. This is a register of who ultimately owns what in a country.

Let me be very clear: As an American citizen, there's no privacy from the IRS. You will be required to report everything to the IRS (except for directly held foreign paper currency, foreign real estate in your own name, and directly held tangible assets such as gold, art, coins, etc.).

Legal developments like the Foreign Account Tax Compliance Act (FATCA), the Foreign Bank Account Reporting (FBAR) form, the Common Reporting Standard (CRS), and Base Erosion and Profit Sharing (BEPS) have made privacy from the taxman a thing of the past.

So, there is no privacy from Uncle Sam... but there may be privacy from the average Joe who wants to sue.

Many jurisdictions' beneficial ownership registries aren't open to the public.

In some countries ("public access" countries), who owns what company is a matter of public record. These countries provide no privacy at all, and the guy suing you can find your assets easily. Several countries in Europe fit this category.

In "restricted access" jurisdictions, foreign law enforcement and tax bodies can gain some access to their registers. This means you can't hide from the taxman, but you can usually find ways to prevent others from finding out if you have assets there. Most of Latin America falls into this category.

However, bear in mind that the U.S. passed the Corporate Transparency Act (CTA) in 2021, which removes full privacy for U.S. citizens abroad...

Americans really do get a raw deal from their government when it comes to the ownership of assets overseas. This is undoubtedly one reason why a record number of Americans have renounced U.S. citizenship in recent years.

Some countries refuse to allow foreign access to their registers, if the register exists at all. These countries are very secret but will be blacklisted, meaning the banks there can't use the conventional international banking systems.

Here's another tip: It's prudent to remember the Panama and Paradise Papers scandals of 2016 and 2017. Even if registries are private, it doesn't mean someone in your law firm or hackers won't leak your financial information like they did to all those billionaires and politicians.

The Tax Justice Network produces a biennial Financial Secrecy Index, which rates countries on the basis of how much financial secrecy they provide.

The Tax Justice Network wants wealthy people to pay more tax, opposes "tax competition" between countries, and advocates for crackdowns on tax havens.

It produces the Financial Secrecy Index in order to name and shame "jurisdictions most complicit in helping individuals to hide their finances."

It's not what they intended... their goal is to shame these countries... but ironically, they've provided us with an excellent tool for judging where to put our money in order to achieve greater privacy.

Basically, the countries that they think are the worst... are the best ones for financial privacy.

From our point of view—we want higher financial secrecy—any score above seventy is good. Any score above seventy out of one hundred means the country is a privacy haven.

However, when you see the list of some of the most secret countries, these aren't places I'd trust to keep my assets safe...

Who would trust Angola or Communist Vietnam with their wealth, no matter how "secret" the country is? Would you trust the courts in the United Arab Emirates if you got into a dispute with a local royal prince?

These are the best privacy jurisdictions—all with scores of seventy or higher in the Financial Secrecy Index:

- St. Kitts and Nevis
- Belize
- St. Lucia
- The Cook Islands
- Panama
- Antigua and Barbuda

## 3. Increase Your "Layers Of Protection"

The real secret to asset protection these days isn't hiding your assets... it's making your assets so unattractive or difficult to acquire by suing that no one will bother going after them.

The best way of doing this is to move those assets offshore to a low-tax jurisdiction that is repellant to litigation.

In other words, protect yourself using offshore banks, corporations, and trusts. There are various levels of asset protection available offshore.

U.S. courts don't have jurisdiction over foreign assets or people.

So, if someone wants to sue you for assets you hold offshore, they must go to the country where those assets are legally held, hire a lawyer, gather evidence that is germane in the jurisdiction, and sue you there.

The best offshore jurisdictions have legal systems set up to protect companies from foreign interference.

To bring legal action in these countries is difficult, expensive, and beyond the scope of most litigants in the United States.

Buying unreportable foreign assets like real estate in your own name and moving out of the United States is the weakest way of protecting yourself, but it does help.

You don't have to report foreign real estate that's held in your own name to the IRS, but if someone searched a property register, they could easily find your overseas property, precisely because it's in your own name.

To get at your assets, a litigant would have to find you and sue you in an overseas country, or get a U.S. court judgment enforced overseas, which isn't that easily done.

Placing your assets in an offshore company and keeping your cash in an offshore bank account is a much stronger way of protecting your assets.

For most ordinary investors, this is all the protection they will realistically need.

To get to those assets, the litigant must know they are there, which can be difficult to learn because most beneficial ownership registries (including most in the EU) are not open to the general public.

If a litigant does find out about them, getting at your assets in a Nevis or Belize corporation—or seizing your cash from your offshore bank account—requires a lot of effort.

The person suing you has to go to each country where you have assets or bank accounts, hire an expensive lawyer, and win a judgment from a court that probably doesn't look favorably at foreigners coming to their country to sue local companies.

## The Pros And Cons Of Offshore Companies

### Pros

- **Privacy.** The right entities can provide strong privacy.
- **Asset protection.** Offshore companies provide strong asset protection.
- **Banking access.** With an offshore company, you can open bank accounts that are not in your name in many offshore havens like Panama, Belize, or the Bahamas (which seems to be the new crypto-protectorate capital of the world, thanks

to having zero taxes).

- **Reduce tax.** Using an offshore company, American taxpayers can avail of the Foreign Earned Income Exclusion ($126,500 in tax-free earned income). You can also avoid the U.S. self-employment payroll tax when overseas, because you legally work for your offshore company. Because it's not a U.S. company, you don't have to pay payroll taxes on that income.
- **Options for your real estate.** Holding real estate through offshore companies provides privacy protection. In many countries, especially in Latin America and the Caribbean, you have the ability to transfer the property to a new owner and avoid stamp duty. This works because you won't be transferring the title of the property; you are merely transferring the shares in the holding company that owns the property.
- **Access to overseas operations.** A foreign corporation can allow Americans to invest in non-U.S.-registered investments.
- **IP protection.** Intellectual property is best held offshore, where it's prospected and not subject to tax. Belize and Nevis are common countries used for IP holding companies.

## Cons

- **Compliance and maintenance.** There will be costs associated with ensuring you're complying with local laws, as well as costs to maintain your company.
- **Blacklisting.** Some countries don't like dealing with companies from offshore havens.
- **Extra Taxes.** Depending on the jurisdiction the asset is in, you might become liable for extra taxes. For example, Portugal imposes a punitive ten percent transfer tax on property bought by offshore companies from blacklisted tax havens, including Panama. Or, some countries will charge VAT on sales made by your company. This is why you should get expert legal and tax advice from a firm that specializes in U.S. expat clients and not buy a cheap offshore company from an online provider. Remember: improperly structured offshore companies or bad legal advice could cost you both your investment and your freedom...

## How To Choose An Offshore Haven

There are many factors to consider when choosing the jurisdiction for your offshore entity (company or trust).

Here's a comprehensive but not necessarily complete list...

Your reasons for incorporating are the first consideration. What do you want to do with the entity? Is it to be a holding entity for intellectual property? A crypto trading entity? Or to protect your real estate holdings?

The level of asset protection is a vital consideration. How difficult does that jurisdiction make it for foreign litigants to sue you? This concern should be near the top of your list.

The reputation of the jurisdiction is important. If you want this entity to do business in the EU, you can't use an entity from a country that is blacklisted by the EU.

What about taxes? Though tax is no longer the main reason U.S. persons go offshore, you still want to incorporate in a country that has territorial, low, or zero taxation, so you minimize your liabilities.

The cost of incorporation is a big consideration too, as are annual maintenance fees. Don't be suckered by the service providers who offer incorporations for $500 but charge you thousands every year to maintain your entity.

If you're in a hurry to protect your assets, how quickly you can form the entity may be a decisive factor. Mauritius is known as a fast offshore incorporation jurisdiction.

Can you incorporate an entity without physically going to the country? This is important. The best offshore havens have mechanisms for you to open companies and bank accounts without physically going there. If not, you face a trip that will likely cost you thousands of dollars and up to a week of your time.

In addition, there may be a requirement to have a company director resident in the country... and this can be a factor to consider. Some low-corporate-tax countries, like Ireland, insist that you have a director who lives in the country. If you don't live in the country personally, you'll have to pay someone to do so and tell them your financial secrets.

Currency controls are an issue in some jurisdictions. There's not much use sending all your money to a place that you can't get the money back out of.

Finally, communication is key. Does your provider speak English? What's the main language of business in the country? You need to be able to communicate clearly with your offshore bank and service provider.

The best jurisdictions for offshore companies include the following:

- Belize, which is a zero-tax jurisdiction where it's very hard to sue.

- Panama, which is arguably the most livable offshore jurisdiction, has a well-developed economy and a diversity of well-heeled lifestyle options. There are a range of low-tax offshore company options.
- Antigua, a Caribbean island and another zero-tax jurisdiction.
- The Marshall Islands, for fast incorporations, for investors in a hurry.
- The British Virgin Islands (BVI) is traditionally considered an excellent haven, but it is pricey and becoming over-regulated.
- St. Kitts and Nevis, where it's extraordinarily hard to be sued.

## Offshore Trusts: The Strategy That Gives You Maximum Protection

The absolute best way to secure your assets and get maximum privacy, is to go a step further than setting up an offshore company, and establish an offshore trust.

Offshore trusts work best when located in a low- or zero-tax jurisdiction, like Belize or the Cook Islands.

However, out of all the options given, they are also by far the most expensive to set up and maintain.

In fact, they are often so expensive to set up that you might decide you don't need that level of protection or cost...

You need to be protecting millions or be at high risk of litigation to warrant setting up an irrevocable offshore trust, as they cost up to and over $50,000 just to set up, and you must pay thousands to maintain your trust every year as well.

For the average investor, a well-planned offshore company structure could provide much of the same protection at a much lower cost.

Bear in mind, of course, I am writing in general terms about the kinds of protections offered by particular entities. What's right for you and your particular circumstances—that I can't say. That's individual to you and likely requires professional advice. It's certainly not the case that everyone needs an offshore trust...

Domestic (onshore) trusts like those offered in Delaware or Wyoming are often touted as better than offshore trusts.

But there is one very important way in which they are not... U.S. trusts are subject to U.S. court orders.

Offshore trusts aren't tied to a U.S. jurisdiction and aren't subject to U.S. laws.

## Trust Terms You Need To Know

- **Deed of Trust or Trust Agreement.** The legal document that dictates how the trust is structured and ad-

ministered.
- **Settlor or Grantor/Trustor/Donor.** The person who sets up and funds the trust (you).
- **Trustee or Trust Company.** The person who is entrusted with protecting the assets transferred into the trust for the beneficiaries.
- **Protector.** Nowadays, there can be a protector who lives outside both the jurisdiction of the settlor or the trustee, who can provide additional protection by watching over the trustee's administration of the trust.
- **Beneficiary.** The person to whom the trust pays out. Some offshore jurisdictions allow you to be both the settler and grantor of the trust and the beneficiary, which literally allows you to have your cake and eat it where asset protection is concerned.

## How Trusts Work

1. You (the settlor) decide on a jurisdiction and find a trust company to form a trust that's designed for your requirements.
2. You appoint the trustee and designate the beneficiaries of the trust.
3. You transfer assets into the offshore trust, so you technically no longer own those assets.

**4.** The trustees protect the assets in the trust on the beneficiary's behalf and pay out dividends as per the trust agreement. You can make yourself a beneficiary or co-beneficiary in some countries.

Just to reiterate, U.S. courts have no jurisdiction over foreign citizens or companies, so your trustee cannot be forced by a U.S. court to hand over the assets in the trust.

If your creditor wants to sue you for your assets, he must initiate the legal action in the country where your trust is incorporated.

Several jurisdictions, such as Nevis and Belize, require you to place a sizable deposit before you can even begin legal action there ($25k to $50k). And hiring lawyers there will cost your opponent hundreds of dollars per hour for months on end.

This is a powerful protective shield against frivolous lawsuits. You're making it very hard and expensive for litigants to get at your assets.

## The "Claw Back" Risk

The idea of transferring your assets to a third party to avoid paying your debts certainly isn't a new one.

In 1571, the English parliament passed the Fraudulent

Conveyances Act, better known as the Statute of Elizabeth.

The law stated that if you transfer property to someone else purely to defraud your creditors, that transfer can be reversed or "clawed back."

This law is still on the books in America today, now called the Uniform Fraudulent Transfer Act (UFTA).

If you transfer assets into a trust to evade your debts, a judge can "claw back" the assets for a number of years afterwards and give them to your creditors.

Some offshore trusts make it nearly impossible for courts in the trust's jurisdiction (or anywhere else) to claw back your assets out of the trust.

The Cook Islands is the most litigation-repellant jurisdiction.

To be able to even begin legal action there, creditors will need to prove beyond a reasonable doubt that you transferred the assets into the trust to defraud the creditor.

The Cook Islands also has a very short statute of limitations, making it very hard to initiate action before the complaint becomes statute barred.

There is a very high burden of proof on anyone looking to sue you in the Cook Islands, and you can sometimes even transfer the assets to the Cook Islands after the U.S. litigation begins and still avoid any fraudulent transfer claims.

Hardly anyone tries to sue in the Cook Islands because it is so difficult to win and expensive to pursue.

Belize and Nevis are also incredibly frustrating places for litigants to try and sue offshore entities.

## How Offshore Trusts Add Extra Layers Of Protection From U.S. Courts

A common question U.S. citizens have about moving their assets offshore is, "If I still live in the United States, why can't a U.S. judge just tell me to bring my assets back onshore so the U.S. courts can seize them? Can't I be held in contempt of court if I refuse?"

If you have your assets in a U.S. trust or an ordinary foreign trust, a U.S. judge could decide to jail you until you agree to transfer the trust or its assets back to the States.

That's not much use to you.

An irrevocable discretionary offshore trust avoids this if the trust is properly drafted with duress clauses.

As you no longer own the assets in the trust, the judge can't force you to hand them back.

If the judge orders you to tell the trustees to return the assets to you, you can legally avoid this too.

If a U.S. court orders you to return the offshore trust's assets to the States, you send a letter to the trustees telling them to release the assets, giving the reason that you have been ordered by the court to repatriate the funds.

**COWBOY MILLIONAIRE—THE NEW AMERICAN PIONEER**
*Chapter X: Do This Before You Get Sued (And You'll Be Safe)*

The trustee will refuse your request because you are acting "under duress" of the U.S. courts, and they are legally bound not to return assets to you in this circumstance.

You can't be held in contempt of court by the American judge as you did what the court told you by requesting the trustee release the assets back to you.

This means there is no willful violation of the judge's order, and therefore you cannot be punished, and the trustee is outside the jurisdiction of the U.S. judge.

Just to state: I'm not recommending you do this; I'm merely laying out how a process like this could go.

Flight clauses are another aspect of offshore trusts that can be used to protect your assets. If there's a flight clause in your trust documents and you are sued—or upon certain "trigger" actions—the trust automatically flees to another jurisdiction and is re-registered there instead.

For example, if my Belize trust comes under attack by court action, the litigant must come to Belize, pay the court deposit, and pay tens of thousands of dollars to a Belize law firm to try and sue the trust; the trust can flee by transferring itself to the Cook Islands or Nevis. It doesn't cost that much to re-register in another offshore trust jurisdiction.

This means the plaintiff must find out where the trust went, go there and hire another lawyer, spend even more money, and start the legal action all over again.

In theory, you could do this again and again until the person suing you runs out of money or patience.

## Flips And Twists With Offshore Trusts

Here are some other things you need to know about offshore trusts... and some other common questions answered...

- Your trust must be compliant with the laws of your country of tax residence.
  Incorporating an offshore trust is one thing, but to make it legally effective in protecting your assets, you must have a lawyer versed in U.S. tax law review or help draft the deed of trust too.
  It's no use if your company or trust is great for protecting your assets in St. Lucia, but it doesn't work with U.S. tax law.
  U.S. tax residents must file IRS Form 3520 for any trust ownership activity, as well as other declarations that your accountant will tell you about.
- Can you protect assets physically located in the U.S. in an offshore trust?
  If you own a house in the States, having it held by an offshore trust might not help you much.
  American courts often just seize U.S.-located assets

owned by foreign trusts, because they decide U.S. law is supreme.

To avoid this, you must use "asset stripping," which would involve taking out a mortgage or placing a deed of trust on the U.S. house.

If the asset is threatened, you have an offshore finance company acquire the debt and lien on the property.

The loan payments are paid to your offshore company, and there is too little equity left in the property to bother suing you for.

These sorts of actions may seem like the dastardly doings of politicians, oligarchs, and billionaires—but any legal asset-protection avenue is potentially available to the rest of us, too.

Don't get mad at the global elite for playing these games—join them and protect yourself.

- Where is the best place to incorporate your trust? Different jurisdictions are better at certain types of trust actions.

Which one you choose depends on your objectives, litigation risk, the amount of money involved, the bank accounts you need to operate, and the types of assets held in the trust.

If you are holding an EU business in the trust, use Luxembourg or Jersey trusts.

For hedge funds, the Cayman Islands.

For maximum litigation-risk avoidance, Belize or the Cook Islands.

The Cook Islands and Belize crafted their offshore company and trust laws to suit Americans, designing their structures to work with the IRS code.

They also offer legal mechanisms to avoid forced heirship of family members—where it mightn't be legal to disinherit certain family members at home.

Nevis and the Bahamas are also popular with U.S. investors. The British Virgin Islands is another common offshore trust location.

- Another thing to be aware of is whether or not the country is a signatory to the Hague Trust Convention and whether the convention is applicable to your trust.

  This is a set of rules that some jurisdictions have agreed to obey, so there are common processes and procedures for governing trusts between the countries. If a country hasn't ratified the treaty, it's not bound by these rules.

## An Example Of A Strong Asset Protection Structure

Here's what a strong asset protection structure might look like...

A Cook Islands or Belize trust, which owns a Nevis LLC plus your other assets.

The Nevis LLC has an offshore bank account with your cash in it.

If you are sued, your trustees automatically take over management of the Nevis LLC, so you can't be compelled by courts to hand over the cash in the Nevis LLC's offshore bank account.

There will be no real legal standing to sue the trust, and if it is somehow attacked, it can flee to another jurisdiction.

After the litigation is over, you revert to being the manager of the Nevis LLC and controlling its bank account.

Visit this link: **cowboymillionairesecrets.com**, or scan the QR code to view what a strong asset protection structure could look like.

## CHAPTER XI

# The "Secret Of The Kings" That Keeps Your Money Safe

When the King of Rock and Roll died in August 1977, his estate was valued at more than $10 million.

Unfortunately, Elvis Presley's will wound up going through probate, and it took three years for the lawyers to work things out in court.

Finally, the court ruled that the estate should pass to his only child, Lisa Marie.

But Lisa Marie Presley didn't get the $10 million. Between taxes and legal fees, Elvis's estate was reduced to just $3 million.

Yes, seventy percent went straight to the taxman and the lawyers, while his daughter was left with just 30 cents on the dollar.

Another king, however, was the Oil King, H.L. Hunt.

His story has a far-different ending...

Just prior to his death in 1974, Hunt's net worth was estimated at $2 billion... that's about $12.2 billion in today's dollars.

This king was better prepared. He had carefully distributed his assets into all sorts of legal structures—funds, trusts, life insurance... you name it.

After his death, the only asset that could be linked to H.L. Hunt was a pick-up truck worth $2,000—hardly worthy of a courtroom battle.

His fortune remained intact, and his heirs received everything he wanted them to...

Frankly, this tale of two kings reflects your two estate-planning options: protect it or give much of it away.

The moral of the story? Only you have control over your wealth.

You—not the government, creditors, litigants, or banks—get to decide what happens to your assets, now and in the future.

The secret that all royalty possess is the ability to pass on the crown to their heirs. That's what kept ancient kingdoms intact.

In the same way, multigenerational wealth means being able to pass on what you've built to the next generation...

And the only way to be sure you're able to do that is to have the right estate plan in place.

Nowhere is this more important than when you've built something on the "new frontiers" overseas.

You'll be dealing with different legal systems, different

standards... and, even if you've produced a will in America, it may not be enough to protect your overseas assets.

As I await the birth of my second grandchild, these concerns are much on my mind.

I grew up relatively poor, the son of a single mother. We never went without dinner on the table, but we were definitely lower middle class.

I saved to be able to buy my first car, and I worked two jobs to cover college tuition... then grad school.

I don't resent it. It gave me a real appreciation for the value of a dollar and made me who I am.

The prejudice is that kids of wealthy parents don't do anything with or for themselves, and I've seen it. Kids from upper-class families do sometimes grow up to be ne'er-do-wells.

Of course, there's no guarantee either way. Children of wealthy parents can turn out to be hard workers, while kids of poor, hard-working parents can grow up to be lazy gits.

In the face of it all, how should you approach your generational wealth aspirations?

Giving money to your kids without first thinking through a big-picture strategy can create big problems... for you and for them.

Take, for example, the proud father who gave his daughter a big house in a nice neighborhood as a wedding present.

He had the best intentions but didn't think through the

consequences of the gift. While the son-in-law made a good living, the young man couldn't afford the property taxes or the maintenance.

So, even though they lived in a paid-for house, the daughter and son-in-law struggled to keep up financially.

One asset-planning attorney I work with tells the story of a client who tried to address the risks of giving a child more than he or she could handle. He set up a trust that allowed his children to withdraw an amount up to the income they generated personally each year.

His son, a teacher earning $50,000 a year, could take out $50,000 a year. His daughter, a Wall Street banker earning $500,000 annually, could withdraw $500,000 a year.

They could each double their income.

The thinking is that the banker would, in theory, know how to manage that kind of income and wealth, while the teacher would struggle to manage ten times the amount of his annual salary.

Maybe he'd figure it out… or maybe he'd squander it. Perhaps he'd even be tempted to quit his teaching job and live off the trust money.

For a long time, my financial objective associated with my children was to be able to pay for college for them. I met that goal.

Now I'm looking ahead and thinking bigger and longer term.

Now I'm beginning to think about legacy planning…

I'm looking at which investments I own that could perhaps be transferred now to my children.

Like for the kings of old, there's a balance to be struck between training the next generation to live responsible lives of their own… and giving them the keys to the kingdom.

But most of us are happy to know that what we've built or owned during our lifetimes can continue to be of benefit to or enjoyed by others after we're gone.

Whether it's a business… a fortune… or even a single property… proper estate planning is the key to ensuring your kingdom remains intact for those who come after you… and that your legacy continues.

In my thirty years of going offshore, I've learned lessons along the way about estate planning.

The one main takeaway I have for my own situation is that it's always changing and becoming more complex… so I need flexibility.

For others, it can and should be simpler.

However, whether your situation is simple or complex, you do have to plan.

Otherwise, you risk leaving a mess for your heirs and attorneys to deal with.

To start out, I'll use my divorced parents' situations as examples of what to do and what not to do.

## Plan, Plan, Plan

My mother's estate is fairly straightforward, and I'm the only heir. A simple will would have been sufficient for me to be able to deal with her assets when she dies, but the estate would have had to go through the full probate process. That process is slow, takes effort, and can end up costing more in legal fees than needed.

With some extra planning beyond a will, I've been able to organize my mother's assets so they'll all be passed directly to me, the sole heir. Probate will thus end up being a simple administrative process.

The two keys to that are being listed as a beneficiary on investment and bank accounts (or co-owner on the bank accounts, if your parents allow it) and transfer-on-death deeds for assets with a title.

Listing beneficiaries on IRAs, 401(k)s, and other investment accounts is easy. You should have someone listed already, whether it's your spouse, your kids, or your siblings.

Twenty-nine U.S. states and D.C. allow for real estate to have a transfer-on-death (TOD) deed registered. Twenty-one states have a similar option for vehicles. These TOD functions allow the heir to take immediate ownership of the property without going through any probate or court process.

Removing assets from an estate by listing beneficiaries or

using TOD options reduces the estate value, which can then eliminate probate altogether or limit it to a minimal administrative process rather than a court process.

Each U.S. state has different value thresholds for probate, but most require probate if real estate is involved, even if the estate value is less than the probate threshold.

Also, if someone disputes a will, the estate is going to have to go through probate anyway. Therefore, getting the real estate out using a TOD deed is beneficial for all estates.

My mom's estate planning is well organized, and she used an attorney to make sure everything got recorded correctly… the will and the TOD deeds.

## What Not To Do

My father, on the other hand, has a DIY will.

When my father died, his original will in his files at home was missing a page…

Fortunately, the attorney my brother hired was able to find the fully recorded will at the county clerk's office.

However, my father's estate had to go through full probate procedures, leaving my half brother to deal with the probate while also dealing with all of my father's stuff and his real estate.

The time required to deal with probate can be significant.

Notifications need to be sent out to anyone who might have a claim on the estate... debtors and potential heirs.

A hearing date has to be set for claims or contesting the will.

After that, the executor can proceed but has to provide documentation of the liquidation process to the court.

I'm simplifying the whole thing here... but I know it's something I'd prefer to make easier for my kids.

## The Offshore Twist

For basic U.S. estates, naming beneficiaries on financial accounts and doing TOD deeds on property where you can will make things simple for your heirs.

Offshore assets will be trickier to deal with.

Joint tenants with rights of survivorship (a form of TOD) isn't something that exists in most countries. Neither do other TOD options for real estate. Financial accounts can have named beneficiaries, but you'll need to confirm that with the financial institution.

Without TOD options for property, the next level of simplification can be holding property in entities from countries that allow a beneficiary option. The level after that is holding assets in trusts or foundations with named beneficiaries.

Full estate planning for an international portfolio of assets can get complicated. But the lesson to take away from my experience with my parents' estates is simple...

Do something, and don't try to do it yourself.

My father may have saved a few hundred dollars by doing his own will. But the mistakes made with that document cost his estate thousands of dollars in unnecessary legal fees for the probate process. Not to mention a lot of time.

## Your Global Estate—How To Build Legacy Wealth

The idea of generational planning isn't new. Families from the Rothschilds to the Duponts and the Kennedys have done it for a long time, and some European families have created plans that have maintained family wealth for centuries.

The idea that those of us with less substantial assets might want to organize our assets and structure our holdings so as to create a legacy of wealth that will carry forward for generations may be newer, but, in the current climate, where it is harder and harder to keep what you've earned, I'd say it's critical.

The bricks and mortar of any legacy plan are the structures that hold the assets in question. The right structures are the key to minimizing inheritance taxes, wealth taxes, and transfer taxes... and those things are the key to being able to transfer wealth so that it can continue to grow over future generations.

Whether you are worried only about the next generation or you are hoping to create a generational legacy that will still be around centuries from now, your plan can become more complicated when you start internationalizing your life.

Bank accounts, real estate, corporations, trusts, stocks, and physical precious metals all held in different countries can create a much more difficult administrative burden very quickly.

You've got to choose the right structures in the right jurisdictions, remembering your big-picture goals and building in flexibility and accommodations for ongoing asset growth and diversification.

## You Need More Than One Will

The starting point for any estate plan is a will.

You know that you need a will in your home country, but you may not have addressed the fact that you also need wills in any other jurisdiction where you own real estate, a bank account, or any other asset. This applies to every country where you own something, be it a piece of property, stocks, a bank account, or gold in a private vault.

Your will in your home country won't always prevail in another country. The law and maybe the language will be different (even from the United States to Ireland, for example, legal terminology varies), and a local will prepared by a local attorney in accordance with local laws is the best way to cover your assets in that country.

Most countries have specific rules related to the distribution of assets when the owner of those assets dies. Many countries adhere to ancient methodologies that don't fit in a modern world.

France is the best (extremely complicated) example. Like anything bureaucratic in France, there are the rules, the exceptions to the rules, and the exceptions to the exceptions that get you back to the original rule. Die without a will in France, and your assets get distributed according to your blood line.

This means that, in the case of joint assets owned with a surviving spouse, your share will be distributed in a manner that could mean your spouse ends up with as little as one-quarter of the assets overall if you have three or more children.

In truth, if you have children, your surviving spouse could technically end up with nothing. Following the rules a bit further, your spouse could, in fact, end up with nothing if you have a surviving parent or siblings.

Other countries also use this "follow the bloodline" method for inheritance distributions, but none have mastered the complexities of it as well as the French.

The good news is that having a will or other planning document in place in France can bypass the French inheritance laws. Further, if you're a non-resident, the bloodline laws apply only to real estate, and these can be gotten around by holding your real estate in a special French entity designed specifically for this purpose (it's called a Société Civile Immobilière, or SCI).

Take possession of any real estate in France in the name of an SCI rather than your own name or the name of some other kind of corporation, and the shares of that entity can be accounted for under the will of your country of residence.

The specifics of planning for the distribution of any French real estate holdings aside, there's a bigger picture here... In today's world of second wives, stepchildren, adopted children, and unmarried life-partners, following the bloodline doesn't work for most people anymore.

But without a proper will in each country where you hold assets, you run the risk of inheritance going to some third cousin you've never met rather than your adopted child (for example).

A will on its own may work for your initial planning as you begin working to set up your plan for diversification offshore... but it's only one tool in the toolbox that you're going to need if you intend to do more than simply open a bank account in another jurisdiction.

In fact, in many cases, a bank account in another country can be a simple matter in the context of your legacy plan. Most banks in most places allow you to name a beneficiary or beneficiaries. So, if you have just a single bank account in one offshore jurisdiction and no longer-term planning to coordinate, you may be able to get away without a will.

But, bigger picture and longer term, I'd suggest that you probably still want one covering that bank account just to be safe. What happens if one or more of your beneficiaries predecease you? A will could cover that.

One benefit of naming the beneficiaries of an offshore bank account directly (assuming you're not looking for intergenerational planning) is that it does one thing a will doesn't: it avoids probate.

Probate is the process of "proving" the will. With beneficiaries named for your bank account, all they have to do to have access to the funds in most cases is to show a death certificate. Other assets, unfortunately, must go through the probate process.

As I've said already, probate can take a long time and cost a lot of money.

Let's imagine that, by the time you pass on, you've done a great job internationalizing your life, and you hold assets in four or five countries. Furthermore, you have wills in place in each country designating who gets what when you're gone.

All of that is great, but it won't get around probate. Your heirs will still have to go through the probate process (assuming the assets are above the minimum probate thresholds, which are typically low) in each country where assets are being transferred.

You have to decide whether you want some extra administration and costs on your side while you're still alive or whether you want to pass the administration and costs on to your heirs.

To achieve a Rothschild level of planning (that is, multigenerational planning), you'll have to do more than put wills in place in every country where you hold assets. I'd say this isn't an issue, though, unless you have a lot of assets to work with.

In other words, your entire estate plan might be accomplished by making sure you have a will in place in every jurisdiction where you own some assets.

## Beyond A Will... The Benefits Of Trusts

The way to obtain the third level of estate planning after the probate and tax question is to set up an offshore trust in a jurisdiction that will protect the trust assets should you—as the grantor and primary beneficiary—be sued back home.

Offshore trust jurisdictions organize their laws to specifically protect trusts in their country from frivolous lawsuits. As we saw in the last chapter, the barriers to piercing a foreign trust by a U.S. attorney are effectively insurmountable, including rules that require the plaintiff to pay the defendant's legal costs if the plaintiff loses.

Most U.S. attorneys will take on a frivolous lawsuit on a contingency fee basis, knowing they'll at least get some settlement out of most suits, whether it's just the defendant taking the hit to save legal fees or an insurance company paying out to make the suit go away.

Those same contingency fee attorneys won't risk their time by filing a suit in another country. They'll want to be paid by the hour, which generally forces the plaintiff to abandon the frivolous suit.

For an offshore trust to work most effectively, you'll need to move the assets in the trust out of your home jurisdiction. That gets you to the topic of offshore investing, which is beyond the scope of estate planning.

Simply moving assets outside of your home jurisdiction and holding them in an offshore entity that isn't an offshore trust gives you a barrier to someone trying to attack your assets, but the assets are yours in that case, so the protection is limited.

Nevertheless, holding offshore assets in an offshore entity does give you some estate planning benefits if your assets are in different countries. You can hold real estate, for example, in Panama, Belize, and Colombia all in the same Nevis LLC.

When you die, your estate won't need to go through probate in each of the three countries where the real estate is based, as the titles are in the name of the entity. Your estate simply deals with Nevis.

In that scenario, you wouldn't need a will in each of the three countries to outline your wishes for who gets your properties.

If you held title in your own name, without a will in each country, each property would be allocated to heirs based on the laws of each country.

As we've seen, most countries look to blood relatives first, including children. And for people with second marriages with stepchildren and halfsiblings, those rules may not be what you want.

So, take the time to structure your estate in a way that will meet your goals for who inherits what.

## Do Something—Today

Whatever you do when it comes to estate planning… do something. And do it sooner rather than later.

Even if you don't have much when you die, the process of getting whatever assets you do have into the hands of those you want to inherit them can be a big hassle for those heirs if you leave no instructions. Asset thresholds as low as $25,000 trigger probate in some states. Real estate assets of any value will likely trigger probate in most states.

At a minimum, have a will created in each country where you own property so that the people you want to inherit your assets will get them... even if they do have to go through a probate process.

Considering the future deeply and planning for the long term are easy to put off. But, when you get down to it, it's the difference between the most successful family names in history... and being at the mercy of events—and broke.

## CHAPTER XII

# The Three Most Important Things To Know Before You "Go Offshore"

In high school, my best friend moved from Phoenix to Milwaukee. His family kept their house in Phoenix and turned it into a rental.

When he moved back to Phoenix a few years later, we drove by the property to check on it. He talked about problems with tenants and the management company his parents had hired.

The management company didn't do anything for their money, and the tenants simply damaged the house. In his and his parents' minds, the income from the rental wasn't worth the expense and hassle.

Years later, as I was shopping for my first rental property, I couldn't understand why more people didn't own rental investments. If you bought right and could use leverage, real estate seemed like the best thing since sliced bread.

## COWBOY MILLIONAIRE—THE NEW AMERICAN PIONEER
*Chapter XII: The Three Most Important Things To Know Before You "Go Offshore"*

But as I put my spreadsheets together in my search and started adding expense lines for repairs, maintenance, rental management, etc., I recalled the conversation with my friend back in Phoenix...

The hassle factor was the reason more people didn't own rental properties.

I was willing to deal with the hassles of owning a rental property... so, being young, I pushed ahead with my search and found a property that fit my requirements.

The hassles started before I moved in.

Over the two-and-a-half years of owning the building, the small hassles were plenty, but then the payday came when I sold and ended up with thirty times my initial down payment.

All the repairs and maintenance had been paid for by rent... or security deposits in the case of a broken window. That made all the hassle worthwhile.

More recently, friends told me they were selling a second home that they don't use often enough to justify keeping. When I asked why not set it up for short-term rental, the hassle factor reared its head. The overriding hassle in this case wasn't tenants or dealing with a rental manager. It was taxes.

They didn't want to deal with the tax filing and all that entailed—not so much the actual taxes they may have to pay, but the hassle of the paperwork. So they'll sell instead.

I didn't understand their position until I spoke with another

**COWBOY MILLIONAIRE—THE NEW AMERICAN PIONEER**
*Chapter XII: The Three Most Important Things To Know Before You "Go Offshore"*

friend who's older than me. He was talking about his business and wanting to pass it along to his children.

They have ideas for expanding, but those ideas would require new permits and a few other hassles. The friend isn't interested, but he's happy to let the kids run with their ideas.

Turns out you have less tolerance for hassle as you get older.

That helps explain the other friends wanting to sell rather than rent their apartment.

Over the years, I've selected which hassles I'm willing to take on and which I'm not. You can't deal with everything, so focus on areas that you have an interest in or that are at least entertaining.

For Kathleen and me, renovating a property is fun... fun that can turn into profit. Others might rather wait until a renovation is done to buy a property. Fair enough—they don't want the hassle of the renovation and understand that they'll pay more for the convenience of buying a renovated property.

The hassle factor can come into play with most aspects of life. I prefer to not wake up at 2:00 a.m. the day after Thanksgiving to save $50 on a new TV set that I don't need. I'd rather just pay the normal price. Others, however, are happy to deal with the hassle of waiting in line in the freezing dark to get those savings.

We all choose which hassles to deal with. Recognizing

## COWBOY MILLIONAIRE—THE NEW AMERICAN PIONEER
*Chapter XII: The Three Most Important Things To Know Before You "Go Offshore"*

that's what we're doing and factoring it into our overall risk assessment of an investment, business, or life decision helps you make wiser choices.

I'm willing to go through some hassles in order to make a big profit... I'm also willing to go through some hassles to make sure my wealth and my future are protected.

And I'll tell you quite plainly: There are plenty of hassles when it comes to offshore living. Dealing with bureaucracy. Managing overseas investments. There are lots of service providers and people who can help you... but you also have to stay on top of it all.

Globalizing your life is about more than planting flags. Banking, establishing residency, obtaining second citizenship, and investing overseas are the big picture, but all these things come with administration, and you're going to need some "global" administration as well. None of this is sexy or timely (except when it comes time to file tax returns), but it's all very necessary.

Unlike in the days of the Old West, you don't usually have to put up with physical attacks and bandits, dangerous critters, etc., on the new frontier (unless you count lawyers). It's the administration that can sometimes make you think twice about the pioneer's life...

But it doesn't have to be hard...

So, let me share with you some of the top things I've learned

**COWBOY MILLIONAIRE—THE NEW AMERICAN PIONEER**
*Chapter XII: The Three Most Important Things To Know Before You "Go Offshore"*

to do (and not to do) when it comes to offshore living...

## 1. You Need Your Own Personal "A-Team"

Developing an advisory infrastructure—that is, legal, financial, tax, banking, and structures resources—in the places where you want to live or invest overseas is critical to building a globally diversified portfolio and a globally diversified life.

Here's the most important thing to know if you're just getting started at this: It takes time.

Before you engage an advisor, start with an interview. I've spoken with hundreds of attorneys and accountants in the twenty years I've been living and investing overseas.

Most of them I've met with once and decided, after that initial conversation, that this wasn't the guy (or gal) for me. Others I've worked with for specific investments or structure set-ups and not needed again. A handful have become long-term advisors and trusted friends.

What's the difference between the guys I spoke with once and knew I didn't want to work with and the advisors I've cultivated personal relationships with?

That is, how should you go about choosing your own advisors?

Make your selections based on these three criteria:

1. This doesn't have to be complicated, and I recommend

you avoid any potential advisor who suggests otherwise.

Over the years, I've interviewed attorneys who've insisted on preparing memos on my situation. I prefer personal meetings if possible and casual one-on-one conversations when trying to source new advisors.

In my experience, the attorneys and tax advisors who prefer more formal getting-to-know-each-other strategies aren't for me. That's just not how I'm most comfortable operating.

In addition, a more formal, memo-like approach usually means more complicated recommendations. I don't want pages of legalese on different options.

I want a straightforward recommendation of the best option with simple facts to support it. That way, I can make a quick determination as to how to proceed.

2. This doesn't have to be expensive. Offshore attorneys and tax advisors cost money, of course, but they needn't cost as much as you might fear they'll cost. And you don't have to go with the most expensive.

As with all things, you get what you pay for... but you can also overpay.

I've found that the guys who want to deal in lengthy memos and multiple options and scenarios prefer those complicated tactics because they can justify higher fees. Simple is not only better; it takes less time... and so it costs less money.

3. Finally (and perhaps most importantly), any offshore ad-

visor you engage should be a person you feel comfortable with.

Base your comfort level on two things: First is the advisor's practical experience working with people like you trying to do the things you're trying to do. Local experience isn't the same as expat experience.

Second is your gut reaction during the interview. If you don't like the guy, fair enough. If he makes you feel confused or uncertain about your situation, pay attention to that. Don't ignore your instincts when making these important choices.

Taking a step back, what infrastructure, exactly, are we talking about?

First, an American going offshore needs a U.S. accountant who understands offshore tax situations for U.S. persons. The CPA exam includes a section on taxes, but that doesn't mean someone with a CPA certification knows much about taxes.

CPAs who are fluent in U.S. tax matters often specialize in certain areas, such as corporate taxes. Most CPAs who specialize in personal taxes have never heard of the Foreign Earned Income Exclusion, let alone prepared a tax return that included the required forms.

My point is that you shouldn't expect your current U.S. tax preparer to understand anything about how to manage or report your tax obligations associated with offshore investments or structures.

Over the years, readers have told me that their tax advisors in the States have told them such crazy things as having a bank account in another country is illegal or that they aren't eligible for the Foreign Earned Income Exclusion because they are self-employed (have Schedule C income).

You need to find a U.S. tax preparer who specializes in expat tax matters. They aren't easy to find, but they do exist. I've spoken to and worked with dozens of them over the years. One observation I'd pass along is that you're better off with someone who is an expat himself.

The other core advisor you need is an offshore attorney. Typically, it's your offshore attorney who helps you set up whatever offshore structures you want.

Most formation companies and registered agents in other jurisdictions require you to come to them through an advisor, typically an attorney. Sometimes, you can go directly to a formation company, or you can use an online service.

However, going direct or using an online service means you are doing this on your own, without personalized legal advice or support. You'll be getting a cookie-cutter entity that you'll need to know how to deal with. You can save money by going this DIY route, but when you're just getting started, this may not be the best idea.

This is particularly true if what you want is an offshore trust. Trusts are complicated documents that require personalization to be most effective. An off-the-shelf trust document

## COWBOY MILLIONAIRE—THE NEW AMERICAN PIONEER
*Chapter XII: The Three Most Important Things To Know Before You "Go Offshore"*

will cost less, but it won't likely do what you need it to do.

Whether you're putting your offshore investments into a trust or holding them in an offshore LLC, you'll need a place to deposit the capital. That's where offshore investment or private banks come in.

The challenge here can be minimum account balances, which can be as much as $1 million. Some investment banks allow you to open an account with as little as $250,000.

If you're working with less, you do have options, including brokerage houses offshore.

With this basic infrastructure in place, you can expand organically and over time as you grow and diversify your holdings. The majority of my offshore investments are in real estate and direct investments in different countries. This means an important and ever-evolving part of my advisory infrastructure is local attorneys in every country where I've invested.

Critical when choosing a local attorney is language. Unless you are fully fluent in the local language, you need a local attorney who is fully fluent in English. No matter your language skills, you want a local attorney who has experience working with foreigners.

At a minimum, your local attorney will review contracts and carry out due diligence for any investment you're considering in his country.

I've found, though, that my in-country attorney advisors

often become much more involved in my local activities over time. They provide references for other resources, provide insights into the local market, alert me to emerging opportunities, and even send me deal alerts that I'd otherwise never have access to.

## 2. Think "What" Before "Where"

One question lands in my email inbox more than any other... Where is the best place to set up an offshore entity?

The quick and simple answer can include Belize, Panama, Nevis, and the BVIs. (See Chapter IX for more.)

These are my preferred jurisdictions. You have dozens of other options.

However, where to establish an offshore entity isn't the question you should be asking.

The question you should be asking is... What kind of entity is called for?

Using the wrong type of entity can create tax and administrative issues that can be costly to remedy... especially for Americans.

If an American uses an S.A. (Sociedad Anónima) from Panama to hold passive-income-producing investments, for example, he can create a U.S. tax liability for himself.

Use a Belizean IBC to hold property in Belize, and you can

**COWBOY MILLIONAIRE—THE NEW AMERICAN PIONEER**
*Chapter XII: The Three Most Important Things To Know Before You "Go Offshore"*

have a tax problem on the Belize side.

Generally speaking, Americans want to use a pass-through entity (or one that can be elected to be a pass-through entity) to hold assets that produce passive income.

For an active business, you want an entity that isn't pass-through. A corporation or its equivalent in most countries can't be used for pass-through activity even if you wanted to, which is why corporations are generally ideal for active businesses.

Once you've answered the "what" question, then you can move on to the "where."

The right "where" depends on many things, including where your attorney likes to do business. Offshore attorneys have favorite jurisdictions, depending on the needs of the client and the attorney's knowledge of local laws.

Some people like the idea of using a jurisdiction far from where they live.

If you're an American, an entity in the Seychelles can seem attractive simply because you figure no U.S. attorney trying to locate your assets in connection with a lawsuit is going to be able to find the country on a map, let alone your entity and assets based there.

For the most part, distance isn't important. Jurisdictions closer to home or where your investment activity is located probably make more sense.

The most important thing is to use the right entity for the

**COWBOY MILLIONAIRE—THE NEW AMERICAN PIONEER**
*Chapter XII: The Three Most Important Things To Know Before You "Go Offshore"*

right purpose.

Don't get talked into setting up an entity just because some attorney in a country where you're considering investing says you need an entity in that country.

I've told a story that makes this point so many times that the lady who features in it wrote to ask if she should be getting a royalty every time I publish the tale.

The story goes like this…

Lady came to Panama on a real estate scouting trip. She didn't end up buying any real estate but left with a Panamanian corporation.

I met the lady years later at a conference, where she approached me to ask what she should do with her Panamanian corporation.

She'd been carrying it for years… paying the associated fees… but had never known what to use it for. She formed it because the attorney she met with during her years-ago property scouting trip in Panama had told her she needed it.

Unfortunately, that lady isn't the only one I can tell the same story about.

Panamanian attorneys sell Panamanian entities. Specifically, they sell Panamanian corporations.

Every Panamanian with any money puts his real estate in a Panamanian corporation. It's an effective strategy for Panamanians on many levels. It provides asset protection should someone sue them personally in Panama, and it can save on transfer and property taxes.

However, a Panamanian corporation can have negative tax implications in the United States for an American.

Alternative entities are available for holding property in Panama that don't create a potential U.S. downside, including, for example, an SRL (Sociedad de Responsabilidad Limitada).

Many countries have SRLs. It's the civil law equivalent of an LLC.

However, the requirements to set up an SRL in Panama mean they rarely make sense.

You can, though, use a non-Panamanian entity to hold property in Panama. It's legal and doesn't present a problem unless your Panamanian attorney doesn't understand Panamanian law.

You don't need to register your non-Panamanian entity in this country... though some Panamanian attorneys will insist you do, either out of ignorance or a desire to get some extra cash out of you.

Some countries do require a foreign entity to be registered to do business, but many (in fact, most) don't require you to register your foreign entity if you're using it only to hold property.

Some foreign attorneys may advise you that you can't hold property in their countries with a foreign entity... registered or not. They'll tell you that you need to set up a local entity to hold title to property in that country, and that the local entity can then be owned by your foreign entity.

It's true that your foreign entity can own your local entity. However, in most cases, you don't need that extra layer. It's just another way for your local attorney to get more money out of you.

Start by asking what you need an entity for... but also ask why. Always question why someone is telling you that you need a specific entity.

The lady who was told she should have a Panamanian corporation when she was scouting for property years ago did ask why. The answer she got was, "Because everyone in Panama has one."

That kind of answer should make you wonder about who you are working with.

In the end, the lady in my story let her Panamanian corporation fall off the register.

She never did buy any real estate in Panama. If she had, that corporation wasn't the entity she needed anyway...

## 3. Don't Be Tempted By Workarounds

Here's a case where wanting to avoid hassle overseas can get you in big trouble...

## COWBOY MILLIONAIRE—THE NEW AMERICAN PIONEER
*Chapter XII: The Three Most Important Things To Know Before You "Go Offshore"*

Throughout the years, I've had people tell me I've been wrong when I've suggested to them that certain things couldn't be done.

They've insisted I was wrong because, as they've assured me, they've been able to do whatever it was I was saying couldn't be done. They'd done it themselves, no problem.

For example, someone wrote in to tell me I was wrong to say that foreigners can't own land in the Philippines. As the reader explained to me, he had been able to buy land in the Philippines himself... no problem.

As I continued to read his letter, I realized the problem.

Yes, indeed, he'd bought land in the Philippines... by using a workaround that some local attorney had told him would be fine. And it will be fine right up until the point when it isn't.

I've known foreign buyers who've used similar workarounds to buy land in Thailand. They've bought land in that country in the name of the Thai corporations they've set up.

While Thai corporations can own land in Thailand, foreigners can't own the majority of shares in a Thai corporation.

"No problem," some local attorneys will tell you. "We can work around that..."

One workaround can be to issue forty-nine percent of the shares of the Thai corporation in the foreigner's name and the other fifty-one percent in a Thai person's name... then have that Thai person sign over the shares in blank.

## COWBOY MILLIONAIRE—THE NEW AMERICAN PIONEER
*Chapter XII: The Three Most Important Things To Know Before You "Go Offshore"*

The attorney holds onto the share certificates. Many Thai attorneys have become wealthy landowners thanks to this handy workaround.

Another workaround involves some convoluted structuring that has the foreigner owning forty-nine percent of company A and company B owning fifty-one percent of company A. The buyer then also owns forty-nine percent of company B, with company A owning the other fifty-one percent. Again, this works until it doesn't.

Eventually, the Thai government began cracking down on the various workarounds foreigners were using to own land. The same will happen in the Philippines at some point.

In the offshore world, workarounds are common, not only when it comes to property ownership.

You'll encounter workaround options to do with establishing residency... acquiring a second passport... paying taxes on income from your rental property...

Whenever you find yourself presented with and considering the idea of a workaround to help you achieve some objective, ask yourself if the risk (as in the case of buying land in Thailand) or the liability (as in the case, say, of ignoring filing a local tax return to report your rental income) is worth it.

A friend used a workaround to get his oversized dog to Costa Rica. He told the airline that it was a seeing-eye dog. My friend isn't blind, and I have no idea how he convinced the airline that the dog was a service dog, but it worked.

His risk was low, as, had his sham been exposed, he simply would have missed his flight and taken his dog back home with him. Missing a flight isn't as big a risk as losing the property you thought you owned in Thailand.

Another common workaround for expats in many countries for many years has been the border run...

This is a way of staying beyond the length of time allowed by a tourist visa without investing in establishing longer-term residency formally. You just leave the country (run across the border) and then return, in a day or two, say, to renew your tourist visa.

Historically, some countries ignored the multitudes of tourist stamps in some passports and allowed this workaround to continue. Meaning that, again, this was a fine strategy... until it wasn't.

Eventually, countries got more serious about formal residency requirements... especially in the wake of the COVID-19 pandemic, when no country wanted more people inside their borders than they legally had to accept.

Border running was so common in Thailand that service industries sprouted up. Locals would charge a fee to take your passport to the border for you and get you a new stamp. They used part of your fee to bribe the immigration officers at the border and kept the rest of it for the service.

**COWBOY MILLIONAIRE—THE NEW AMERICAN PIONEER**
*Chapter XII: The Three Most Important Things To Know Before You "Go Offshore"*

Expats were happy to use these services because they saved them money. The risk to the expat ranged from overstaying his tourist visa if the courier wasn't able to get a new stamp for him in time… to having his passport stolen.

I used this workaround myself when I lived in Argentina for five months. I was working in the north of the country for a drilling company that hadn't decided how long I would be staying and therefore did nothing to get me legal residency.

I was only thirty minutes from the Bolivian border, so I drove to the border to exit Argentina before my tourist visa expired and then re-entered to get a new tourist stamp and another ninety-day visa.

Unfortunately, the Bolivian immigration worker said I had to spend the night in Bolivia for him to stamp me into that country. Without the stamp from Bolivia, I wouldn't be able to get the new entry stamp in Argentina that I needed.

I had no intention of wasting a night in Bolivia, so I had my Argentine assistant tip the Bolivian immigration guy. We were then allowed to turn around and go back across the river back into Argentina… where I got a new stamp.

That worked once, more than twenty years ago, and could still work today once or twice, but it's not a strategy for remaining a resident long-term in Argentina… or anywhere else.

The risks if you're caught include being banned from the country where you're trying to remain for as long as a decade. That would be a problem if you had a business or property investments in the country.

Workarounds can be common in the world of offshore banking, too. It's not easy to open a bank account in Colombia as a non-resident foreigner. Banks in this country are going to want to see your Colombian cédula (national ID) before opening an account for you.

One practical reason for this is that, to open a new account, Colombian banks' computer systems require an ID number with the same number of digits as a cédula number. Otherwise, the system won't accept the new account application.

Nevertheless, I was able to open a bank account in Colombia without a cédula. However, it was only because I had a personal introduction to the branch manager by my attorney... and because that branch manager was clever and open-minded enough to make up an ID number for me that included my passport number so it would fit in the cédula field.

Did I then go around telling everyone that it's possible for a non-resident foreigner to open a local bank account in Colombia, no problem? Nope.

Because it's not... my workaround experience notwithstanding.

## PART III

# The Ultimate "Backup Plan" For Your Lifestyle

# CHAPTER XIII

# The "Master Key" That Allows You To Escape Lockdowns And Travel Restrictions

The virus came from China.

All of a sudden, it seemed like the whole world was shut down... Lockdowns, stores closed, people trapped in their homes by government order...

I'm sure you remember the COVID-19 pandemic of the early 2020s perfectly well.

I'm not one for conspiracy theories... but I know many people decided to put a rush on setting up their backup plan—their "get out of dodge" plan, their "bug out" plan—after COVID...

They did not want to be trapped and stuck—their freedoms restricted—ever again. They wanted options.

And, as I hope you understand by now from reading this book so far, when you cast your view as wide as can be, you'll

**COWBOY MILLIONAIRE—THE NEW AMERICAN PIONEER**
*Chapter XIII: The "Master Key" That Allows You To Escape Lockdowns And Travel Restrictions*

always find options to increase your freedom...

COVID is what prompted my friend, real estate investor, and speaker, John Palumbo, to seek a second passport.

John says, "I think we will see another COVID effect, so to speak, somewhere in our lifetimes. We've been trained on how to shut countries down in the blink of an eye.

"The next time something serious comes, they can literally close borders in days.

"And unless you're sitting on a second passport, you'll be frozen out.

"Even though I had a home in Europe, I couldn't go. They said it didn't matter. You're not a citizen."

And that's why John decided to become a citizen of the European Union...

During the pandemic, I was able to travel freely between the United States and Europe—even when Americans were banned—because I hold a European passport as well as my U.S. passport...

This is the power of a second passport, and why I call it the "Master Key" that can help unlock so many other aspects of an internationalized life...

With a second passport, not only do you enjoy greater travel freedoms, but all the rights of citizenship in a whole other country—including the automatic right to live there permanently, work there, start a business, access banking and free

**COWBOY MILLIONAIRE—THE NEW AMERICAN PIONEER**
*Chapter XIII: The "Master Key" That Allows You To Escape Lockdowns And Travel Restrictions*

nationalized health care, and much more.

Kathleen and I both hold Irish citizenship and Irish passports, thanks to the time we spent in Ireland. We became naturalized Irish citizens.

When I first suggested to Kathleen that we get naturalized in Ireland once we were eligible, she wasn't terribly interested in the idea. It required paperwork, and she dislikes administrative tasks.

Her attitude changed when having Irish citizenship allowed us to live in Paris full-time when we decided to move there (because both countries are part of the EU).

When the pandemic closed off travel routes, she was even happier that we had options and were able to make travel plans thanks to this decision made more than a decade before...

My immediate family all came together for Christmas during the pandemic in Chamonix, France. We followed the lockdown rules in France, but the fact that we were all able to be in France during the pandemic is a testament to the thirty years of internationalization I'd done... including—and most importantly—getting second citizenship.

Our granddaughter was able to take in her first sledding experience in the shadow of Mont Blanc because her parents moved to France before she was born. Our daughter wanted to live in the culture and art that overflow in Paris.

## Chapter XIII: The "Master Key" That Allows You To Escape Lockdowns And Travel Restrictions

Our son, thanks to the pandemic, skipped his classes at NYU Shanghai since he wasn't interested in taking remote classes. He used that time to work on various music projects, including his first album. Then he was able to take in-person classes from NYU in Paris the next semester, thanks to his Irish passport.

Kathleen and I were able to go to the States to help my mother with some work on her house over the summer and return to Paris via Ireland… again, thanks to our Irish passports.

We had residencies, citizenships, properties, and bank accounts organized to allow us this very flexible international life… even in the most inflexible times.

## Why This Is The "Master Key"

One of your ultimate goals should be to get yourself a second passport… to give yourself more options and a backup plan in case the situation in your home country turns sour due to politics or some other government pestilence.

A second passport expands horizons and fosters opportunity. It allows you to live, work, and invest more freely. With an EU passport, for example, you could get a job in any EU country and move around the European Union at will.

A second passport can also allow you to visit more destinations without needing a tourist visa. My EU passport came

## COWBOY MILLIONAIRE—THE NEW AMERICAN PIONEER
*Chapter XIII: The "Master Key" That Allows You To Escape Lockdowns And Travel Restrictions*

in handy when I had to make a research trip to Brazil. U.S. passport holders needed a visa to enter Brazil, but with my Irish passport, I could sidestep this requirement, saving time and expense.

As I've said, we all remember the lockdowns and travel restrictions during the pandemic. Americans were banned from entering Europe, and Europeans were banned from entering the United States.

But, as I've already covered, because I hold both an EU and a U.S. passport, I was free to enter either jurisdiction. The bigger issue for me at the time was finding flights.

There are other benefits to holding a second passport, too...

Want a bank account in Europe? Your chances as an American are poorer, but another passport will open the doors of many bankers who otherwise might ignore your knocks.

A passport for an EU member country brings special advantages, but it can also be the hardest to come by these days (with important exceptions related to genealogy).

You have a number of other good alternatives, as well, in the Americas and the Caribbean.

Information on residency, citizenship, and second passports is easy to come by in this internet age. The trouble is, googling "foreign residency" or "second passports," you don't know whether you can trust the information you find.

**COWBOY MILLIONAIRE—THE NEW AMERICAN PIONEER**
*Chapter XIII: The "Master Key" That Allows You To Escape Lockdowns And Travel Restrictions*

There are three main ways to go about getting a second passport:

1. You might be entitled to a second passport because of your heritage. Up to forty percent of Americans could actually be entitled to a European passport, according to Bloomberg. If your parents or grandparents were born in Ireland, for example, and you can prove it, you can be entitled to Irish citizenship. The same applies in many other countries.
2. If you live in a country long enough, you will usually be entitled to apply for citizenship after a certain number of years. The length of time varies widely, depending on the country. This is how Kathleen and I got our Irish passports.
3. You can legally buy second citizenship and a passport in certain countries.

    OK, technically speaking, you are not buying citizenship or a passport. But multiple countries have so-called citizenship-by-investment programs (CIPs). Make a substantial investment in the country... which can include buying real estate... and you will be entitled to fast-track citizenship.

    If you can afford them, these programs will grant you a new passport within as little as a few months.

## COWBOY MILLIONAIRE—THE NEW AMERICAN PIONEER
*Chapter XIII: The "Master Key" That Allows You To Escape Lockdowns And Travel Restrictions*

In this third and final part of my book, we're going to cover all the different ways and means to get yourself a second citizenship and second passport... and why this is the "Master Key" that unlocks so many other opportunities.

As I mentioned, you could already be entitled to a second passport through your genes, your heritage... This is the first route you should explore to get a passport, because, if you can prove your case, you get citizenship immediately (well, once the bureaucratic process is complete), without having to move anywhere, and at relatively little expense. So, this is covered in the next chapter, Chapter XIV.

For most people, however, getting residency in a particular country—and actually living there for a period of time—will be a necessary interim step before you can become a naturalized citizen in that country and acquire the country's passport. Your best options for overseas residency are covered in Chapter XV... and the pathway from residency to citizenship is covered in Chapter XVI.

For some people and in some countries, residency alone may satisfy their needs. They never go the extra step of acquiring citizenship. I have permanent residency in Panama, for example, but I haven't sought citizenship here. One reason is that Panama technically requires you to give up your other citizenships once you acquire citizenship there... it does not allow dual citizenship.

**COWBOY MILLIONAIRE—THE NEW AMERICAN PIONEER**
*Chapter XIII: The "Master Key" That Allows You To Escape Lockdowns And Travel Restrictions*

Some countries have special programs for investors, known as "Golden Visas," that allow you to acquire residency there if you invest a particular amount (usually several hundred thousand dollars) in a local business, government bonds, or real estate.

These often come with a minimal requirement for the amount of time you actually must spend in-country... and can offer a shorter route to a second passport than the traditional naturalization route. This is covered in Chapter XVII.

Finally, in Chapter XVIII, you'll learn about countries where you can "buy" citizenship outright (perfectly legally) through their citizenship-by-investment programs. A small number of countries offer these direct-to-citizenship options. It's the most expensive, but certainly the fastest route to your second passport.

But... not all second passports are created equal. Some provide more travel freedom—visa-free access to more countries. Some (like an EU or CARICOM passport) give you the automatic right to live and work in countries other than the country the passport is from.

So, you'll want to pay close attention to the differences between particular programs to understand the right option for you.

## Residency Versus Citizenship—What's The Difference?

With citizenship, you get the right to vote as well as permanently live and work in a country and enjoy all the protections and rights that citizenship affords (such as protection from the state). Getting citizenship also means that you can acquire a physical passport from that country.

Residency is typically more temporary, subject to renewal and changing conditions, depending on the government of the day. Residency can give you a residency card, but not a passport.

However, residency can often be converted into citizenship if you spend long enough in the country. Typically, five years or more... this is called acquiring citizenship through naturalization.

## CHAPTER XIV

# The "Inheritance Gift" You Never Knew About—That You Could Be Entitled To (Here's How)

What do you know about your family history?

If you're like most Americans—probably quite a lot. Stories passed down through the generations...

Did your family come from the Old Continent?

If so, you could already be entitled to a European passport and just not know it yet. You can "inherit" citizenship through your bloodline...

Europe offers many opportunities for second citizenship through ancestry. If you aren't sure of your heritage, find out. Your second passport could be a family tree search away.

The blood flowing in your veins, or, in other words, your family ancestry, is just as valid in the eyes of many nations regarding citizenship as the act of being born in those countries.

Based on the laws of nationality in the following countries, you are eligible for citizenship regardless of where you were born by virtue of your father, your mother, or both being citizens of that country... and, in some cases, generations much further back than that.

It's worth it to brush up on your family history and see what adventure could await you overseas.

## These Countries Will Grant You Citizenship Based On Your Ancestry

Two terms that are important to understand when researching citizenship through ancestry are *jus soli* (right of the soil), which means citizenship based on where you were born, and *jus sanguinis* (right of blood), which means citizenship based on your ancestry.

About sixteen percent of the world's countries, nearly all of them in the Western Hemisphere, grant *jus soli* citizenship. If a child is born in the territory of one of these countries, say, the United States, Argentina, Mexico, or Canada, boom, he or she is a citizen of that country.

Most of the rest of the world grants *jus sanguinis* citizenship. Rather than as a result of country of birth, *jus sanguinis* citizenship is passed through blood relation. That is, the parents' citizenship(s) determines the child's.

So if a child is born in a *jus soli* country... say, Canada... to parents from *jus sanguinis* countries... say, a Thai mother and an Irish father... right out of the womb, the newborn would have *jus soli* citizenship from Canada and *jus sanguinis* citizenship from Thailand and Ireland. Lucky kid.

Many countries in the Old World extend *jus sanguinis* rights deeper into the bloodline, beyond parents. With these programs (usually referred to as citizenship by descent or ancestry programs), grandparents, great-grandparents, and, in some cases, the deepest family roots you can dig up can qualify you for citizenship.

Although ancestral citizenship is a birthright, you must apply and prove the qualifying family ties before citizenship is granted.

Nevertheless, for those who qualify, citizenship through ancestry is the easiest, quickest, and cheapest route to a second citizenship and passport.

Among the most interesting ancestry programs on offer are those from European Union-member countries. Holding a passport from one of these nations comes with big benefits, including the right to live and work in any of the twenty-seven EU-member nations.

At the most practical level, a second citizenship is useful for travel, and it can also mean residency and work options.

**COWBOY MILLIONAIRE—THE NEW AMERICAN PIONEER**
*Chapter XIV: The "Inheritance Gift" You Never Knew About—That You Could Be Entitled To (Here's How)*

The following are countries that follow the practice of *jus sanguinis* to some extent...

- Armenia
- Austria
- Canada
- China
- Czech Republic
- Estonia
- Germany
- Haiti
- Iceland
- India
- Iran
- Ireland
- Israel
- Japan
- Malta
- Mexico
- Norway
- Philippines
- Poland
- Romania
- Slovakia
- South Korea
- Switzerland
- Thailand
- Tunisia
- U.K.
- Ukraine

Another form of *jus sanguinis* called leges sanguinis offers immigration privileges to those with ethnic ties to a country (ancestors having left due to diaspora, war, etc.).

You might not get full citizenship, but if you can prove ties to the countries below based on their criteria, you might benefit from expedited naturalization times or easier paths to citizenship than you'd have otherwise.

These countries include:

- Afghanistan
- Armenia
- Bulgaria
- Croatia
- Finland
- Greece
- Hungary
- Ireland
- Israel
- Italy
- Kiribati
- Liberia
- Lithuania
- Rwanda
- Serbia
- South Korea
- Spain
- Turkey

Here's a closer look at some of your top options…

## Greece

Greeks believe in bloodlines. You're eligible for Greek citizenship if you have at least one biological parent or grandparent of Greek origin, i.e., born in Greece.

The name of the game is "Find As Many Supporting Documents As You Can"—birth, marriage, and death certificates; baptismal records, IDs, passports, even college records… extra points for a Greek municipality certificate certifying the ancestor's birth and municipality number.

Along with the family supporting documents, you'll need to

provide a clean police report.

You can apply in Greece at a registry office in Athens, or you can apply at the Greek consulate in your home country.

A common concern with Greek citizenship is military service. Males ninteen to forty-five can circumvent the requirement by maintaining foreign resident status (possible as a Greek national), which permits up to six months of residency in Greece per year. Anything beyond six months automatically renders the citizen a permanent resident and may require up to fifteen months of military service.

## Ireland

Thinking you'd like to live or work in the EU? Good luck, my fellow North American. No problem, though, dear citizen of the Emerald Isle.

Interested in traveling in the Middle East? In some countries, your blue passport with the eagle on the cover might be a liability, but your red one with the harp on the front won't raise anybody's eyebrows. The luck of the Irish...

For a country of only five million, Ireland's overseas presence is remarkable. In the United States alone, nearly thirty-five million souls claim some Irish descent. The worldwide number is estimated at around seventy million.

If either of your parents were an Irish citizen at your birth or any of your grandparents were born on the island of Ireland (thus including Northern Ireland), congratulations! You're entitled to Irish citizenship and an EU passport.

All you have to do is enter your birthdate into the Register of Foreign Births and apply for a passport. To add your birth to the Foreign Births Registry, apply online at **dfa.ie**.

You'll need the following documentation… from your Irish-born grandparent:

- Marriage certificate (if applicable);
- Passport or copy of the death certificate;
- Full, long-form civil Irish birth certificate or baptismal registers if born after 1864.

From the parent from whom you are claiming Irish descent:

- Marriage certificate (if applicable);
- Passport or official ID;
- If deceased, a certified copy of the death certificate;
- Full, long form civil birth certificate.

From you:

- Full, long-form civil birth certificate;
- Notarized copy of passport or official ID;

- Proof of address (bank statement, utility bill).

The registration process takes about nine months. Once registered, you're an Irish citizen and can apply for a passport.

## Italy

Italy's citizenship through ancestry program is even more generous than Ireland's.

If either of your parents were born in Italy, you have a right to Italian citizenship.

You can use any of your Italian-born grandparents, as well. There are categories for great-grandparents, too—basically, if you have an ancestor from Italy at any point since the unification of the country in 1861, you could be in the running.

### Case Study: "How I Got My Italian Citizenship Through Ancestry"

My friend John Palumbo acquired Italian citizenship through his bloodline…

"In Italy, it's called 'law of blood,'" John says.

It sounds ominous… but it's actually a law that could

benefit millions of Americans.

It's the law that allows foreigners with Italian bloodlines to gain citizenship in Italy through their ancestry.

John recently acquired his Italian citizenship through digging into his heritage... with the assistance of italMe, a company that helps Americans do just that.

"They told me as I started my journey: Assuming that everything works out for you, you're already an Italian citizen, John. We just need to prove it.

"Because of your blood, you were born an Italian citizen. As of right now, though, you've never gone back there to document it. And so we're just going to take back what is already yours.

"You don't get granted Italian citizenship, you get recognized as an Italian citizen. There's a big difference."

## It All Started At A Conference...

John first got the idea to pursue a second passport at a Live And Invest Overseas conference...

"I wanted a second passport because of my heritage. That was truly my first desire for having it. Because, born into an Italian family, yes, we ate spaghetti every week, and yes, we had meatballs and all the good stuff that goes with it.

## COWBOY MILLIONAIRE—THE NEW AMERICAN PIONEER
*Chapter XIV: The "Inheritance Gift" You Never Knew About—That You Could Be Entitled To (Here's How)*

"And so I was very proud of my Italian heritage. And even my daughter today is proud of her Italian heritage and her last name, Palumbo.

"The speaker at the conference gave different options for getting a second citizenship and second passport—you could spend six or seven years in a country and get naturalized.

"Or for some countries, you could fast-track it by spending $400,000 or $500,000, and I could buy my way in. I just thought, those were not really options for me.

"The real clincher was that, at the very end of the program, the gentleman on the platform said, 'Now, if you have bloodlines that go back to these certain countries, that's the path of least resistance. That's a piece of cake. All you've got to do is just prove your bloodline, and boom, you're in.'

"And I thought, this is a piece of cake. Because I am Italian. My grandparents on my mother's side and my father's side both came from Sicily."

John alludes to the three primary ways that people can get citizenship in another country and a second passport: There's citizenship by investment, which some countries have. And that's a route that can cost hundreds of thousands of dollars. There's also naturalization, which is spending long amounts of time in a particular country, multiple years, to get a passport.

But then there's the route that John took and which I think every American really should look into for themselves—because there are so many tens of millions of Americans with European heritage, and they could be entitled to, like John, citizenship by ancestry.

People sometimes think you can only go back one generation to acquire citizenship—in other words, that your parents had to be citizens of that country.

But that's not the case in lots of countries, like Italy…

"That's more of a myth," John says. "For some people, going back one generation may be their only option because they usually can't find their relatives' records going back further.

"My grandfathers on both sides of the family, who came over to the United States, were born in the 1800s. So part of this process is that they've got to go back to these small towns to find the original birth records. And in Italy, they're typically going to a small church. It's kind of like in the movies… they're blowing the dust off of these old books to go into them and find the ledgers of birth.

"My daughter and I, we did this process together, by the way. And it's funny because I told my daughter not to have any children until we got citizenship here. So that way, once you've got your citizenship in Italy, your child will be born instantly into citizenship in Italy. If you have a child before then, we'll have to go through the process for them. She just kind of laughed. She said, 'I'll see what I can do, Dad, but I'm not making any promises!'"

## Getting Help

"There are a lot of companies out there that will help you," John says.

"They're law firms, mostly, or firms that have attorneys with them that will take you through the process. I found that some of them had 1900 numbers for you to call. And if you're not familiar with what a 1900 number is, that's when you start paying the minute they answer the phone. It's 50 cents, a dollar, or maybe even a couple of dollars a minute.

"So I did my homework till I found what I felt was the most suitable match for me, from their fee structure, how they did it, and everything from there. The gentleman that helped me was named Ray Rapallo, and he's with a company called italMe."

Ray ran what italMe calls a "blueprint," creating a timeline and history of John's family and tracing it back...

"Here's what's interesting," John says. "I was almost one hundred percent sure we were going to go through my grandfather on my father's side, and that's what I told Ray... I'm going to say it took maybe thirty or sixty days to come back with the 'blueprint.' And Ray said, 'I've got good news and bad news.'"

John asked for the bad news first.

Ray told him they wouldn't be able to use his grandfather as his gateway back to Italian citizenship...

"And I was, like, but that's impossible. My grandfather came over on the boat, and I can remember his stories of what happened when he got off the boat and how he was treated and, unfortunately, mistreated and taken advantage of in many ways.

"I just didn't understand. How could this be possible?"

It turned out that when John's grandfather returned to the United States after fighting in World War I, he raised his right hand and took an oath of citizenship to America, thus rescinding his Italian citizenship. This was two years before John's father was born.

"Becoming a citizen of the United States automatically voided his Italian citizenship back then."

Such a thing does not happen today...

"Ray said, you're not going to be able to use your grandfather's bloodline because when he voided his citizenship, that cut off your bloodline. If my father had been born two years prior to him doing that, the line would have been open."

Luckily, there was also good news...

John's great-grandmother on the other side of his family never rescinded her Italian citizenship.

"I had no idea that I was able to go back to my great-grandmother on my other side. This was the value of the blueprint."

Things did not turn out the way John thought they would based on his family history and family stories... but he still had a pathway to citizenship.

## Should You Do It Yourself?

John says that working with Ray and his team and the blueprint they created really made everything simple. He didn't want the hassle of doing the whole process himself...

"I had talked to some people that had done it on their own, one hundred percent on their own, and they said it was a little bit miserable for them.

"First of all, you have to get every speck of documentation together, which means you'll need to go to Italy. You'll need to know what to get. And if you don't speak Italian, you'll need someone there with you to explain what you're getting and why you're getting it.

"Second of all, once you feel like you've got all of

that together, you have to make an appointment at the Italian embassy.

"If you get there and you don't have one T crossed or one I dotted, you go to the back of the line and start over again.

"And so I kind of got the impression that it wouldn't be as easy a process, and I don't know that I really wanted to go through that.

"Because, yes, I'm Italian, but I don't speak Italian. Maybe a few tiny words. *Bonjourno. Buonasera.* I would have been at a loss.

"I ran all my numbers, and by the time I would have made several trips over and had to hire someone to do documentation and certifications, I was coming up with $30,000 or $40,000 by the time hotels and rental cars and airplane fares had been taken into account."

John did not have to make a trip to Italy or even to the Italian embassy in the United States. Once he had filled out as much of his family history and details as he could remember, the professionals took over from there...

"I remember they were sending me reports in the early days of what they found, and they literally were coming back with where certain family members were buried, when they were born, when they died, and all the connections.

"So I found the blueprint to be fascinating. It's not like you're spending $10,000 to get a blueprint done—but I would have spent $10,000 just by the time I'd have bought an airplane ticket or two and gone over there.

"And by the way, I hear the time necessary to get into these embassies can be as much as twelve to thirty-six months for appointments."

## Don't Delay

John originally got the idea to pursue a second passport at a Live And Invest Overseas conference years ago…

But one of the main reasons he finally decided to go for it, he says, was COVID, travel bans, and everything that happened as a result of the pandemic.

"I was an avid traveler to Europe to begin with. I travel a lot, all over the world, regularly. And Europe was shut down."

John realized that if he had a European passport, he would have been able to travel to Europe, even when "ordinary" Americans were banned… because EU citizens (including dual citizens) were always welcome…

That's why John decided to become a citizen…

An Italian passport doesn't just mean John can live in Italy. He can live permanently in any of the twenty-seven

> European Union countries.
>
> "I'll give you a great example. I don't own a home in Italy, but I do own one in Greece. Having an Italian passport is just as good for living in Greece.
>
> "In Greece, they have a saying about the Greeks and the Italians, which translates to, 'One Face, One Nation.' Yes, the Greeks and the Italians are pretty much commingled together because the countries are so close, especially Sicily. A lot of the Sicilians came from Greece, and a lot of the Greeks came from Sicily.
>
> "I enjoy being able to be a part of the European Union as well as maintaining my U.S. citizenship.
>
> "I've had a lot of people ask me, Are you going to get rid of your U.S. citizenship? And I'm like, Are you crazy?
>
> "No. People struggle to get these. I would never let go of this. I enjoy being a part of the United States, and I enjoy having my second home—or really, it's my primary home—which is being part of Europe.
>
> "It's great to have that flexibility and freedom."

## Germany

German citizenship by descent is an option for those with German parents, grandparents, and great-grandparents.

**COWBOY MILLIONAIRE—THE NEW AMERICAN PIONEER**
*Chapter XIV: The "Inheritance Gift" You Never Knew About—That You Could Be Entitled To (Here's How)*

A child is automatically a German citizen from birth if they are born to at least one German parent, whether the child was born in Germany or abroad.

With an estimated population of forty-four million, German-Americans are the largest of the self-reported ancestry groups in the United States.

In order to qualify for German citizenship by descent, you have to have a German ancestor in your family so you can prove a family link. You can do this by filling out a form named "Appendix V" where you can prove all of the family generations that link up to that ancestor.

The rules can be somewhat convoluted...

The main criteria to be eligible to reclaim your German citizenship by descent are:

- You were born before 1975 as the legitimate child of a German citizen father;
- You were born after 1975 as the legitimate child of a German citizen (father or mother);
- You are a descendant of German Jews who had their citizenship taken away under Nazi rule between January 30, 1933, and May 8, 1945 (your descendants would also be eligible for German citizenship);
- You were born in wedlock before April 1, 1953, to a German mother—whose citizenship had been revoked—

and a foreign father;
- You were born out of wedlock before July 1, 1993, to a German father and a foreign mother. If you were born out of wedlock after June 1993 and your father is German, you are eligible if paternity was proven before you turned twenty-three.

You'll need the following documents to start your application process:

- Your passport;
- Your apostilled birth certificate;
- A completed application form in German;
- The birth certificate and copies of passports of the relevant ancestors;
- Your marriage certificate (if applicable);
- The marriage certificate of the relevant ancestors;
- Any documents related to your ancestor's political persecution (if applicable).

Becoming German comes with one caveat: a German citizen who voluntarily applies for and accepts another nationality in other countries except European Union countries automatically loses their German citizenship.

To start the application process, visit your nearest German

consulate for more guidance. You'll need to submit all your documentation in German.

## Latvia

Known as "the pearl of the Baltic Sea," Latvia is situated in northeastern Europe and shares its coastline with the Baltic Sea and the Gulf of Riga. It shares land borders with Lithuania, Estonia, Russia, and Belarus.

Latvia is one of the greenest countries in the world, with forests covering half of its territory. There are many castles and old palaces. The capital, Riga, is the most populous and largest city in the country. In addition to the official language of Latvian, Russian and Lithuanian are also spoken.

Latvia's nationality law is based on the Citizenship Law of 1994. It is primarily based on jus sanguinis and allows dual citizenship.

To be eligible for Latvian citizenship, you have to meet these two general criteria:

- One of your parents, grandparents, or great-grandparents was born in Latvia from 1918 to 1940 and had Latvian citizenship;
- This ancestor withdrew or was exiled from Latvia during or after World War II.

**COWBOY MILLIONAIRE—THE NEW AMERICAN PIONEER**
*Chapter XIV: The "Inheritance Gift" You Never Knew About—That You Could Be Entitled To (Here's How)*

You don't have to know Latvian and can keep your current citizenship if you meet these two general criteria.

You must have documentation that proves your connection to your Latvian parents, grandparents, or great-grandparents and proof that they withdrew or were exiled during that time period.

If your ancestor left Latvia before 1940, you are still able to qualify for citizenship but will not be allowed to have dual citizenship.

Your kids can apply for Latvian citizenship, too, if they were born before October 1, 2014. But if you're able to secure your Latvian passport first and then decide to have children, they would be eligible for Latvian citizenship at birth.

Prepare the following documents to start your application process:

- Your passport;
- Your birth certificate;
- One of your parents or grandparent's birth certificates;
- Your application form;
- Marriage certificate, if applicable.

You can visit Latvia's Office of Citizenship and Migration Affairs website (**pmlp.gov.lv/en**) for more information on the application process and how and where to submit your application.

At the time of writing, you can either submit your documents through your nearest Latvian consulate by mail to the Citizenship and Migration Affairs office in Latvia, by email, or electronically by using their e-service portal.

According to their website, you'll know if you have been granted Latvian citizenship or not within one month from the day the Migration Affairs office receives your application.

## Lithuania

Lithuania is situated in the center of Europe on the eastern shore of the Baltic Sea, surrounded by Poland and Kaliningrad (Russia) to the southwest, Belarus to the east, and Latvia to the north.

This gem of the Baltics is famous for its ancient history, fascinating pagan roots, and archaic language.

It's a country of gently rolling hills, forests, rivers, and lakes. Lithuanians are known for being nature lovers. This ancient nation attracts tourists for its unique culture and mix of Baltic heritages.

You are eligible to apply for Lithuanian citizenship if you meet these criteria:

- One of your parents, grandparents, or great-grandpar-

ents was a citizen of the Republic of Lithuania from 1918 to 1940;
- Your ancestor left Lithuania before March 11, 1990, when Lithuania restored its independence from the Soviet Union;
- Your ancestor left for any country that was not part of the former Soviet Union.

Besides these general rules, there are some other nuances that apply to Lithuanian citizenship eligibility.

For example, one of the cases is related to changing borders. If a person can prove that they or their ancestors were born in the territory of present-day Lithuania after 1918, then they can get Lithuanian citizenship.

If the place where your ancestors were born is not a part of Lithuania today (but was previously), then you should find other proof that your ancestor was a Lithuanian citizen.

## The U.K.

In spite of no longer being part of the European Union due to Brexit, a British passport is still one of the most coveted in the world.

As a British citizen, you can still travel visa-free to the EU for a ninety-day period. After that, you'd need a waiver via the Eu-

**COWBOY MILLIONAIRE—THE NEW AMERICAN PIONEER**
*Chapter XIV: The "Inheritance Gift" You Never Knew About—That You Could Be Entitled To (Here's How)*

ropean Travel Information and Authorisation System (ETIAS).

You may be able to claim British citizenship if you weren't born in the U.K. but you have a parent who was, as British citizenship is automatically passed down one generation to children born outside the U.K.

You may be eligible to claim British citizenship by ancestry if:

- You were born outside the U.K. to a parent who was a British citizen otherwise than by descent;
- You were born or adopted in the U.K. before January 1, 1983;
- You were born in the U.K. on or after January 1, 1983, to a mother or, if your parents were married, a father who was already a British citizen;
- You were born in the U.K. on or after July 1, 2006, and either of your parents were British citizens.

If you were born before January 1, 1949, you may be able to acquire British citizenship in the following circumstances:

- You and your parents were born in a Commonwealth country;
- You or one of your parents were born in a former British territory;

- One of your parents or grandparents married a British citizen before 1949.

If you were born before January 1, 1983, your British citizenship eligibility can be based on one of the following:

- You or one of your parents were born in a former British territory and registered as a British citizen;
- One of your parents was in Crown service when you were born;
- Your parents married before 1949, and your father was born in the U.K.;
- Your mother's father was born in the U.K., but you were born outside the EEA (European Economic Area).

If you were born after January 1, 1983, you can claim your eligibility if:

- You have a British-born grandfather who was in Crown service at the time of your parent's birth;
- You or one of your parents were born in a former British colony;
- Your mother was born in the U.K. and was registered as a British citizen between February 2 and December 31, 1982.

**COWBOY MILLIONAIRE—THE NEW AMERICAN PIONEER**
*Chapter XIV: The "Inheritance Gift" You Never Knew About—That You Could Be Entitled To (Here's How)*

Typically, the documents required to qualify for citizenship are a current passport, your full birth certificate, and the full birth certificates of your British parent or grandparent.

There may be other documentation involved in your application process, depending on your circumstances. For more information on application requirements, visit the U.K.'s government website (**gov.uk**).

It is important to understand that if you acquire British citizenship through ancestry, you won't be able to automatically pass on citizenship to any children who are born outside the U.K.

## Luxembourg

The Grand Duchy of Luxembourg—the only remaining grand duchy in the world—is a tiny country sandwiched between Germany to the east, Belgium to the west, and France to the south.

Luxembourg's estimated population is six hundred forty thousand, making it the second least populated country in the European Union. It has the highest number of expats among European countries, with more than forty-six percent of the population consisting of foreign residents.

With an area of two thousand five hundred eighty-six square kilometers (one thousand square miles), Luxembourg is also the second-smallest country in the European Union after Malta.

What is not small about this country is its economy—according to multiple sources, Luxembourg is the wealthiest country in the world with a GDP per capita of $133,590.

You can apply for Luxembourgish citizenship in two ways…

- If you have a male ancestor who was a citizen of Luxembourg after 1815 and before April 19, 1944. This date changes each passing year, i.e., if applying in 2026, your male ancestor must have been a Luxembourgish citizen before April 19, 1949.
- If you have a male or female grandparent born in Luxembourg. Having only great-grandparents won't qualify you for citizenship.

This route requires you to travel to Luxembourg in order to finish your application.

You'll need the following documents:

- Each ancestor's birth certificate;
- Each ancestor's marriage certificates;
- Each ancestor's death certificates (if applicable).

If your certificates are in French, German, or Luxembourgish, you won't need to have them translated, as these languages are widely spoken in this country. If your documents are not in one of these languages, you should have them translated to any of the abovementioned.

For more information on how to start your application process and trace your Luxembourgish lineage, visit Luxembourg's government website (**gouvernement.lu**).

## Israel

In Hebrew, the word aliyah means "ascent"—physically and spiritually. The word can mean that you are physically moving to Israel and is also used in religious services, i.e., when you're "called up" to the Torah reading.

Israel's 1950 Law of Return establishes that you are eligible to make aliyah to Israel and acquire Israeli citizenship if you're Jewish.

You are required to prove that you're both Jewish by heritage and that you practice the faith in order to qualify.

The documents required to start the process are your original passport and birth certificate to prove your connection with your Jewish parents and grandparents.

If you don't have the originals, then have your copies apostilled at your Israeli consulate.

**COWBOY MILLIONAIRE—THE NEW AMERICAN PIONEER**
*Chapter XIV: The "Inheritance Gift" You Never Knew About—That You Could Be Entitled To (Here's How)*

Bring your spouse's birth certificate and your marriage certificate with you to Israel, too, if you're married. Bring your kids' birth certificates as well, if you have any.

Israel also requires a criminal background check as part of the process. Americans can get theirs at the FBI.

What documents will you need in order to confirm that you're a practitioner of the Jewish faith? The truth is, there's not a specific list of documents for those making aliyah—not even provided by Israel's Ministry of the Interior. This is a case where the more supportive documents you can provide, the better.

Some acceptable documents to prove your Jewish faith are:

- Your Jewish marriage certificate;
- Your bar mitzvah or bat mitzvah certificate;
- Membership in a synagogue or Jewish organization;
- A letter submitted to Israel's Ministry of Interior by your rabbi that proves you're a practitioner of the faith;
- Proof of your parents' or grandparents' burial in a Jewish cemetery;
- Anything that proves your ties to the Jewish faith and community, such as speaking Hebrew.

## Romania

Romania, the largest of the Balkan nations, is situated between Moldova, Hungary, Serbia, Ukraine, and Bulgaria. The Black Sea also borders Romania in the southeast. It joined NATO in 2004 and has been a member of the EU since 2007.

The country's citizenship-by-ancestry program is one of the easiest to qualify for. To know if you're eligible, you must find out if:

- Your parents or grandparents were Romanian citizens, and
- If they renounced their Romanian citizenship voluntarily or if it was withdrawn involuntarily by Romanian authorities.

There are several articles in the Romanian Citizenship Law that support *jus sanguinis*. According to Article 5, any child who's born to at least one Romanian parent automatically becomes Romanian, regardless of where the child was born.

Article 10 says that any Romanian citizen who lost their Romanian citizenship has the right to regain it.

Many Romanians emigrated and lost their citizenship during the end of the nineteenth and twentieth centuries. If this is the case with your relatives, i.e., if you're the child or grandchild of a Romanian citizen who emigrated and lost their citizenship, you're entitled to Romanian citizenship by descent.

Article 11 says that Romanians who lost their citizenship unwillingly due to circumstances beyond their control can regain their right to a Romanian passport.

Before World War II, there was "Greater Romania," which included parts of present-day Bulgaria, Ukraine, and Moldova. After WWII, Romania lost considerable territory, and many Romanian citizens became Bulgarians, Ukrainians, and Moldovans.

To determine whether you have relatives who were Romanian citizens, you must take into account the fact that the old territory of Romania also includes parts of today's Ukraine, as well as parts of Moldova and Bulgaria.

You'll need to submit your application in person at the Ministry of Justice in Romania's capital, Bucharest, along with the following documents (apostilled and translated to Romanian, if applicable):

- Your passport;
- A clean criminal record in your country of origin;
- Birth, marriage, death, or divorce certificates of your relatives;
- Written statements and proof of loss of Romanian citi-

zenship (the more, the merrier).

If you live abroad, you can submit the documents to the Romanian embassy or consulate in your home country, but taking this step could extend the approval time for about a year.

In order to obtain Romanian citizenship, it's not required to know Romanian or take a history test—it is enough to prove the existence of your relatives with Romanian citizenship. You will have to say the Oath of Allegiance in Romanian in front of Romanian officials, but it's just two lines long.

Romania allows dual citizenship. You can include your children in your application if they are under eighteen years old. After you become Romanian, any descendants you may have will become Romanians at birth.

# Hungary

Hungary is one of the oldest countries in Europe, with a complex history as well as beautiful architecture, rich cultural traditions, and incomparable thermal baths.

It joined the EU in 2004. Bordered by Slovakia, Ukraine, Romania, Serbia, Croatia, Slovenia, and Austria, Hungary is a land-locked country, but it's well-connected to Europe through excellent rail networks.

Hungary's citizenship law is also based on jus sanguinis.

## COWBOY MILLIONAIRE—THE NEW AMERICAN PIONEER
*Chapter XIV: The "Inheritance Gift" You Never Knew About—That You Could Be Entitled To (Here's How)*

And Hungary has made it easy for its descendants to qualify.

You can apply on the basis of your parents, grandparents, great-grandparents, or even generations further back. In fact, if you can prove an ancestor of yours lived in the territory of the Hungarian Empire going back as far as the Middle Ages, you could get citizenship. You will also have to prove you can speak basic Hungarian, however.

You'll need documents from the Hungarian archives to verify that you're a descendant of immigrants who departed Hungary or that one or both of your parents or grandparents are of Hungarian origin.

Once you determine that you're eligible to apply, you'll need to submit the following documents:

- An application form in Hungarian (an aid in English is available);
- Your birth certificate;
- Your parents' marriage certificate;
- The birth certificates of the relevant parents, grandparents, or great-grandparents;
- Any other relevant official Hungarian documentation, i.e., old passports, civil, or military records, ID booklets, etc. It's key to establish a paper trail of your connection to the country.

*Chapter XIV: The "Inheritance Gift" You Never Knew About—That You Could Be Entitled To (Here's How)*

Once all of the documents have been put together, you can apply for Hungarian citizenship at your nearest Hungarian consulate. You must apply in person.

CHAPTER XV

# How To Live Anywhere You Want For As Long As You Want

It was once easy enough to get by under the radar in many countries, especially in Latin America and Asia—to be living in the country without going through the process of obtaining legal resident status...

In some cases, this meant doing a border run... staying only as long as your tourist visa allowed, crossing a border, then returning with new tourist status. I've known expats who have lived this way in some parts of the world for years or decades.

In other cases, it meant simply coming and going as you liked, largely without concern, because the country was lax in enforcing immigration restrictions.

Those days are over.

Today, you don't want to take the chance of not having proper status in whatever country you plan to spend significant time in overseas.

That means you'll need a residency visa... which can be a pathway to second citizenship and a second passport, depending on the nature of the visa and how much time you spend in the country...

Your options for residency overseas are many. Some countries offer a dozen different programs or more, including what I refer to as "self-sufficiency" options (that you qualify for by showing a guaranteed minimum monthly income) and investor options. And you can have residency in more than one country.

Maybe you simply want to know you have a place to retreat to if things get too bad in your home country...

Or perhaps you want to be able to spend more time each year in a country than that country's tourist visa allows...

Or maybe you're looking to move to another country full-time...

While most countries offer viable options for taking up full-time residency, some countries make more sense than others as backup residency options.

Be warned, though, that residency rules can and do change quickly and often. So, my strong recommendation is that you take steps toward establishing a backup residency in another country as soon as you are able to.

Don't wait until you think you need it. Getting the documentation together to apply for residency in another country can take weeks or even months. In that time, the rules can change. Panama provides a good historical example.

For several months in 2008 in Panama, all new residency applications were put on hold as the government changed the requirements for most of the country's residency permits, including the required investment amounts for investor visas.

When the smoke cleared after the changes, the investment amount to qualify for its reforestation visa had doubled, and other requirements were virtually impossible to comply with.

One company I know spent months reworking its reforestation program to meet the new requirements. Meanwhile, everyone who had applied or who wished to apply to use that option had to wait.

Jumping forward to 2012, Panama's then-President Ricardo Martinelli issued a decree that opened the door to ease residency for citizens of twenty-two countries… which became twenty-four countries with an amendment issued a month later and, in the years since, has risen to fifty.

The government also put in place mechanisms to allow applicants for residency under this Friendly Nations Visa to be issued work permits as well.

It's not that residency or citizenship rules change often in any single country. However, when they do change, they change quickly, typically within a few months. That leaves you with little time to take action to get in under existing rules, as you may have been intending.

Acquiring a second citizenship is typically a later step in any go-offshore plan. Most people don't start here—unless you have the option for citizenship by ancestry, covered in the previous chapter, or want to buy a passport, covered in Chapter XVIII.

As I say, for most people, residency will be their first step toward ultimately getting a second citizenship and second passport.

But there are also good reasons to pursue overseas residency as an end in itself—maybe in a different country from the country where you'll acquire your second passport. More options means you have more choices in the event of a crisis...

Like I alluded to, there are several broad types of residency visas available to you around the world. There are investment visas (Golden Visas), where you get a residence permit for spending a certain amount of money in the country, usually hundreds of thousands of dollars—whether you invest in the country's culture or sport or shares, start a business, or buy property. We'll discuss this route in extra detail in Chapter XVII.

Then there are more regular methods of acquiring residency, open to those without lots of money to spare—the subject of this chapter. You have work visas, often linked to having a job in-country; passive income and retirement visas, where proving a certain level of passive income every month will qualify you for residency; and various other permutations.

Generally speaking, work visas are linked to specific jobs, and your employer will help you with that—it's not a subject that I cover.

The exception is self-employment visas, which some countries offer, or the raft of "digital nomad" visas that have sprung up in recent years to attract remote workers.

We're primarily interested in visas that allow you to live in-country by showing a basic level of income or savings…

Let's look at some of your options for residency in some of my favorite countries around the world…

## Portugal

Right now, I'd call Portugal the easiest European residency option.

### The D7 Visa

You can qualify for the D7 visa by showing sufficient means. You need to prove you have an income, whether from financial investments, a pension, or rental income. Any provable passive income qualifies.

The minimum income requirement for the main applicant

is one hundred percent of the annual minimum wage in Portugal (820 euros per month). If a spouse or parent is included, the requirement is fifty percent of the minimum wage per person, and for each dependent child, it's thirty percent.

These are the bare-minimum figures... but my attorney in Portugal recommends showing income of 1,200 euros or more per month to smooth the application process.

The D7 Visa requires you to spend at least six consecutive months or eight non-consecutive months in Portugal to be able to renew your permit. It's intended for people who wish to live in Portugal, rather than pure investors.

It also makes you tax-resident in the country, as anyone who spends more than one hundred eighty-three days in Portugal is considered resident for tax purposes.

When you become a D7 Visa holder, you benefit from the following:

- The right to live, work, and/or study in Portugal;
- The right to include dependents in the application, including your spouse or partner, your children (including those over eighteen if they're single and studying at a Portuguese university), your parents or your spouse's parents, and siblings;
- Visa-free access to the Schengen area;
- Access to Portugal's public health care and education;

- After five years of permanent residency, you are eligible to qualify for citizenship.

The D7 visa is valid for two years, after which it can be renewed for three years.

## Mexico

Mexico is one of the easiest places to become a resident. This is one place where you don't need a monthly pension or income minimum requirement, but where you can qualify with your savings.

In our experience, this is a unique situation. Even though you can qualify for residency based on a real estate investment, it is not necessary.

These are the benefits of residency in Mexico:

- Once you become a resident, there is no minimum stay time in-country;
- Mexico has lenient rules for tax residency;
- It's easy to apply yourself, in English, at the nearest consulate.

The residency process begins at your home-country consulate. When requesting the visa at the consulate, you can file

**COWBOY MILLIONAIRE—THE NEW AMERICAN PIONEER**
*Chapter XV: How To Live Anywhere You Want For As Long As You Want*

your documents in English.

You will start as a temporary resident for four years, after which you will become a permanent resident without needing the specified financial criteria. You will first get a one-year temporary residency, which can be extended for an additional three years.

A temporary resident can qualify with just $45,000 in savings or $2,400 per month in pension income. For permanent residency, you'll need $180,000 in savings or $4,300 in income.

The qualification thresholds vary by consulate, and they're based on Mexico's minimum wage.

You could upgrade to permanent residency at any time while you are in the country if you meet the financial criteria. But you also have the option of jumping right to a permanent resident visa—without serving the normal four years as a temporary resident—by having slightly more income or savings.

You do not need to live in Mexico to maintain residency. However, you do need to be there to renew your residency when it expires.

After your visa application, you must enter the country within six months. Make sure you don't get processed as a tourist and are registered as a new resident. This will get you a thirty-day entry, while the visa is still unprocessed.

Within these thirty days, you must register at the Instituto

Nacional de Migración to get your card. You might not get your card before the thirty days are up, but it's important to start the process during this time.

Besides qualifying for residency based on your savings, it is possible to qualify through a real estate investment with a minimum value of $254,000 (this value can change slightly depending on the consulate where you are applying for the visa).

## Panama

To get residency in Panama, you have four main options: Panama's Friendly Nations Visa, the Retirement (Pensionado) Visa, the Self-Economic Solvency Visa, and the Qualified Investor Visa.

The procedure to get any residency visa is carried out at the central offices of the National Immigration Service. You need to be present in the country at the moment you apply.

First, you'll need to register your passport with the Affiliation Department of the National Immigration Service. Your passport will get a seal with a sequential registration number. After this is taken care of, you will file for the residency application.

All of this will be carried out by your lawyer, even if you do need to be here for the application. Your lawyer will make sure you have met all the requirements for the specific visa you are applying for.

You will then go with your lawyer to the Migration Department, where you will get an ID card, valid for six months. In this moment, your status as a foreigner will change from tourist to resident-in-process.

During this six-month period, you need to stay in the country while your application is being processed. If, for some reason, you need to leave the country, applying for a special permit can be granted.

It's recommended that you apply immediately for authorization to leave the country as you are applying for your visa to save you the trouble in case of an emergency. Traveling out of the country during the processing period without the special authorization carries a $2,000 fine.

### Friendly Nations Visa

Panama had the easiest residency program to qualify for out of any of the countries that I know.

Until August 7, 2021, if you were from one of the fifty countries on the Friendly Nations list (including the United States and Canada), you qualified for residency by opening a bank account with a minimum of $5,000 plus one of the following: a Panama corporation, a job offer from a company in Panama, or property in Panama owned in your own name.

The biggest change today is that either an investment or employment contract is required to qualify for a Friendly Nations Visa. The investment can be in real estate (you will need to acquire a Panamanian property worth at least $200,000) or a time deposit (again, a $200,000 minimum investment) in a Panamanian bank.

A valid employment contract with a Panamanian company can also qualify you for the Friendly Nations Visa. This needs to be approved by the Ministry of Work and Labor Development (Ministerio de Trabajo y Desarrollo Laboral), which can be a lengthy and bureaucratic process.

The Friendly Nations Visa used to grant you permanent residency with the first application. Today, you will first get a provisional residency card that is valid for two years. After the two years are up, you will need to apply for a permanent residency card.

Non-Friendly Nations Options

For people from countries other than the fifty on the list of friendly nations, Panama still has a long list of residency permit options...

The most straightforward is the permit called the Self-Economic Solvency Visa, which allows you to invest $300,000 and apply for residency.

The $300,000 investment can be in real estate (again, you have to hold title in your own name) or a bank CD in any combination you like. For example, you could buy a $200,000 condo and put $100,000 in the CD.

If you're retired, you can apply for the Pensionado Visa, which is the only residency permit that grants you permanent residency, with the first application.

The Pensionado Visa works for anyone who is receiving a pension—private or government. For Americans, that means if you're on Social Security, you can qualify for this residency permit. The minimum pension income required is just $1,000 for a single person and then $250 for each dependent, i.e., $1,250 for a married couple.

The government fees are cheaper for the Pensionado Visa than they are for the other options.

For the Qualified Investor Visa, you will need to make an investment of $300,000 as an individual or a legal entity in a property purchase. This amount is slated to increase to $500,000. You can also invest $500,000 in securities as an individual or a legal entity. Or you can invest in a CD with $750,000 for a five-year period.

The Qualified Investor Visa has two benefits compared to the $200,000 investment requirement for the Friendly Nations residency option: The first is that the Qualified Investor

Visa gives you permanent residency with the first approval... no temporary residency period.

The second is that you don't have to be in Panama to start the process, and the approval process is fast-tracked to be completed within thirty days (still, it's Panama, so don't hold your breath on that special timeline).

## Colombia

Colombia has a transparent process with easy documentation requirements, including—very unusually—no need for a background check from your current country of residence.

My friend and colleague Lee Harrison is a do-it-yourself kind of guy when it comes to residency and other offshore tasks for which some may prefer to pay an attorney. Lee likes to get his hands dirty, so to speak, partially to save money but also to understand the process inside and out.

Lee started his residency process in Colombia while living in Uruguay. He went to the Colombian embassy to get the list of requirements and to find out how long approval would take.

It was the most pleasant embassy experience he's had in his decades of living and investing overseas. They brought him Colombian coffee, he met with the Colombian ambassador to Uruguay, and he walked out with everything he needed to proceed with residency.

All residency permits in Colombia are issued out of the immigration office in Bogotá. Once Lee had submitted all his documents, the embassy delivered his temporary resident's visa in two business days.

The following year, he decided he wanted a permanent resident's visa. He copied the requirements from the immigration website, collected the documents, and hopped on a plane from Medellín to Bogotá.

Expecting to stand in lines all day, he got to the immigration office early... standing in line when they opened at 7:00 a.m. He was out of there by 7:50 a.m. with his visa in hand. He had the rest of the day to kill before his flight back to Medellín.

Lee has gone through the residency process in Mexico, Ecuador, and Uruguay, as well, and none of them were as easy as Colombia. What sets Colombia apart is not only the simplicity but also the clarity and transparency of the process. All requirements are clearly spelled out on the immigration website, and the requirements don't change when you get to the individual agents.

To be a do-it-yourselfer for residency, you need to speak Spanish well enough to get through the process. However, if you don't speak Spanish and end up using an attorney, the process is still very easy.

Along with the easy process, Colombia has several residency permit options that are easy to qualify for.

Its Pensionado Visa income threshold changes with the exchange rate and annually with any increase in the monthly minimum wage, but the number in U.S. dollars currently is about $995. (The specific threshold is three times the monthly minimum wage in Colombia.)

Colombia also has several residency permits through investment. The lowest one is one hundred times the monthly minimum wage, or about $33,355 at the current exchange rate in a Colombian business.

Investors also have the option to invest in real estate for a value that amounts to three hundred fifty times the minimum wage, or about $116,760 at the moment. Those investments get you temporary residency that has to be renewed each year.

Bump up your investment to six hundred fifty times the monthly minimum wage, about $216,645 right now, and you can obtain permanent residency through your investment.

Temporary residency comes with a requirement to be in the country at least once every six months, while permanent residency has a requirement of being in the country only once every two years. Other residency permit options are available as well, but whichever you qualify under, Colombia has the easiest process I've seen so far.

## "Digital Nomad Visas"... Are They Right For You?

Nomad visas have been around since before the COVID-19 pandemic. Estonia introduced the first official program going back before 2020.

But the number of programs has risen dramatically post-pandemic. More than fifty countries around the world now have digital nomad visa programs, with more on the way. It includes many countries that also have investor programs, like Malaysia.

The rise of nomad visas reflects the changing world of work since the COVID-19 pandemic, and the boom in remote work. Countries are competing for mobile, relatively well-off workers.

Digital nomad visas offer opportunity... if you meet the criteria. The income requirements, while not huge, can be relatively high—multiples of local wages.

For example, for Portugal's digital nomad visa (D8), you must show you have a monthly income of about four times the local minimum wage, or roughly 3,000 euros per month. In Greece, the number is 3,500 euros per month after taxes.

The programs can be relatively restrictive, too. Unlike when you make a Golden Visa investment and typically get at least five years of residency... nomad visas are typically valid for one year initially but are renewable.

The Czech Republic's nomad program is specifically for skilled IT professionals and available only to applicants from eight countries: Australia, Canada, Japan, New Zealand, South Korea, Taiwan, the U.K., and the United States.

Unlike a Golden Visa, which gives you a longer residency term and something tangible in-country like a property... nomad visas are shorter-term and more precarious.

On one hand, it might seem attractive that so many countries are competing for remote workers to spend time there. But there's another way to look at these programs...

The rise of digital nomad visas could be seen as a crackdown on unauthorized work—visitors coming and going from countries across the world and working on their laptops while just in possession of a tourist visa.

"Digital nomad visas" don't honor the idea of being a digital nomad in the traditional sense—hopping from country to country every few months.

Countries instead want remote workers to register with the authorities, get official status, and stay longer in-country so they become eligible to pay taxes...

It's not laptop-slinging backpacker artists or writers;

these visas are aimed to attract... but better-off tech workers. Still, in most cases, if you can show the right levels of income, that's what matters.

If you've got the right knowledge or the right income, you have your pick of countries competing for you right now.

With a more senior remote worker in mind (like myself, perhaps), here are three digital nomad destinations worth a closer look.

As well as a digital nomad visa, each offers excellent health care, English-speaking locals, affordable rentals, warm weather, low crime, and a more mature expat community.

## Malta

While the Maltese archipelago (consisting of three main islands) may be small—taking up just three hundred sixteen square kilometers (one hundred twenty-two square miles) in the southern Mediterranean—it has a lot to offer.

You'll find a beautiful natural landscape, a warm climate, large expat communities, and friendly locals. Along with Maltese, English is an official language here and is widely and fluently spoken.

Malta's medical care ranks among the best in the world, and the island is home to several state-of-the-art facilities staffed by highly trained English-speaking personnel.

For digital nomads, Malta offers a Maltese Nomad Residence Permit, which is valid for one year. To be eligible, you need to have a work contract from an employer that is registered in a country other than Malta, be a partner or shareholder in a company that is registered in a foreign country, or offer freelance services to clients based outside of Malta.

You will also need to show proof of a property rental or purchase agreement, a certificate of good health, and a clean criminal record. The application fee for the Maltese Nomad Residence Permit is 300 euros.

## Panama

Panama is blessed with beautiful islands, palm-fringed beaches, mountain retreats, and colonial towns. The locals are welcoming, the climate is tropical, and your dollars really stretch here.

It's also home to some of the best and most modern hospitals in Central and South America and is ideally located for travel to the United States and Canada.

In 2021, Panama launched the Remote Worker Visa.

Among the criteria required to qualify are an employment letter and a letter of responsibility issued by your contracting company (a non-Panamanian company).

You'll also need a clean criminal record, a certificate of good health, and proof of at least $36,000 a year in income.

The Remote Worker Visa is valid for nine months and can be renewed once, for a further nine months. As Panama has a territorial taxation system, digital nomads are not taxed on any income from outside the country.

The fee is $250 payable to the National Treasury plus $50 for the visa card.

## Malaysia

Rich in history and natural beauty, offering a high standard of living at a low cost, first-rate health care, a low crime rate, and welcoming visa programs, Malaysia has long been one of Southeast Asia's most appealing retirement havens. Plus, as a former British colony, English is widely spoken, particularly in expat hot spots like Kuala Lumpur, Penang, and Johor Bahru.

Malaysia's digital nomad visa launched in 2022. Known as the DE Rantau Nomad Pass or the Professional Visit Pass, the visa allows location-independent workers in the digital sphere to stay in Malaysia for up to twelve months, with the possibility of renewing for a further year.

Under the terms of the visa, you can work as an employee, business owner, or freelancer for companies or clients outside of Malaysia. To qualify, you need to prove an income of at least $24,000 per year, have a clean criminal record, and have a valid passport with a minimum of fourteen months of remaining validity and six blank pages.

Under the terms of the visa, a dependent spouse or children can accompany you. A further requirement is health or travel insurance, which covers you and any dependents for the duration of your stay.

The visa application can be completed online and costs around $220 for the main applicant. The fee for each dependent is around $110.

## Will Your Old Pot Conviction Stop You From Living Overseas?

To obtain legal residency in most countries in the world, you have to provide a report from your current country of residency showing that you have no police record.

Outstanding warrants for speeding tickets may not

keep you from qualifying for a residency permit in another country, but any felony conviction probably will.

It used to be the case that an American with a felony record in a state where he used to live could get a report from his local sheriff or police in his current state of residence.

That game doesn't generally work anymore.

Most countries now require a clean report from the FBI, meaning any felony in any state will be flagged.

Some countries also run an Interpol check on any residency visa applicant.

For most people, an Interpol review isn't a concern. However, in the last couple of years, I've been asked by at least a half-dozen readers and conference attendees if an old drug conviction (typically marijuana) would make it impossible for them to qualify for legal residency in XYZ country.

Well, that depends. In some countries, such as Portugal, it depends on whether what you were convicted of is also a felony in the country where you're seeking residence. Portuga has decriminalized the possession and use of all drugs, including marijuana. So an old pot conviction should not hold you back in this case.

But there are other countries... and, of course, other crimes... that might be a problem for you. In these cases, you need to look for a country where your record won't matter.

There aren't many of these, but one country that currently doesn't require a police background check is Colombia.

This creates an opportunity... even if you're not interested in relocating to Colombia.

As I've explained, to apply for residency in most any country, you need to provide a clean police report from your current country of residence. So, if you have a felony conviction on your record, you could apply for residency in Colombia (which isn't going to care about your felony conviction because they aren't going to find out about it)... become a resident of Colombia and maintain that residency for a reasonable period, say two years... then get a background check from Colombia to use for your application for residency in the country where you really want to go.

Of course, this strategy presumes that you don't get arrested for something else during those two years as a resident of Colombia.

Obviously, acquiring residency in a country where you want residency by first establishing and maintaining residency in an interim country will take longer and cost more, but your alternative would be to live in the country you want to live in without obtaining legal residency. (I don't recommend this.)

If, for whatever reason, you don't establish legal residency in a country where you remain beyond the term of your tourist visa, you'll typically have to do a border run every ninety days to renew it.

"Border runs" used to be a common strategy for many American expats... but most countries have now cracked down on border runners.

Following this strategy, you run the risk of not being allowed to re-enter the country where you're "residing."

In addition to the tourist visa time limit, most countries also impose limits on the total days a foreigner can remain in the country in any twelve-month period; typically, this is six months.

The Schengen countries in Europe (most of the EU and Switzerland except Ireland and Romania) impose this six-month within a twelve-month period rule.

Someone I met on a plane once had been returned to the United States when trying to enter the Netherlands. This guy worked thirty days on, thirty days off as an engineer in Amsterdam.

When he kept to that schedule and returned to the United States for his thirty days off, he was OK. However, one off period, he took a vacation in Europe with his wife.

During that trip, they never left the Schengen region.

When he tried to return to work for his next thirty days, the immigration office at the Amsterdam airport took the time to count the guy's days in the country over the previous year. His vacation with his wife put him over for the rolling twelve-month period, so immigration sent him back.

On the other hand, I know people who have lived in France for twenty years or longer without establishing legal residency and who have never had a problem coming and going from that country. Is it that the French don't care as much as the Dutch? Maybe.

The risks associated with not having legal residency in a country where you're "residing" indefinitely range from not being allowed to re-enter the country for ninety to one hundred eighty days following a border run up to being banned from entering the country for as long as a decade.

A Canadian I knew years ago spent a year in the Caribbean on a boat; technically, she never left the United States (she never went through a border check), meaning she overstayed her U.S. visa. She was banned from entering the United States for ten years.

This made traveling to Latin America complicated, as most flights to the region at that time went through the United States and required clearing U.S. immigration.

> Staying on top of residency rules can be complicated.
>
> But, as these stories show, you do not want to get caught out.

## CHAPTER XVI

# The Easiest And Cheapest Way To Get Your "Master Key"

The reality, if you want to get a second passport... and you want to get it from a country that you like spending time in... is that you're going to have to put in that time.

Kathleen and I did that in Ireland decades ago. We didn't intend to leave Ireland. Life had other plans, but our Irish passports have allowed us lots of flexibility along the way.

When acquiring citizenship through residency, it's typically the duration of residency that matters; however, the type of residency can play a role as well. Pensionado residents in Panama, for example, used not to be able to qualify for naturalization no matter how long they lived in the country.

Also important is the difference between temporary and permanent residency. For those residency options in Panama, for example, that can qualify you for citizenship, the citizenship clock doesn't start ticking until you have achieved

**COWBOY MILLIONAIRE—THE NEW AMERICAN PIONEER**
*Chapter XVI: The Easiest And Cheapest Way To Get Your "Master Key"*

permanent residency status.

The point is to make sure you're aware not only of the different residency and citizenship choices available to you country by country but also of the particulars of each, as some can be limiting.

Before applying for a second (or third) citizenship, understand the rules of the countries where you already hold citizenship and those of the countries where you want to obtain it.

Following a series of Supreme Court cases and legislation passed in the 1970s and 1980s, the United States allows for dual citizenship. In fact, the United States really doesn't want you to lose or give up your citizenship. Give up your status as a U.S. citizen, and they can't keep taxing you.

Other countries have different rules. Singapore, for example, doesn't allow dual citizenship and proactively ensures that anyone who is naturalized gives up his previous citizenships.

Panama has a similar rule for anyone naturalized in this country; however, it doesn't proactively enforce the rule. Note that an exception to the rule is made for Panamanians born with dual citizenship (usually Panamanian and American). In this case, it's possible to keep both legally.

Some countries don't allow you to be naturalized in another country after you've been granted citizenship by them. Uruguay is an example.

If you're naturalized in Uruguay and then become a naturalized citizen of another country, Uruguay can take away your Uruguayan citizenship.

Again, the point is to check the rules for all countries you're considering before getting too far into the process with any one of them, remembering that the particulars of one citizenship could affect the others and that it can be advisable, advantageous, or even necessary to gain your new citizenships in a certain order.

## Easy Options

Many countries make it possible to acquire citizenship through residency. After you've been a full-time resident of the country for a specific number of years, you become eligible to apply for citizenship and a passport.

In some countries, if you have pension income over a certain threshold—generally $1,200 or more monthly—you can acquire a residence visa that eventually may lead to your eligibility for second citizenship and a passport. In all cases, applicants must pass a strict vetting process.

While economic citizenships (covered in Chapter XVIII) go for hundreds of thousands of dollars, the cost of obtaining a passport by being resident in the country for a specified period is usually a few thousand dollars. The much bigger investment requirement in this case is your time.

The catch can be the required period of residency, which varies from country to country. Most countries require a minimum of five years of legal residency before you can apply for naturalization. And most countries require you to be physically present in the country for most of that time. The idea is that you assimilate.

The specific requirements vary depending on the type of residency permit you have and how long you've held it, but most countries require you to be a permanent resident for at least three to five years before you're eligible to apply for citizenship, meaning that time in the country while you hold a temporary residency visa doesn't typically count toward the years of residency required before you can be naturalized.

In this chapter, I have identified some of the world's easiest countries to acquire a second citizenship through naturalization. Whether it's the length of time you must spend in the country (shortest is best)... or the simplicity of the application process... the countries covered here all rank highly compared to others, in my view.

The goal of this chapter is to make you aware of good-to-hold second passports you may not have considered before... and that are realistically available to you. These may or may not be places that you personally would want to live... that is an important factor and definitely something to be evaluated.

But my point here is to show you some of the shortest and easiest routes to citizenship by naturalization, if acquiring a second passport is one of your offshore goals (as I believe it should be)...

This is not something you can do overnight, but the first step is to educate yourself on the options available to you so that you can determine which country best fits your needs. And I want to make it easy for you.

To successfully becoming a dual citizen!

# Portugal

Portugal is a top global retirement destination because of its low cost of living, easy residency, slower pace of life, and beautiful surroundings. It also has great food, great weather, a large English-speaking population, and easy, cheap access to the rest of Europe. This is a great base from which to explore the whole of the continent.

In addition to the right to live, work, and do business in Portugal, one of the most stable economies in the world, you will receive a passport from an EU member state when approved for naturalization.

The Portuguese passport is one of the most widely accepted in the world, providing a great incentive to those who can claim citizenship. For example, since Brexit, the number of people applying to obtain Portuguese citizenship has surged.

Before Brexit, many British citizens would not have considered changing their status. Now, however, wishing to maintain their right to free travel in the EU, British citizens are seeking dual citizenship.

## How Many Years Of Residency Are Required?

Any person aged eighteen or over can apply to be naturalized as a Portuguese citizen after five years of legal residency (or three for those who are married or in a common-law partnership with a Portuguese citizen).

Anyone who has lived ten years as an illegal resident can also apply for Portuguese citizenship. I don't recommend going the illegal way, but it is possible if you can show proof you've been in the country that long.

## Are Tests And Interviews Required To Get Citizenship?

To qualify to become a citizen of Portugal, you'll have to pass a test in Portuguese.

You don't have to be fluent, but you'll need to be able to hold a conversation with the interviewer and take the Portuguese language test to ensure that you have a basic understanding of Portuguese. This is known as the A2 Level Certificado Inicial de Português Língua Estrangeira (CIPLE) test.

Five years is enough time to pick up the language if you're living in the country full-time.

A test on the history or constitution is not required.

## How Long Does It Take To Get Citizenship In Portugal After Applying?

The whole process of obtaining Portuguese citizenship by naturalization, from start to finish, takes about a year. The Minister of Justice makes the final decision on the application for citizenship.

If the application is approved, they will notify the National Archives of Portugal that your citizenship has been granted. You'll be notified via the contact details you provided.

You'll receive an ID card that includes a fingerprint chip and their personal information, such as social security, health insurance, and a tax identification number. After receiving the ID card, you can apply for a passport at the nearest passport authority office with your ID card.

## What Is The Naturalization Process Like?

Start by applying in person at the nearest registry office, the offices of the National Center for the Integration of Immigrants (Centro Nacional de Apoio à Integração de Migrantes, or CINAIM) in Lisbon and Porto, registration centers of the Institute of State Registration and Notaries (Instituto dos Registros e do Notariado, or IRN), or at Portuguese consulates and embassies.

If you can't apply in person, mail your application to the Central Registry Office (Conservatória dos Registos Centrais).

Your application must be submitted along with these documents:

- An identity document, such as the Portugal residence permit card;
- A copy of your birth certificate, apostilled at the Portuguese Consulate;
- A clean criminal record;
- A certificate of proficiency in Portuguese.
- An application form filled out in Portuguese with:
    - Your name, date and place of birth, nationality, marital status, profession, and names of parents;
    - Your name, number, and issue date of your passport or ID;

## COWBOY MILLIONAIRE—THE NEW AMERICAN PIONEER
*Chapter XVI: The Easiest And Cheapest Way To Get Your "Master Key"*

- Your current place of residence plus the list of countries in which you've lived before applying.

Note that the application form must be signed before a notary or an officer of the Portuguese Migration Service.

The Central Registry Office will do a preliminary review of your application. This can take up to thirty days. They'll notify you if your application is incomplete, and you'll have twenty days to provide any missing information.

After reviewing your application, the Central Registry Office sends a request to the Immigration and Border Service (Serviço de Estrangeiros e Fronteiras, or SEF) and the police.

The Immigration and Border Service will confirm if you've been a legal resident for the past five years, and the police will provide information about your criminal record in the country.

When your information is cleared by both institutions, the Central Registry Office decides whether or not to accept your application. This process takes about forty-five days.

Assuming your application is approved, the registry office will send your documents to the Minister of Justice. If your application is rejected, you still have twenty days to provide any additional proof and request a second review of your application.

After receiving your ID card, you can request the issuance of your Portuguese passport and get it by mail.

## Does Becoming A Portugal Citizen Make Sense For You?

Portugal is a great place to live, and Portuguese citizenship carries multiple benefits, one of which is the ability to travel, live, and work freely within the EU.

A Portuguese passport is one of the most widely accepted passports, giving citizens the right to visa-free travel or visa-on-arrival in more than one hundred eighty countries. It doesn't have the common visa restrictions imposed on other passports.

Portugal offers excellent opportunities for those looking to invest in real estate in Europe. You won't find any restrictions on the purchase of real estate, and most land and property are sold freehold. The country's property system is centralized and very reliable. The law protects property, property rights, and the right to access and use one's own property.

While Portugal is not a no-tax or even a low-tax jurisdiction, it does offer easy-to-get visas and has focused on initiatives that invite foreigners and foreign companies to come and spend, including tax breaks for the individual, the investor, and businesses.

If you have your eyes set on a European passport, Portugal may be your best bet. It's one of the best places on Earth to retire—a place where a top-notch lifestyle meets unique real estate opportunities.

## Uruguay

Uruguay has a spectacular coastline featuring some of South America's most luxurious beach resorts. Despite Uruguay's abundance of natural attractions, it remains largely undiscovered by North American expats.

Located on South America's eastern seaboard, Uruguay is surrounded by Brazil and Argentina; the South Atlantic Ocean forms its eastern and southern borders, while La Plata River makes up the western border.

The capital city of Montevideo—the southernmost capital in the western hemisphere—is home to almost half of Uruguay's three-and-a-half million residents. Roughly the size of Missouri, Uruguay occupies about the same latitude in the southern hemisphere as the state of Georgia does in the north.

The Uruguayan people are primarily of Spanish and northern Italian descent, with Italians having the most significant cultural influence. The first European settlement on La Plata River, on which Uruguay's capital, Montevideo, sits today, was founded by an Italian (Venetian) explorer, Sebastiano Caboto, during the Great Age of Discovery in 1527. Almost half of

Uruguay's population claims Italian descent, and ninety thousand Italian citizens live in the country.

Despite being a former Spanish colony, present-day Uruguay has a culture without significant Spanish influence, aside from the language.

Uruguay's colonial heritage and strong economy give it a European feel. This, combined with its pleasant climate, high standard of living, and beautiful natural features, makes Uruguay a prime retirement and investment spot for North American expats.

Once you've established foreign residency, Uruguay is one of the easiest places in the world to obtain citizenship and a second passport. The Uruguayan government is a stable democracy, and the country enjoys a solid banking system, which grants it the nickname "the Switzerland of South America."

## How Many Years Of Residency Are Required?

Married couples only need to keep their legal resident status in the country for three years before they can apply for citizenship.

Single individuals have to be legal residents for at least five years. For both options, applicants need to be physically present for at least six months a year.

## Are Tests And Interviews Required To Get Citizenship?

You must have a basic understanding of Spanish, as applicants will be tested on their Spanish-language proficiency. You will not be required to take an exam on famous people, government or constitutional affairs, or historical facts.

## How Long Does It Take To Get Citizenship In Uruguay After Applying?

It can take twelve to eighteen months or longer to be granted citizenship from the moment of your application. The decision is made by Uruguay's Electoral Court.

## What Is The Naturalization Process Like?

After you've been a resident for five years and spent at least six months in Uruguay per year, you can start your naturalization process.

This period is reduced to three years if you have underage kids who are legal residents or if you're married. The start date is the day that you file for residency.

You'll need the following to start your naturalization process in Uruguay:

- Your birth certificate;
- Copy of your passport or ID;
- Your residency certificate proving that you've lived in the country for the past five years (three if married);
- A certificate of entrance to the country issued by the National Migration Office (Dirección Nacional de Migración);
- Proof of any familial ties in Uruguay;
- Marriage certificate (if applicable);
- Your employment history issued by the Social Security Bank (Banco de Previsión Social), if applicable;
- Two witnesses registered in the Civil Registry. They must be at least twenty-five years old;
- A clean criminal record;
- Proof of social ties to Uruguay (property titles, utility bills, bank accounts, being part of an association or organization, volunteering activities in Uruguay, if you have children in school, any documents that support it). The more documents that support your ties to Uruguay, the better;

Once you've gathered all of the necessary documents (and all required documents must be notarized), make an appointment with Uruguay's Electoral Court and file your citizenship application on the date of your appointment.

The Electoral Court will review the documents and proceed to open a file. They'll set up a hearing that will be scheduled ninety days later. On the day of the hearing, you need to show up with two witnesses and pass an interview.

Citizenship is granted within six to twelve months. You won't have to take an oath of allegiance. The Electoral Court will issue the Naturalization Certificate as proof that your legal citizenship has been approved.

Thereafter, you must renew your ID as a legal citizen, and once your ID has been issued as a legal citizen, you can immediately apply for the Uruguayan passport.

## Does Becoming A Uruguayan Citizen Makes Sense For You?

Uruguay is a great country to become a citizen of if you don't mind being physically present for at least six months a year for five consecutive years.

The country has a sound banking system. It has one of the lowest crime rates in Latin America, one of the lowest poverty levels, and the longest life expectancy. Uruguay also offers a high quality of life for a fraction of what you would pay in North America.

For investors looking to buy real estate in Uruguay, it's a straightforward matter. This country has an excellent system of property registry and a well-organized process for property purchases. You can buy property in U.S. dollars, euros, or any major currency.

When it comes to individual sovereignty, Uruguay is a top choice. For those who want to fly under the radar, diversify their financial assets, obtain a second citizenship, or even live off the grid, you won't beat Uruguay.

With a solid financial system, First World infrastructure, and a stable and consistent democratic government, there are few better places to establish yourself.

## Paraguay

Paraguay is perhaps the least known, least understood country in the Americas. It's a country with a twisting, turning, complicated past that, at one point in its history, almost ceased to exist.

In the mid-nineteenth century, Paraguay was a wealthy nation thanks to protectionist dictators who happily exported tea and wood to the outside world but taxed imports heavily, creating a self-sufficient, wealthy, and (unlike Brazil and Argentina) debt-free country.

In fact, at the time, Paraguay was flush enough to pay cash for technology that allowed it to own its railroad. Elsewhere in the region, it was the British who owned and profited from

**COWBOY MILLIONAIRE—THE NEW AMERICAN PIONEER**
*Chapter XVI: The Easiest And Cheapest Way To Get Your "Master Key"*

the railway operations.

According to locals, that healthy economy inspired an attempt to interfere with Britain's tea monopoly in Europe, which led to the War of the Triple Alliance in 1864 (between Paraguay and the Triple Alliance of Brazil, Argentina, and Uruguay). Other stories about the start of this devastating conflict include that Paraguay was just trying to protect Uruguay's independence and got tricked into a much larger-scale conflict.

Still others say Paraguay's dictator at the time, Francisco Solano López, was delusional enough to attempt to take over South America.

Whatever the reasons for the war, the results were disastrous for Paraguay. By the end of the fighting in 1870, the population was decimated, and twenty-five percent of its territory was lost. Brazil occupied the country for six years.

A century-and-a-half later, Paraguay is back on the path to prosperity. The country has the fourth-lowest GDP per capita in South America, but its economy is growing. It's the world's eleventh-largest beef exporter, tenth-largest exporter of corn, sixth-largest producer of soy, and tenth-largest exporter of soy oil.

There are other compelling reasons to be paying attention to this little-thought-of country right now. Paraguay doesn't boast mega-tourist attractions, but it's got something that should catch your attention as a global investor—a burgeoning agricultural industry and oodles of fertile land. Plus, residency in this country is one of the easiest to get on Earth.

Paraguay's capital, Asunción, is located on the country's western edge alongside the Paraguay River (think Mississippi River) and serves as a regional hub.

You can fly from Asunción to most anywhere you'd want to go in South America—Buenos Aires, Montevideo, São Paulo, La Paz—within two hours. The country beyond the capital is divided into seventeen departments, and the country overall is natural disaster risk free.

---

## The Laws Of Dual Citizenship

Although every other country in this chapter formally allows dual (or multiple) citizenships, according to its constitution, Paraguay technically only allows dual citizenship with Spain and Italy, as those are the only countries with whom they have a dual citizenship treaty.

This could lead to the conclusion that, by not having an international treaty with other countries, dual citizenship would not be possible in Paraguay.

However, in practice, this is not the case.

An example given by a Paraguayan immigration attorney is Argentinians who have acquired Paraguayan nationality. They are still able to keep their Argentinian nationality because Paraguay does not demand the renunciation of the applicant's previous citizenship.

That would not be the case in Singapore, as the authorities in that country will request proof of renunciation of previous citizenship if you ever wanted to become a Singaporean.

To put it simply, if your country allows taking foreign citizenship, you can keep your previous citizenship and, at the same time, become a Paraguayan citizen.

For example, Canadians can keep their citizenship because Canada recognizes dual citizenship. Same with U.S. citizens—the Supreme Court has ruled dual citizenship constitutional.

## How Many Years Of Residency Are Required?

You can apply for naturalization after only three years of permanent residency.

## Are Tests And Interviews Required To Get Citizenship?

You have to take a test in Spanish to be approved, but you don't have to be completely fluent to pass.

There's also a test about Paraguayan history and culture.

## How Long Does It Take To Get Citizenship In Paraguay After Applying?

While you are eligible to apply for naturalization after three years of legal residency, the approval process can take anywhere from twenty-four months to five years, depending on the bureaucracy at the time of your application.

The volume of applicants in the queue when you apply, as well as the current mood of the Supreme Court (all naturalization applications go through the court), have an impact on how long it takes for your application to get through the system.

Even if it takes two years for your application to be approved, a total of five years to get your second citizenship (three years of residency and two years for the naturalization process) is no longer than the five-year residency requirement for most countries.

Thanks to the short residency requirement, Paraguay is one

of the quickest noneconomic citizenship options available.

## What Is The Naturalization Process Like?

Paraguay has a super-simple residency process. You don't need to make an investment or prove any amount of income; you can simply apply for residency, and as long as you're in good health, have a clean background, and supply the necessary documents (passport, birth certificate, etc.), you can get residency.

With such an easy residency program, it's not surprising that Paraguay also has one of the best citizenship options available anywhere. One important rule is that you must not be physically absent from Paraguay for more than six months during that three-year period.

The downside is that you have to prove your assimilation into local society. In other words, to be approved for naturalization, you have to show you have a connection to Paraguay.

While that should be easy enough if you move to Paraguay during the three-year residency requirement, it's harder if you get your residency but continue to live wherever you originally came from.

Simply put, to qualify for citizenship, you need to put some effort into creating some kind of life in Paraguay to help your case.

Buying property in Paraguay helps... as does having friends, speaking Spanish, and spending time in the country on a regular basis. The more support you can provide to show the effort you have made to establish a connection with Paraguay, the better.

After completing three years as a permanent resident, the next step is applying at the Supreme Court.

You'll need to submit the following:

- A birth certificate;
- ID-sized photos;
- Original passport and a photocopy (authenticated);
- Immigration card;
- Paraguayan *cédula*;
- Permanent residence permit stating the date of entry to Paraguay;
- Health certificate:
- Certificate of good conduct from your home country;
- Certificate of life and residence;
- Police background check;
- Paraguayan police certificate;
- Letter of employment (if you're working for a Paraguayan company);

- Marriage certificate (if applicable);
- Ownership certificates (if you own property in Paraguay).
- Any documents, such as bills, utilities, or rent, that serve as proof of your physical presence in Paraguay during the last three years.

Any documents from abroad must be notarized, apostilled, and translated to Spanish.

Your petition must be signed by all nine ministers of the Supreme Court. This is the tricky part of the process and why it's hard to establish a timeline to obtain Paraguayan citizenship. If one of the ministers who have already signed your petition retires or dies, the new minister has to re-evaluate whether or not they'll sign your petition.

Assuming that your application passed the review phase and was signed by all nine ministers, the Supreme Court will grant you the "Carta de Naturalización," which is a certificate of naturalization. You'll receive this certificate during the oath of allegiance ceremony at the Supreme Court.

After taking the oath, armed with your certificate of naturalization, you can request your Paraguayan passport and receive it ninety days later.

To maintain citizenship, you cannot live outside the country for more than three years after obtaining it.

**COWBOY MILLIONAIRE—THE NEW AMERICAN PIONEER**
*Chapter XVI: The Easiest And Cheapest Way To Get Your "Master Key"*

## Does Becoming A Paraguayan Citizen Make Sense For You?

Paraguay is generally overlooked by tourists and retirees who don't imagine it has much to offer, but Paraguay is a land of opportunity.

Historically, Paraguay has been a place to disappear. Folks on the lam from far and wide have sought out this country because it has something people who don't want to be found appreciate: super-low population density, at least in parts.

Paraguay is divided in two by the Paraguay River. To the east of the river is the Oriente; to the west is the Chaco.

Paraguay is home to seven million people. About three hundred thousand people live in the Chaco, a region larger than the entire country of Uruguay. That's about two people per square kilometer.

There is only one real road in the Chaco, the Ruta de Chaco, that travels from Asunción to the Mennonite town in the center of the Chaco and then on to Bolivia.

Easy in a place like that to get lost and never be found again if you don't want to be... That reality has contributed to Paraguay's reputation as a kind of global hideout. There are decades-long expats in Paraguay who were probably attracted to this country initially for reasons that fall into this category.

Other expats have come not to escape but to prosper.

## Chapter XVI: The Easiest And Cheapest Way To Get Your "Master Key"

Paraguay has a whole lot of undeveloped land. More important to some than the lack of population living on the land is the quality of the land itself. The global boom in agriculture (see Chapter III) makes acquiring land in Paraguay an excellent investment.

In the current global climate, a country with such an impressive agri-track record is definitely worth focused attention. Paraguay is a country of farmers.

Agriculture represents about twenty-eight percent of the country's economy, while nearly half the population depends on agriculture for its livelihood, making it a place for agricultural opportunities appropriate for the small individual investor.

Paraguay qualifies right now as a "blue ocean" market, an investment arena awash with opportunity. Besides agricultural opportunities, there are emerging urban and rural property investment opportunities. The very young population, as it matures, is all going to need places to live, making the local housing market an interesting bet.

This country is also a competitive and tax-friendly investment hub. You pay no tax on yields earned from an investment in the Asunción stock exchange, and both the value-added (or sales) tax and the rate of corporate tax are ten percent—the lowest in the region. Elsewhere in South America, earners are paying thirty to forty percent.

This place is also a bargain. Everything is cheap.

If you're hoping to acquire a second citizenship and a second passport through residency, Paraguay is one of your best choices.

## The Dominican Republic

The Dominican Republic is the Caribbean, but so much more—a melting pot with an eclectic population and a diverse history informed by Afro-Antillean, European, North American, and Latin cultures. The country also enjoys strong European influence. This not-so-little island nation has a lot to offer and a long history of welcoming foreigners.

The Dominican Republic first came onto my radar in the 2000s. It was the country's undervalued beachfront property that got my attention back then. These days, though, I focus on the DR's diversification opportunities in a bigger-picture way, as the DR checks nearly every box:

- It's one of the world's best residency-for-citizenship options;
- It has a strong, stable, and growing banking industry that still welcomes Americans;
- It has an approach to taxation that favors the expat;
- It's one of the world's top real estate investment markets.

The DR is the largest democratically run country in the Caribbean. It's increasingly accessible, with daily flights to and from the United States, Canada, Europe, and Latin America. Economic growth is being driven by tourism, primarily, and agriculture.

The Dominican Republic offers you a rich, relaxing, and truly diverse lifestyle. This is a bona fide Caribbean paradise that you don't need a big budget to enjoy, and recent infrastructural developments mean it's never been safer or easier for foreigners and investors to stake their claims.

## How Many Years Of Residency Are Required?

The Dominican Republic requires only two years of permanent residency before you can become a citizen… although that can be fast tracked if you purchase property worth $200,000.

## Are Tests And Interviews Required To Get Citizenship?

An interview is required before naturalization is granted, so you'll need to have a decent level of Spanish. During the interview, the officials will ask you why you want to become a

Dominican citizen.

You will also be asked to demonstrate knowledge of the country's traditions, culture, geography, and history.

How Long Does It Take To Get Citizenship In The DR After Applying?

After the Director of Immigration accepts your application for citizenship, the government process of approving your request can take a year-and-a-half to two years.

## What Is The Naturalization Process Like?

The DR has what is probably the easiest residency permit to maintain, with no time-in-country requirements. Once you have permanent residency, the only requirement you have is to renew your residency card every four years.

After two years of permanent residency, if you have all the required documents for your citizenship application and your application is accepted by the Department of Interior, you'll have your first interview on that same day. The director will meet with you to discuss your plans in the DR and why you're interested in becoming a citizen. This interview will be in Spanish.

Assuming you pass the first interview and your documents are in order, you'll be called to take a test on the history and geography of the DR.

**COWBOY MILLIONAIRE—THE NEW AMERICAN PIONEER**
*Chapter XVI: The Easiest And Cheapest Way To Get Your "Master Key"*

It's a ten-question multiple-choice test where you should have seven correct answers in order to pass. This test is taken around twelve to eighteen months after the first interview.

If you pass the second test, you'll be summoned to take the oath of allegiance about a month later. During the oath ceremony, you're given a certificate of naturalization. You're also given a sealed envelope (which must only be opened by the competent authority) containing a certification indicating your file number and instructions for the Director of Passports to issue your new DR passport.

You should make an appointment and bring both documents on the day of the application for the passport.

The documents you'll need to apply for Dominican citizenship are:

- Letter addressed to the Dirección General de Migración (DGM) requesting your certification of residency. It must be done in person, as you'll need to fill out a form with your signature and fingerprints;
- Certificate by the DGM indicating you've been a resident in the DR for the past three years;
- Birth certificate (apostilled);
- Curriculum vitae;
- Recent passport-sized photos—front, right, and left. Your arms and shoulders should be covered;

**COWBOY MILLIONAIRE—THE NEW AMERICAN PIONEER**
*Chapter XVI: The Easiest And Cheapest Way To Get Your "Master Key"*

- Copies of your cédula and passport;
- A copy of your residency card. Your residency card should be good for at least six months prior to the application. For example, if your residency card is expiring in June, you should apply by December at the latest.
- Clean criminal record from both your country and the Dominican Republic;
- Marriage certificate (if applicable);
- Certification of migratory movements (evidence of your comings and goings from the country);
- A guarantee letter from a Dominican guarantor with property and a car owned outright and a bank letter addressed to the Ministry of Interior and Police (Ministerio de Interior y Policía). Some exceptions are acceptable if you're unable to comply with all three mandatory qualifications;
- Affidavit of domicile in the DR (this could be the domicile of your attorney);
- Publication of the main page of your passport in an official newspaper;
- All certifications, the affidavit, and the publication in the newspaper must be issued within the last twelve months.

These are submitted to the Ministry of Interior and Police for processing, approved by the Directorate of Naturalization (Dirección de Naturalización), and signed by a Presidential Decree.

## Does Becoming A Dominican Republic Citizen Make Sense For You?

This island nation is your best option for an affordable life in the Caribbean and one of the best places in the world right now to invest in a rental property, both because of the growing demand and also because the property market is still accessible.

Agricultural investment is one of the biggest advantages this country has. Its export markets are not limited to the United States. The United States buys about forty-five percent of all exports from the Dominican Republic, and the country is working to expand its markets in the EU, China, and elsewhere.

Their approach to residency makes it a no-brainer.

You don't have to live in the country to be a resident and enjoy the associated benefits, making this a great choice for a backup residency.

Plus, the DR is the country that requires the least amount of permanent residency time in this chapter—after you've been a permanent resident for two years, you can apply for naturalization.

## Poland

Poland is a fascinating country that serves as the geographical and cultural crossroads of Eastern and Western Europe. Once the largest state on the continent during the Polish-Lithuanian Commonwealth, it was partitioned by Russia, Prussia, and Austria and ceased to exist on maps for one hundred and twenty-three years. It returned to European maps after World War II.

Poland has been a nation of survivors since the foundation of the first Polish state more than one thousand years ago, and, although the country has had a turbulent history, Poles have managed to maintain their identity.

Today, the country enjoys a crucial position as the largest of the former Eastern European states. It's the sixth most populous member of the EU and one of the most economically developed.

Poland offers one of the best passports in the world. It's a NATO and EU member and, since 2019, a member of the Visa Waiver Program. This means Polish citizens can travel to the United States visa-free upon obtaining approval from the Electronic System for Travel Authorization (ESTA) online.

Poles are friendly, and the country welcomes foreigners from all over the world. The country offers low housing prices and lower taxes compared to other EU countries. Renting

**COWBOY MILLIONAIRE—THE NEW AMERICAN PIONEER**
*Chapter XVI: The Easiest And Cheapest Way To Get Your "Master Key"*

or buying an apartment in Warsaw, Krakow, or another large city is much more affordable than in big European cities like Paris or Berlin.

Based in Poland, it's easy to travel all over Europe. Regular buses and trains run from the main cities of Poland to neighboring countries like Germany, Slovakia, the Czech Republic, Hungary, and other Baltic countries. Flights to all major cities in Europe are also extremely accessible—a one-way ticket costs anywhere from 30 to 60 euros.

Poland's economy has progressed rapidly in recent years, making it attractive to both entrepreneurs and investors.

Many of the foreign nationals living in Poland today come from neighboring countries. However, entrepreneurs and investors from around the world are welcome, and there are no restrictions regarding nationality.

Poland boasts a stable economy, and more foreign investments from Western Europe as well as from the United States and Asia are choosing to incorporate in Poland. Poland's geographic location facilitates logistics activities, and the Polish business environment is supportive of start-ups and entrepreneurs.

One of the most important factors in the rise of Poland's economy has to do with Poland's highly skilled labor force. Polish academic traditions date back to the fourteenth century—some of Europe's oldest universities can be found here. The Jagiellonian University of Krakow, for example, was established in 1364. Nicholas Copernicus and Marie Curie are among the great names of Polish scientists known and revered worldwide.

## How Many Years Of Residency Are Required?

The requirement is five years of temporary residency plus three years of permanent residency. If you're unable to get permanent residency, you can apply after ten years of temporary residency.

This is a long period, compared to other countries in this chapter. However, the key here is to compare all aspects of the Polish option to your other options in the EU...

With the exception of some EU countries, such as Portugal and Spain, it's much easier for non-EU citizens to obtain legal status in Poland. I covered Portugal earlier; I don't include Spain here because it does not allow dual citizenship with a few exceptions.

There are plenty of programs to establish yourself in Poland through work, study, family reunification, or investment.

This is not the case in every EU country. And an EU passport is a highly valuable document, which may be worth the wait...

COWBOY MILLIONAIRE—THE NEW AMERICAN PIONEER
*Chapter XVI: The Easiest And Cheapest Way To Get Your "Master Key"*

## Are Tests And Interviews Required To Get Citizenship?

A Level B1 Polish language certification is required for your naturalization application.

## How Long Does It Take To Get Citizenship In Poland After Applying?

The processing time can take up to twenty-four months from the moment your application is submitted at the local governor's office (the Voivodeship).

## What Is The Naturalization Process Like?

Prepare all the required documents and bring them to your nearest Voivodeship.

They'll review your case, and if all your documents are in order, they'll forward them to the Chancellery of the President in Warsaw, as it's the president who grants the citizenship.

You'll need to submit the following documents:

- An application form stating your reasons for obtaining Polish citizenship;
- Copy of your passport and/or ID;

- Passport-sized photos (thirty-five by forty-five millimeters taken over the last six months on a white background);
- Copy of your permanent residence card;
- Copy of birth certificate;
- Copy of Polish language certification;
- Proof of income in Poland;
- Copy of marriage certificate (if applicable);
- Copy of criminal record from Poland and your home country;
- Curriculum vitae with a short biography. It must be signed and state your name, surname, place, and date of birth as shown in your birth certificate, parents' names, profession, domicile, marital status, place and date of marriage, details of your spouse and children (if applicable), and any other information proving ties to Poland;
- Receipt of payment of stamp duty.

All copies must be certified, and all foreign documents must be translated into Polish by a sworn translator. The local Voivodeship will contact you if any additional documents are needed.

Assuming your application is accepted and citizenship is granted by the President, they will send your naturalization certificate by mail.

## Does Becoming A Polish Citizen Make Sense For You?

Poland is one of the most dynamic and fastest-growing markets in Europe due to the increasing number of new investment projects in the country.

As a member of the EU, it offers its citizens one of the most powerful passports in the world. It also offers entrepreneurs the opportunity to have easy access to the world's biggest free market area.

Furthermore, it provides foreign investors with competitive labor costs, a considerable size of the market, and industrial diversity. With almost five hundred academic centers, the Polish are well-educated and highly skilled.

Poland provides investors with a consumer market of thirty-eight million—one of the biggest in Europe—as it's one of the most populated countries on the continent.

It's also located in the heart of Europe, meaning you can easily reach over five hundred million consumers. It facilitates import and export activities while at the same time lowering the cost of transportation. Among Poland's major trade partners are Germany, France, the U.K., Italy, Hungary, Ukraine, Spain, Russia, and China.

Poland also boasts Special Economic Zones that provide investors with the opportunity to run a business with preferential terms and attractive tax benefits. What's more, if you're looking to establish a business in Europe, Poland's nineteen percent corporate tax rate is among the lowest.

Real estate investors can profit from Polish tourism, as it's a well-developed sector. This country attracts impressive numbers of tourists due to its landscape, history, and cultural heritage. Poland also provides high-quality roads as well as good social and urban infrastructure.

The only con when considering Poland for naturalization is the time you have to invest to eventually be able to apply for citizenship.

## Why My Daughter Didn't Get An Irish Passport

My family and I moved to Ireland years ago for personal and business reasons. At the time, I hadn't even considered the concept of obtaining a second citizenship. In fact, it wasn't until after my son Jackson was born that the idea of a second citizenship crossed my mind.

Jackson was born while we were living in Ireland. As a result, he was both a U.S. citizen and an Irish one automatically. In fact, he obtained his Irish passport well before he had his U.S. one. And it was that event—receiving Jackson's Irish passport—that prompted me to begin looking into the Irish naturalization process.

As it turned out, at the time and still today, Ireland's naturalization rules are fairly straightforward and generous.

You simply need to have sixty months (in fact, they actually count the total days rather than months or years) of "reckonable" (a term the Irish like to use) residency in a nine-year period. Reckonable means formal, legal residency.

After living in Ireland for the requisite sixty months, Kathleen and I applied for naturalization. It took the immigration officials in Ireland more than a year to reject our application.

We hadn't met the reckonable residency requirement at the time we sent in the application. Why it took sixteen months to make that determination is unclear, but at that time, Irish immigration was overloaded.

The problem was that, although we had moved to Ireland in December and gotten our first residency stamps in March, those stamps were temporary in nature. It wasn't until May that we obtained our first official residency documents.

Those first residency cards issued to us by Irish immigration were passport-sized pieces of folded construction paper with our photos stapled into them and an official seal stamped over the photo.

Eventually, a few years later, the system was digitalized, and ID cards similar to U.S. driver's licenses replaced the 1950s-style residency card we'd originally been issued.

As we had continued to maintain our residency status in Ireland after we'd made our original naturalization application, we were allowed to update our applications and resubmit them.

The final naturalization process took another year. So, all in all, it was close to seven years after we'd first established legal residency in Ireland before we received official naturalization.

## Another Problem

Not understanding the reckonable part of this country's residency rules caused another problem.

Our daughter, who was eight when we moved to Ireland, wasn't required to have a formal stamp or registered residency; as a minor (under the age of sixteen), she was able to piggyback on our stamps.

We thought this was a positive thing. It means she didn't have to miss school for every appointment with the immigration officer.

However, knowing what I know now, we should have forced the immigration officer to register her residency officially.

Because we didn't, as it turns out, we left Ireland before she had the required sixty months of registered residency.

She ended up with just two years of reckonable residency, between the ages of twelve and fourteen, by which time we'd wised up a bit.

This wasn't enough, though, for her to qualify for the naturalization process… meaning that, while my wife and I both obtained Irish citizenship and passports as a result of our years of residency in that country, our daughter did not.

Now, when looking at the residency and naturalization options a country offers, I know to ask more questions and to take a broader perspective.

## Ask The Right Questions

You need to look at more than just the immediate requirements in front of you and try to consider your situation long term.

For example, for years I was told that it was possible to be naturalized in Panama after five years of residency. The actual requirement is five years of permanent residency.

**COWBOY MILLIONAIRE—THE NEW AMERICAN PIONEER**
*Chapter XVI: The Easiest And Cheapest Way To Get Your "Master Key"*

Before the Friendly Nations visa program came into play, the only residency program in Panama that offered permanent residency from the first approval was the Pensionado Visa, which didn't allow for naturalization at all. Every other residency option required between three and five years of temporary residency before you could obtain permanent residency.

Therefore, the minimum amount of time you'd have to be legally resident in Panama to qualify for naturalization was eight years, not five. Even most Panamanian attorneys didn't understand this distinction back when Panama was just coming onto the offshore world's radar.

What other kinds of things should you think about before committing to a residency-for-naturalization process?

Check to find out whether, if you were naturalized in the country, you would be required to relinquish citizenship from another country where you hold a passport.

If serial naturalization is in your plans, you should check with attorneys in the countries where you're considering being naturalized before you start the residency process anywhere. Many countries retain the right to cancel your naturalization if you've pursued naturalization elsewhere.

I learned the questions to ask too late in Ireland. Don't make that mistake.

Make sure you have a clear understanding of what's

## Chapter XVI: The Easiest And Cheapest Way To Get Your "Master Key"

> required both before and after being naturalized by a country.
>
> Remember that some countries require all citizens of a certain age to perform military service...
>
> You don't want to find out too late that you have to spend two years serving in the armed forces of your new homeland.

CHAPTER XVII

# The Investment With "No Profits" That's Still A Good Buy

Residency by investment comes with many investment options, but the most straightforward and lowest cost is usually through real estate.

Golden Visas are associated with real estate investment programs in Europe and now other countries, but they also cover other investment options for residency in places like Portugal and Spain.

These residency programs are often confused with citizenship-by-investment programs (CIPs) because marketing groups sell them both.

However, they are each a different animal.

Citizenship by investment (covered in the next chapter) means just that. You invest in a country—real estate or a donation to the government being the main option for that investment—and the country will grant you citizenship. Typically, you'll have your new passport in less than a year after all the paper-pushing is done.

Residency by investment programs grant you residency—not citizenship—although after some period of residency, you may apply for citizenship. You have to ask yourself what your end goal is when looking at the residency program.

If you simply want residency so you can live in the country, buying real estate to obtain your residency permit can make sense, but check what other residency options the country has and the rules of those other options before jumping in and buying a property for your residency.

However, if a second passport is your goal, don't just seek out the cheapest investment threshold and apply for residency in another country. The naturalization requirements and processes will be different in each country.

The below is not an exhaustive list, but each of these countries has something worth considering for residency—whether it's a second passport or full-time living.

Here are some options in Europe that could ultimately lead to that coveted EU passport...

## Portugal

Portugal's Golden Visa program has multiple categories to qualify for residency. Two of them are donations to either scientific research or Portuguese art and culture. You can also invest in or start a business and create jobs.

However, although it was an investment option for many years, real estate purchases no longer qualify for Portugal's Golden Visa…

Because of a shortage of affordable housing for Portuguese nationals, Portugal's government announced major changes to the program in 2023. After months of deliberation, the changes became law.

Contrary to some reports, Portugal's Golden Visa was not terminated. It continues, but with changes to its investment options…

Property has been eliminated as an investment option. Prior to the changes, you could have qualified for residency by buying property for as little as 280,000 euros (albeit an older renovation property in a low-density area).

Your main options for qualifying for a Portugal Golden Visa today include: cultural heritage and artistic contribution (250,000 euros); scientific contribution (500,000 euros); VC and investment fund (500,000 euros); or start or invest in a business with at least ten local employees (500,000 euros).

Residency under the Golden Visa program requires you to spend just seven days in the country the first year and fourteen days every two years after that. It's a manageable time-in-country requirement for those simply looking for a backup residency option or a path to an EU passport that doesn't require an extensive amount of time in-country.

Portugal also lowered its required residency time for naturalization from six to five years, making it even more attractive.

Think about what this means: With this residency permit, you only have to spend, on average, a week a year in the country in order to keep your residency. And then, after five years of residency (although you'll need to spend more than just a week a year to show you've established a connection with the country), you can apply for citizenship.

It's a very sweet deal for anyone looking for an easy EU passport...

Portugal gives a test for naturalization that requires you to be conversant in Portuguese (A2 level) and answer basic questions about the country. You're not likely to pick up enough Portuguese by visiting a week a year, so you'll need to make an effort to obtain the required language skills.

Portuguese is a romance language, but out of the four main romance languages (Portuguese, Spanish, Italian, and French), Portuguese is considered the toughest to learn.

## Greece

Greece's Golden Visa allows you to invest in real estate or

other investment categories (Greek government bonds, alternative investment funds, etc.) to qualify for residency. It has some of the lowest investment thresholds among Europe's programs, starting at 250,000 euros.

To qualify for a Greek Golden Visa through a real estate purchase, you must invest 800,000 euros if the property is in the Administrative Region of Attica, the Regional Units of Thessaloniki, Mykonos, and Santorini, or on an island with a population of more than three thousand one hundred people.

In all other regions of Greece, the investment threshold is lower, at 400,000 euros. Properties must have an area of at least one hundred twenty square meters.

A lower investment threshold of 250,000 euros is available if you invest in a property (of any size, in any location) that has been converted from commercial to residential or if it's a listed building (of historical or cultural significance).

There are some restrictions on your use of the property. You can't place it on the short-term rental market or use a property that has been converted from commercial to residential as company headquarters.

Real estate prices in many areas of Greece remain low, as the country is just starting to recover from its decade-plus-long national debt crisis. You can find great value for your Golden Visa investment in Greece.

Greece's program imposes no physical presence requirement. That means you can invest in Greece, get and maintain your residency without ever returning to Greece. (You do have to go at least once to complete your paperwork and get your permit.)

However, if you want to get a Greek passport—as opposed to just keeping your residency permit—you'll need to actually live in Greece for a minimum of seven years.

And, if you want a Greek passport, you'll also need to learn the language—a requirement for naturalization.

You don't need to be fluent... just proficient (B1 level), but, with a new alphabet to learn and most Greeks under forty able to speak decent English, it's best to take some classes and immerse yourself.

You'll have seven years to obtain your language skills, as that is the time required to be a resident before you can apply for naturalization.

One thing to keep in mind is that Greece has mandatory military service for men. While it's not likely to be a problem for most primary applicants seeking naturalization due to the upper age limit of forty-five years, it might affect children you might include in your plans for naturalization.

Greece reduced the time of service years ago to just nine months in the Army or twelve months in the Navy or Air Force, and there are rumors the EU is trying to get them to abolish the practice.

**COWBOY MILLIONAIRE—THE NEW AMERICAN PIONEER**
*Chapter XVII: The Investment With "No Profits" That's Still A Good Buy*

# Spain

Spain is probably the most popular European country overall when it comes to expat living. However, its Golden Visa program is not the most attractive compared to others...

The minimum investment threshold is 500,000 euros (to qualify with a real estate purchase), which is among the highest in Europe. In addition, you have to renew your residency permit every two years, whereas for most other programs, it's five years.

In April 2024, Spain's government announced its intentions to do away with the real estate investment option of its golden visa program, citing pressures in the housing market and the ability of locals to afford property.

Another downside of Spain's Golden Visa program is the fact that Spain taxes non-tax residents on the imputed rental income of properties owned in the country. Therefore, if you buy a property for the Golden Visa program and don't rent it out, you'll still be taxed as if you did if you're not living in Spain for enough time to be considered a tax resident (although the imputed rental income tax doesn't end up being onerous).

Of course, if you're in the country long enough to qualify as a tax resident, you'll likely be staying in the property you bought for the program.

Spain allows for naturalization after ten years of residency, which is the longest waiting period mandated by any country I know of trying to attract people to invest through Golden Visa programs. You must be proficient in Spanish to qualify for naturalization.

However, you won't be able to keep your current citizenship unless you're from one of the countries for which Spain specifically allows dual nationality. Those are Andorra, Portugal, and Spain's former colonies, including the Philippines (and, interestingly, Puerto Rico). People from those places only have a two-year residency requirement.

Spain doesn't require a renunciation certificate, so, in practice, Americans can effectively hold both Spanish and U.S. passports (although Spain won't recognize your U.S. citizenship).

## Cyprus

Cyprus has two administrative regions: the north and the south. The Republic of Cyprus, in the south, is a member of the European Union.

Establishing residency in the Republic of Cyprus is about as easy as it gets with the Cyprus Golden Visa.

With this program, you fast-track your residency by purchasing property worth at least 300,000 euros (plus tax). The

## COWBOY MILLIONAIRE—THE NEW AMERICAN PIONEER
*Chapter XVII: The Investment With "No Profits" That's Still A Good Buy*

investment can be split between two properties.

You must also prove an annual foreign income of at least 50,000 euros, plus additional income if you have dependent children (who can be included for residency).

Going this route, the process usually takes just a few months. You'll be granted immediate permanent residency.

Applicants must prove on a yearly basis that they are still receiving the minimum income requirement according to family size.

Investors are also required to prove that they still maintain their original 300,000-euro minimum investment asset.

As a permanent resident, you're eligible to apply for citizenship after five years of living in the country. You must have remained in Cyprus continuously in the year prior to applying.

Believe me, it's not that hard a task—living on a subtropical island with three hundred forty sunny days per year, ample cultural events, and even a ski resort high in the Troodos mountains. This is one of the few places in the world where you can ski in the morning and take a dip in the Mediterranean Sea in the afternoon.

Citizenship through the naturalization route described above is generally granted easily. But you will need to pass an interview about Cypriot culture and current affairs.

After several years in-country, that will be an easy task,

I'm sure... And then you'll have your EU passport.

## Italy

Italy has a Golden Visa program, but it has flown under the radar and is not often considered alongside other programs in Europe.

This is probably because it does not include real estate, and the investment amounts are pretty high...

It is not one of the continent's most popular programs...

Historically, that honor was held by Portugal, which was also the first country to launch a Golden Visa in the wake of the 2008 crisis, in order to lure foreign capital... the idea then became popular across the continent.

But with real estate now removed from Portugal's program, Greece has taken over the top spot...

Currently, you can acquire Italy's Golden Visa either by investing 2 million euros in Italian government bonds, 1 million euros in "projects of national interest," 500,000 euros in an Italian public company, or 250,000 euros in an innovative Italian start-up.

After five years of temporary residency, you can apply for permanent residency and then sell your investment if you wish. After ten years, you can apply for citizenship through naturalization.

**COWBOY MILLIONAIRE—THE NEW AMERICAN PIONEER**
*Chapter XVII: The Investment With "No Profits" That's Still A Good Buy*

# Latvia

Latvia was once touted as the best and easiest place in the EU to qualify for residency. At that time, their real estate purchase requirement was 160,000 euros. Today, it's 250,000 euros, in line with Greece.

On top of the real estate investment, the government charges you a five percent fee based on the property price for the residency application.

You only have to visit the country once a year to maintain your residency, but if your goal is a second passport, you'll have to spend more time in the country, including living there full-time for the last twelve months before applying for naturalization.

Five years as a permanent resident, and you can apply for citizenship, but your initial residency permit is temporary for the first five years. That means the advertised five-year timeframe before qualifying for naturalization is actually a minimum of ten years.

In addition to the longer residency requirement, Latvia requires fluency in Latvian to become a citizen, and they don't recognize dual citizenship. Therefore, getting residency in Latvia only makes sense if you want to live there.

Some people who work remotely have taken up residency to save on taxes, but Latvia's individual income tax rates reach thirty-one percent quickly, meaning the effective tax rate—while good for Europe—is lower elsewhere, including Malta.

## Montenegro

Perched on the eastern edge of the EU, Montenegro is a little gem on the Adriatic and a mecca for investors and billionaires.

Montenegro is a new democracy striving to meet the requirements to join the EU. It's expected to join the world's biggest trading block soon.

The developments this former war-torn country has made since its independence in 2006 are impressive. Some of them include:

- Accession to NATO in 2017, vouching for the country's safety and stability…
- The development of Porto Montenegro at Tivat as a world-class yachting destination is contributing to the overall growth of the tourism sector…
- It's well connected to the rest of Europe. Montenegro has two international airports, offering two- to three-hour flights to European centers located in Tivat (for access to coastal regions) and Podgorica (for central and

northern regions). Flights to the United States usually go through Frankfurt and London. There's also a direct route between Paris and Podgorica. You can travel by ferry from the port at Bar to Bari, Italy...
- It is both a ski and beach destination, thus bringing good economic stability thanks to year-round tourism...

While it doesn't have a Golden Visa program per se, Montenegro offers residency to anyone who buys property in the country. You can invest any amount you like, as there is no minimum amount stated to qualify.

Of course, you'll probably hit a practical minimum of 50,000 euros to find something you'd be happy to live or invest in. The downside is that you have to renew the residency permit annually, making the administration for residency one of the highest.

For those looking to reduce their tax burden, Montenegro has just two tax bands—nine percent and fifteen percent. All earned income over 12,000 euros is taxed at fifteen percent.

Investment income is taxed at a flat rate of fifteen percent.

With three luxury marinas and even ski resorts (you can swim in the warm Adriatic waters and go skiing on the same day)... Montenegro is an up-and-coming destination.

Plus, the whole European continent is on your doorstep.

If you've traveled or done business elsewhere in Europe,

you're probably familiar with the rules of the Schengen Area. Put simply: You can spend a maximum of ninety days in any of the twenty-seven Schengen countries (anywhere in the zone) in any one-hundred-eighty-day period, and you have to be outside the zone for the other ninety days.

But because Montenegro is not in the Schengen Zone, you could base yourself here for the ninety days you're not in the zone, if you wanted. You would never have to leave the European continent, and you would never have to get a visa.

Awesome coastal lifestyle... low costs... profit potential... easy residency...

Montenegro's pending acceptance into the EU also makes this a possible path to an EU passport. Your Montenegrin residency would become EU residency...

Take advantage of a country that's headed for European Union living standards but still currently has the flexibility of being outside the bloc...

## How To Know What's Right For You

With residence by investment (as well as citizenship by investment), the "return" on your investment is the residency permit. If you buy right, or a particular fund does well... you might actually see your capital returned plus a bit more.

But residence-by-investment and citizenship-by-invest-

## COWBOY MILLIONAIRE—THE NEW AMERICAN PIONEER
*Chapter XVII: The Investment With "No Profits" That's Still A Good Buy*

ment programs are not typically touted for their profit potential or ROI. Governments are looking to attract capital to their countries... and willing to allow you to live there if you invest capital. Enabling you to make money or actually profit from your investment is not their priority.

Real estate is typically the best use of your cash. However, if you have the wealth to spare and no desire to deal with real estate, making a 250,000-euro donation to the arts in Portugal could be the most administratively simple option.

Obviously, if you want to live in a country full-time, you'd pursue a residency option in the country you are moving to. In that case, non-investment options may be a better alternative.

Again, using Portugal as an example, you can get residency there by showing you meet their income requirements, which aren't onerous at around 1,200 euros per month per person.

Golden Visa programs are best for those looking to establish residency in a country for either a backup residency or to run the time towards getting naturalized.

The question then becomes: What are the best routes to achieve those goals?

Some countries, like Spain, don't allow dual citizenship. If a second passport is your goal, you can take those countries off the list unless you want to renounce your current citizenship.

Some countries require as few as five years of residency

before you can be naturalized. Those should be at the top of your list.

Language requirements and the required investment are factors to consider. If you're not up for becoming proficient in another language, Greece and Latvia aren't attractive options for naturalization, even if their investment requirements are lower than for other countries.

With the Schengen-country restriction of no more than ninety days allowed as a tourist in any one-hundred-eighty-day period, the only way to spend more time in the region is to get residency in a Schengen country.

You can spend up to ninety days at a time in most other Schengen countries once you put residency in place. That is, the one-hundred-eighty-day rule for the region disappears, and you then apply the rules for the country where you're resident.

For example, become a resident with the Golden Visa in Portugal, and you can then spend ninety days at a time in Slovenia if you like.

Just be sure to not spend one hundred eighty-three days or more in any one country, or you technically become a tax resident of that country.

The bottom line is that you have many options for residency in Europe. You just need to choose one that fits your personal goals. Take a look at my comparison chart of Europe's

**COWBOY MILLIONAIRE—THE NEW AMERICAN PIONEER**
*Chapter XVII: The Investment With "No Profits" That's Still A Good Buy*

Golden Visa programs at this link: **cowboymillionairesecrets.com**, or view it by scanning the QR code below.

# CHAPTER XVIII

# The Fastest Way To Get Your "Master Key"

My friend and colleague in the offshore business, Mark Nestmann, once wrote for my *Simon Letter* service:

"Occasionally, I meet someone who's offended that I'm in the citizenship and passport business.

"'Citizenship shouldn't be bought and sold like a pair of shoes,' a man once told me. 'I think it's scandalous that some countries are selling their citizens' birthright.'

"I disagree. We live in a world where governments have assigned themselves the authority to prevent people from traveling if they don't have the right papers.

"One hundred years ago, you didn't need a passport to travel the world.

"Today, hundreds of millions of people can't leave their own country. Billions more have very limited travel options.

"Are you surprised that a market has developed to provide qualified applicants with the documents needed to travel more freely? I'm not, and I'm proud to be part of a business that, in the end, gives people greater personal freedom."

I wholeheartedly agree.

## "Economic Citizenship": The Quickest Route To A Second Passport

Put simply, "economic citizenship," or citizenship by investment, is a passive, one-time investment or contribution leading to a second citizenship and passport.

Last century, several countries had legitimate buy-a-passport programs that became corrupted and eventually stopped because the passports of true citizens were being questioned when they traveled.

In the new century up to 2013, only St. Kitts and Nevis and Dominica had realistic and legitimate options for obtaining an economic passport (that is, a passport through investment).

However, citizenship by investment programs (CIPs) are back up and running big time—many countries have launched programs since then, particularly in the Caribbean. Europe mostly launched residency-through-investment programs instead.

Many countries, including the United States, offer easier residency (not necessarily citizenship) if you invest $1 million or more, again, in a local business.

However, for straightforward give-the-country-some-cash-and-get-a-legitimate-passport programs, Dominica and St. Kitts and Nevis were, for a long time, the only two players in the game.

The sensible options available right now for true economic citizenship leading to a second passport are in Dominica, St. Kitts and Nevis, Antigua and Barbuda, Grenada, Malta, St. Lucia, and Vanuatu.

You should know, though, that not all passports are created equal, if a passport is your main goal for secondary citizenship. Some passports offer more visa-free travel than others.

You can check online to see the rankings of different passports for visa-free travel as well as compare countries. The Henley Passport Index is the gold standard comparison index in this regard.

The list changes regularly as countries offer or take away visa-free travel for other countries, so nothing is guaranteed. Ultimately, you are buying into one country, and their foreign relations may change over time. You are not, for example, buying automatic access to Europe, as that depends only on Europe. That said, countries with high rankings generally remain high.

On the other hand, it might not matter to you to have the highest number of visa-free countries if your current passport (say, a U.S. passport) offers a high number of visa-free destinations, and you are instead looking for a backup citizenship and a place to put down roots in the event you have to get out of dodge… In this case, outliers like Vanuatu, far from the U.S. sphere of influence, become more attractive.

## Caribbean Citizenship Options

The Caribbean island nations have much in common, although each has its own character.

They are all located in the string of islands known as the Lesser Antilles of the Caribbean West Indies, stretching between Puerto Rico and Venezuela.

They were all originally inhabited by native tribes—the Arawak, Carib, or Ortoiroids—and subsequently conquered by European colonists.

Spanish, French, and British invaders all left their marks, and slavery contributed to their economic and cultural development.

Since achieving independence, each country has established incentives for foreign investment and residency, including their respective CIP options.

Let's look first at what they have in common…

- Antigua and Barbuda, Dominica, Grenada, St. Kitts and

Nevis, and St. Lucia all offer at least two options for economic citizenship. One involves the purchase of real estate in a government-approved development. The other requires a donation or deposit in a government-sponsored fund. In some cases, business investment options also exist, but these tend to require substantially larger investments and longer approval processes. They are aimed at people who truly intend on living and establishing businesses on the islands. For that reason, we rarely recommend these business investment options.

- They all offer permanent lifetime citizenship that can be passed on to your descendants.
- These countries impose no income, inheritance, or wealth taxes on international revenue. Some impose taxes on revenue generated in the country.
- In all cases, it is not required that the applicant travel in person to the country during the application process, though an in-person interview may eventually be required. Since 2024, interviews by video conference have become the norm.
- In all cases, the application process is expedited, with completion in two to six months once all documentation has been submitted.
- They all speak English as the official language.

**COWBOY MILLIONAIRE—THE NEW AMERICAN PIONEER**
*Chapter XVIII: The Fastest Way To Get Your "Master Key"*

# What Do You Get? What Do You Give Up?

Nothing distinguishes an economic citizen from a natural citizen of any of these countries. You'll have the same rights, including the right to vote. In the case of Antigua and Barbuda, all citizens are required to reside in their constituency for at least a month before an election to vote.

Furthermore, as a citizen of one of these Caribbean nations, you'll have the right to live and work in other members of the Caribbean Community (CARICOM: Antigua and Barbuda; Bahamas; Barbados; Belize; Dominica; Grenada; Guyana; Haiti; Jamaica; Montserrat; St. Lucia; St. Kitts and Nevis; St. Vincent and the Grenadines; Suriname; and Trinidad and Tobago).

None of these countries impose taxes on citizens who don't live on their islands, except on income generated by local property or businesses. You will not pay taxes on income generated offshore.

None impose military obligations on their citizens. In fact, these island nations have no enemies and are entirely peaceful.

You do not need to fear losing your U.S. citizenship with any program either. However, if that is a goal, now armed with a second citizenship and passport, you can safely renounce your U.S. or other citizenship without rendering yourself stateless or passport-less.

Although these countries provide straightforward options for obtaining a quick and relatively affordable second citizenship and passport, you'll need to engage an authorized agent registered with the country you select to submit your application.

This adds more fees, so shop around. Each country's website has a list of authorized agents. We work with NTL Trust (**bit.ly/NTLTrust**), an agent who is experienced with all of these programs.

## The Process—Not A Bureaucratic Nightmare

As most of the programs require the use of registered agents, the process is fairly painless. All you do is come up with the documents to submit and attend an interview if required. The agent does all the rest for you.

For any of the countries we list here, you'll need to obtain a medical report, a criminal background check (applicants whose check reveals a criminal record will be denied), and reference letters from your bank, lawyer, or other licensed professional. Some countries require a personal reference letter.

Many countries require an interview with the applicant, even those that allow you to begin the process from abroad.

This is normally completed by video conference.

U.S. citizens may submit notarized copies of their current passport, driver's license, birth certificate, and marriage certificate (if applicable). For non-U.S. citizens or U.S. citizens living abroad, copies of these documents, certified with an apostille, must be submitted (if they originate outside the United States).

## Antigua And Barbuda

Known as the land of three hundred sixty-five beaches, Antigua and Barbuda boasts pristine shores, crystal-blue waters, and celebrity vacationers. Tourism is the dominant source of income, generating about sixty percent of the islands' GDP.

The English-speaking two-island state lies in the Eastern Caribbean's Leeward Islands. Having gained independence from Britain in 1981, Antigua and Barbuda has developed a reputation for judicial and governmental stability.

It's also historically been a great place for offshore investment, a second passport, and citizenship-by-investment benefits.

Antigua and Barbuda offers an attractive personal tax regime with no capital gains or inheritance taxes and no tax on foreign-sourced income, relying instead on corporation and sales tax.

It has a population of about one hundred thousand residents, giving it a vibrant economy and lots of potential investment opportunities.

It has a short application process that can be completed within three to four months, and you can also add dependent children up to thirty years old and parents (or grandparents) who are fifty-five or older.

There is no travel requirement to Antigua and Barbuda during your application period, and you will not have to do an interview to get approved.

With a second passport from Antigua and Barbuda, you can travel visa-free to one hundred fifty-four countries, including the Schengen zone, Hong Kong, Singapore, and the U.K.

You can choose from several investment options with this CIP program...

One of the options is to contribute $200,000 to the National Development Fund (NFD) for a single applicant or a family of up to four members.

You can include your spouse, dependent children, and dependent parents over fifty-five within the application with no additional contribution required (although government and due diligence fees will be payable per member of the family).

Another option is to invest in real estate, which requires the purchase of any government-approved property development with a minimum value of $400,000. You must hold

## COWBOY MILLIONAIRE—THE NEW AMERICAN PIONEER
*Chapter XVIII: The Fastest Way To Get Your "Master Key"*

title through single ownership. This amount doesn't include processing fees and taxes, so it's important to factor that into the pricing of your potential property investment.

If you don't want to invest $400,000 by yourself, you can join forces with a partner by purchasing a property for $200,000 each. Title to the property will be held jointly.

The property can't be re-sold until five years after the purchase, unless you purchase an alternate government-approved property in Antigua and Barbuda.

If you would like to receive your citizenship by investment by owning a business in Antigua and Barbuda, you must invest a minimum of $1.5 million. Much like real estate, two or more applicants can make a joint investment as well, but the minimum investment per individual is $400,000.

The government of Antigua and Barbuda is business-friendly and looks at the citizen-by-investment program as a way to promote economic growth through foreign capital. It also looks to further the infrastructural development of the country and create jobs.

The application process for all the options is straightforward, and application forms can be obtained from a local authorized agent licensed by Antigua and Barbuda's Citizenship by Investment Unit (CIU). Processing fees for the NFD donation as well as the real estate and business investment options are $30,000.

## Dominica

Dominica—formally called the "Commonwealth of Dominica" to distinguish it from the Dominican Republic—is another island in the Lesser Antilles region of the Caribbean.

It's sandwiched between the French-speaking islands of Guadeloupe and Martinique. The French were the first Europeans to settle here, and their influence is still strong, giving the community a distinctly French flavor.

Dominica's citizenship-by-investment program dates to 1992. For the real estate investment option of its CIP, the minimum required investment is $200,000. The property must be authorized by the government and held for at least three years.

However, if you hold for at least five years, you can resell your property to someone else investing in the CIP program. That feature is unique among the Caribbean CIP countries.

Government fees for the program when using real estate are $25,000 for the primary applicant, $35,000 for the main applicant and up to three dependents, or $50,000 for the main applicant and up to six dependents.

For the donation investment option (a nonrefundable, cash contribution to the government's Economic Diversification Fund), the minimum requirement is $200,000 for an individual.

If you want to tack on dependents that are older than eighteen, it's $25,000 each. Again, all contributions are non-refundable, but you aren't required to pay until after the government has provisionally approved your application.

For both options, due diligence fees are $7,500 for the primary applicant, $4,000 for a spouse, and $4,000 for any dependents over the age of sixteen. A processing fee of $1,000 per application (individual or family group) is also collected and $500 for each certificate of naturalization.

> One cool fact about Dominica is that Island Caribs, natives of the Greater and Lesser Antilles, still reside here today. They were the first inhabitants of the island and are known today as the Kalinago people. They named Dominica Wait'tukubuli, meaning "Tall is her body."
>
> Today, there are about three thousand Kalinago people living on the island, representing the largest native population in the region. Most live in the Kalinago Territory, where you can visit the Kalinago Barana Aute, a model village. Just remember to do so respectfully. Handmade crafts are for sale, and you can observe traditional festivals, rituals, and dances.

Generally, the entire process takes up to six months. You can expect provisional approval about halfway through, at which time you'll need to make the agreed-upon contribution or close on the property.

A passport from Dominica allows travel to one hundred forty-three countries visa-free.

## Grenada

As one of the most famous islands of the colonial spice trade, Grenada made a name for itself as the "Spice Island."

It has gorgeous natural resources and picturesque Caribbean beaches, as well as a deep cultural flare that blends old Spanish culture with modern Caribbean charm.

Grenada has long been a hot spot for luxury tourism, and thanks to citizenship by investment, it's become a hot spot for high-net-worth investors as well.

You have two options to apply for Grenada's CIP. The first is a one-time $200,000 contribution to the National Transformation Fund (NTF). That's the amount for a single applicant. For a family of four, a higher contribution is required.

The second option is a government-approved real estate investment. You can choose from a $350,000 investment for full ownership of an approved property or a $220,000 investment for each share in the unit within an approved real estate project.

All investment options incur fees: $1,500 in application fees for all applicants, $5,000 in due diligence fees for all applicants over the age of seventeen, plus $1,500 in processing fees for all applicants over seventeen.

The real estate investment option incurs additional government fees, including $50,000 for a family of four plus $25,000 for each dependent beyond this.

> Grenada is home to the world's first underwater garden—the Molinere Underwater Sculpture Park, located off its west coast.
>
> Opened in May 2006, this was the first underwater garden by Jason deCaires Taylor. You can visit this site on a dive or snorkel trip or by taking a tour on a glass-bottomed boat.

Grenada processes second citizenship applications in just four to six months, which is extremely fast and efficient.

There is no physical residency requirement and no requirement to physically travel to Grenada during the application process.

With a Grenada passport, you can travel visa-free to one hundred forty-eight countries, including the EU. You may also travel to, or do business in, the United States with a special E-2 visa program provision.

## St. Kitts And Nevis

St. Kitts and Nevis's CIP, considered the premier citizenship-by-investment program by many citizenship experts, is the world's oldest (launched in 1984).

It was previously ranked the best citizenship-by-investment program in the world by *Professional Wealth Management*, the magazine published by the Financial Times.

It offers several paths to a second passport: the purchase of authorized real estate, a charitable donation to the government, or an investment in an approved public benefit project.

For the real estate investment option, the minimum required investment is $400,000. The investment can be in a designated unit from an approved development or an approved private home. In either case, the investment must be held for seven years.

Government fees are $25,000 for the primary applicant, $15,000 for a spouse, and $10,000 to $15,000 for additional dependents. If you invest in an approved private home, it

## Chapter XVIII: The Fastest Way To Get Your "Master Key"

can't be resold to a future CIP applicant.

Other ways to qualify for a Saint Kitts and Nevis CIP include a $250,000 donation to the Sustainable Island State Contribution or a $250,000 investment in an approved public benefit project.

In all cases, the government requires you to pay the non-refundable due diligence and processing fees upon submitting your application. For the main applicant, the fees are $10,000 plus $7,500 for each dependent over the age of sixteen.

---

St. Kitts and Nevis is home to some of the world's best-tasting mangoes.

There are thousands of mango trees dotted across the islands. There's such a surplus that locals don't even have to buy them.

Officially, there are forty-four different types of mangoes grown on the island, though local experts will confirm that it's probably closer to two hundred varieties.

---

Generally, the entire process takes six months. However, there's an Accelerated Application Process for those in a hurry. You can pay $42,500 for the main applicant, $32,500 for your spouse, and $22,500 to $32,500 per dependent for your application to be processed within sixty days.

The St. Kitts and Nevis passport allows travel to one hundred fifty-six countries visa-free.

## St. Lucia

St. Lucia is known for its pair of volcanic mountain peaks, the Pitons, which are preserved as a UNESCO World Heritage Site. Its many beaches and dramatic scenery make it a popular cruise ship and yachting destination.

The French and English went to war over St. Lucia no less than fourteen times, and it retains a decidedly French flair while being part of the British Commonwealth of Nations.

Launched in 2015, St. Lucia's citizenship-by-investment program is the youngest among the Caribbean citizenship programs. It offers several investment options, including real estate projects...

The minimum required investment is $200,000 in a government-approved real estate project. The property must be held for at least five years.

Government fees are $30,000 for the primary applicant, $45,000 for a couple, $10,000 for dependents age eighteen and over, and $5,000 for dependents under age eighteen.

St. Lucia also offers a donation-investment option through

its National Economic Fund, which promotes infrastructural improvements on the island. The minimum contribution is $100,000 for an individual, $140,000 for a couple, or $150,000 for the applicant, their spouse, and two qualifying dependents. Additional qualifying dependents can be added for $25,000.

Due diligence fees for all options are $7,500 for the primary applicant, plus $5,000 per dependent over sixteen years of age. Processing fees are $2,000 for the main applicant plus $1,000 for each dependent.

> While Ireland is named after the mythical goddess Éiru, St. Lucia is the only country that is named after a real-life woman.
>
> Although it was named after Saint Lucy of Syracuse by French settlers, it was initially called Louanalao (meaning "Island of the Iguanas") by the indigenous Arawak people as early as 200 A.D.

Another way to qualify for St. Lucia's CIP is by making an enterprise investment of at least $3.5 million for a sole investor or $6 million for a joint venture with a maximum of six investors. Administration fees are $50,000 per applicant.

St. Lucia's passport allows travel to one hundred forty-eight countries visa-free.

## Changes To Antigua And Barbuda, Dominica, Grenada, And St. Kitts And Nevis's CIPs

On March 20, 2024, the prime ministers of Antigua and Barbuda, Dominica, Grenada, and Saint Kitts and Nevis signed a Memorandum of Agreement (MoA) to harmonize aspects of their countries' CIPs.

Specifically, they committed to cooperating more closely on pricing, standards of transparency and information sharing, security screening, marketing and promotion of programs, and regulation.

Most significant among the changes is the agreement to establish a price floor for investment across these four CIPs. The minimum investment threshold for economic contributions will be harmonized at $200,000. Effective on June 30, 2024, this is a notable price increase for most of these programs.

> Of the five Caribbean countries that offer economic citizenship, only St. Lucia did not commit to the MoA.

## Vanuatu... Not In The Caribbean, But A Similar Program

The nation of Vanuatu is an archipelago of volcanic islands located west of Fiji, east of Australia, and north of New Zealand.

As in so many other cases, the islands were inhabited by both French and English settlers, but, in a rare turn, the two countries jointly governed Vanuatu from 1906 until it became an independent country in 1980.

Economic activity centers on cattle ranching and fishing, along with tourism. Vanuatu is renowned as a diving destination with multiple reefs and wrecks. It gained recognition as a "Survivor" TV series location.

Vanuatu amended its constitution in 2014 to permit dual citizenship in order to accommodate its CIP. The program offers immediate citizenship for the entire family in a country with no tax on income, wealth, or inheritance.

Vanuatu's current program is called the Development Support Program, and unlike the Caribbean CIPs, it only offers a donation option. It has modified the donation amounts to undercut the Caribbean programs' cost of entry.

Currently, the donation amounts are $130,000 for an individual; $150,000 for a couple; $165,000 for a couple and one child; and $180,000 for a couple and two children. Each additional dependent is $10,000.

You'll also have a $5,000 due diligence fee per person and an oath ceremony fee of $1,800 if done in Vanuatu and $5,000 if done overseas.

Vanuatu still offers the fastest "time to a passport" of any of the CIP programs. Typically, once documents are submitted, you're looking at about a month before you receive approval.

A Vanuatu passport affords visa-free access to ninety-three destinations. Should you decide to move there, Vanuatu has no income tax on domestic- or international-sourced income except local rental income.

## What's Your Choice?

How should you choose between these programs, given how similar they are?

Nick Stevens of NTL Trust says, "Commentators spend a great deal of time pushing out index after index ranking passports against each other. Rankings are typically based on the number of countries that holders of this-or-that passport can

**COWBOY MILLIONAIRE—THE NEW AMERICAN PIONEER**
*Chapter XVIII: The Fastest Way To Get Your "Master Key"*

travel to without a visa.

"These rankings are highly subjective. Most investors probably don't care about visa-free travel to, say, Malawi... so why care about one Caribbean country having visa-free access to one hundred forty countries and another one having access to one hundred thirty-five?

"What's more, the definition of a visa is blurry these days. Consider e-visas, visas on arrival, and systems like the U.S. ESTA, the U.K.'s ETA, and the European Union's forthcoming ETIAS—basically all online visas, even though they are called something different.

"Visa requirements can and will change. Vanuatu lost its visa-free status to Schengen (EU) in 2022, and Dominica and Vanuatu both lost visa-free access to the U.K. in 2023. Remember, though, that both countries only gained EU visa-free access in 2015, whereas Dominica's CBI program has been going strong since 1993.

"The bottom line is that when you are investing in citizenship, you are investing for a lifetime and for future generations. If you 'buy' a citizenship just because of its visa-free travel, you might be disappointed. There are much more fundamental reasons why you should be acquiring multiple citizenships.

"Here are some other things to consider...

"If you are applying with a family, the cost varies enormously.

**COWBOY MILLIONAIRE—THE NEW AMERICAN PIONEER**
*Chapter XVIII: The Fastest Way To Get Your "Master Key"*

"Another factor is how efficient the application process is. As licensed immigration consultants, we experience this on a daily basis.

"Processing efficiency is partly about speed. All programs carry out stringent background checks, but there is no reason why a normal background check, however deep, should take more than a few weeks, except in very exceptional circumstances.

"Some politicians like to imply that if the process takes six or twelve months, they can somehow do better due diligence, and they are more likely to root out criminals...

"As a qualified due diligence professional myself, I take the view that if the process takes that long, it's just evidence of operational problems and inefficiencies. And organizations with inefficiencies are generally more likely to miss key due diligence issues.

"Let's talk about how your passport is perceived when you travel... or use it for banking, residency, or whatever other purpose you might have in mind.

"The 'Caribbean Five' passports are perceived more or less equally. However, Antigua and St. Lucia have the most developed tourism industries, and this has helped a lot in terms of positive perception, as nearly everybody has at least a friend or relative who has been there and had a pleasant experience. These two countries have closer relationships with

## COWBOY MILLIONAIRE—THE NEW AMERICAN PIONEER
*Chapter XVIII: The Fastest Way To Get Your "Master Key"*

Canada, which is why they recently regained some visa-free travel there.

"Grenada, way down south, has a cozy relationship with China and has gained some notoriety for having many Russian-origin citizens. The more mature among us will recall the U.S. invasion of Grenada in 1983, when the island was turning towards Cuba and the Soviet Union. I enjoy the intricacies of geopolitics. But Grenada might not suit everyone.

"Of course, there are lots of other factors to consider that I don't have time to go into here…

"In which countries do the islands have embassies? Which ones are visa-free for BRICS countries? Which recognizes Taiwan? Which passports might work better in the Middle East? Which has better on-island private banking? Where can you use your asset protection trust to access citizenship?

"These and many other factors all come into play when deciding which is the best citizenship-by-investment program. It really makes sense to sit down with a professional from a firm that truly knows all the programs, as opposed to one where you will be talking to a junior salesperson who is motivated by commission to push one program over another."

As I always say, about every aspect of life as a cross-continental pioneer…

You need your own personal posse of experts you can trust to help you along the way.

## Collecting Passports... How To Get The Maximum Number

How many citizenships can one person have at the same time? I've done various calculations over the years...

Being born with multiple citizenships is the easiest way to get them... and also the least likely for most people.

My son was born with two citizenships: Irish and American. American came from his parents—known in Latin as *jus sanguinis* (right of blood). Irish came from being born in Ireland (*jus soli*, or right of soil), where Kathleen and I lived at the time.

*Jus soli* was eliminated in Ireland after he was born because too many refugees were taking advantage of the system. Women would arrive in the country pregnant, apply for refugee status, have the baby, and then change their status to parent of an Irish child, which gave them an automatic right to stay in the country. I'm not sure why the Irish didn't change the right to stay rather than eliminating *jus soli*.

That's how the United States works. A child born in the United States is automatically a citizen. However, the parents get no rights because of that, like they would have in Ireland.

Ireland was the last country in Europe to offer unrestricted citizenship if a child was born in the country. Most unrestricted *jus soli* countries at the moment are in the Americas. That limits the options for having your child born with two citizenships… unless you and your spouse hold different citizenships.

A friend in Paris has two children who were born with Italian and U.K. citizenship. She's Italian. Her husband was British. The kids were born in France. Even though France doesn't offer unrestricted *jus soli* if you're born there, those two kids were still born with two citizenships—Italian and British.

Having been born in France and living there while growing up, they are eligible for French citizenship under France's rules, but it requires living in the country. They could have three citizenships and carry three passports.

I believe their mother didn't push for the idea of getting French citizenship because "who needs more than one EU passport?" Well, British passport holders would have benefited from that because of Brexit. Her kids will benefit from having that U.K. citizenship if they want to live or work in the U.K.

As it turns out, my son, with his Irish passport, can live and work in the U.K. because he's an Irish citizen, thanks to the special relationship between Ireland and the U.K.

I knew that in the back of my head from my time living in Ireland, but I buried that specific rule because when the U.K. was in the EU, that rule was moot.

So we're up to three citizenships.

## Math Is Fun

If one of my Paris friend's kids has children with someone like them, born with two citizenships, then their kids would be born with four citizenships, assuming there was no overlap. If that child was born in a fifth country that had *jus soli* citizenship, like Argentina, we're up to five citizenships.

That's really the logical end to how many citizenships one can be born with. Maybe that kid born with five citizenships could marry someone with five citizenships, and their kid could end up with eleven citizenships at birth, but that's a stretch... especially when you start to take in the second level rules.

My son got American citizenship from his parents. He can't pass on American citizenship to his kids unless he lives in the United States for at least five years before his children are born. He's only lived in the United States for a year so far because of college.

## COWBOY MILLIONAIRE—THE NEW AMERICAN PIONEER
*Chapter XVIII: The Fastest Way To Get Your "Master Key"*

Being born with multiple citizenships isn't a choice for the child. They're either eligible or not. However, you can gain citizenship by choice if you spend the time to make yourself eligible. That's done in two ways—residency or money.

As someone I knew growing up used to say, do you have more time or money? Maybe you don't have enough of either, which won't get you another citizenship.

However, if you spend enough time living in another country, you can be eligible for citizenship. Alternatively, if you have enough money to invest in or donate to a country that offers a citizenship-by-investment program, you don't have to put in the time as a resident.

Five years of residency is the most common time requirement. Some countries start the clock once you have legal residency. Some start the clock once you have permanent residency (as opposed to temporary residency). Once you're eligible, the approval process can take a year or more.

That means time isn't on your side if you're looking to have a bunch of citizenships. The other factor against you is that many countries have a clause in their naturalization laws that allows them to revoke your naturalization if you become a naturalized citizen in another country.

Assuming you're born with just one citizenship, you aren't likely to work your way up to four or five citizenships. Three is your likely cap... four if you also have the money to go the citizenship-by-investment route. Although, if money is no object, you could buy into more than one CIP. Some have made it their mission to collect all the Caribbean CIPs, for example.

To get beyond two passports in this scenario, you'd need to start with a country that doesn't revoke your naturalization if you get naturalized elsewhere. The Dominican Republic is one such option.

Once you have that first naturalization under your belt, you would move onto the second country for naturalization, and maybe eleven years or so after you got residency in your first country, you'd have three passports.

Some countries have a shorter time requirement for naturalization... Again the DR is one option. Paraguay is another.

Others have longer periods, like twenty years for Andorra.

And some countries make you give up previous citizenships before they'll naturalize you and give you a passport, like Singapore.

Again, being born with more than one citizenship is the easiest path.

Some people were born with more than one citizen-

## COWBOY MILLIONAIRE—THE NEW AMERICAN PIONEER
*Chapter XVIII: The Fastest Way To Get Your "Master Key"*

ship, but they have to claim it. Those are people with grandparents born with citizenship in a country that offers citizenship through ancestry. A few European countries still offer this, like Ireland and Italy.

The only complication is getting all the right documents together, which for an older person whose grandparents have been dead for decades can be difficult. But there are services that will do the research and submit the claim on your behalf.

Two passports are better than one. That should be obvious. However, the benefits of having more than two citizenships start to diminish unless they are geographically unique countries. By that, I mean three EU passports aren't as useful as, say, holding passports from the United States, an EU country, and a MERCOSUR country like Argentina.

Four or five passports are likely more hassle and expense than they are worth. At least that was the conclusion someone I met once came to. She has two passports but is eligible for two more. With one EU passport in hand already, the other EU citizenship she can claim wouldn't be of any real benefit (unless one of the two countries left the EU). She's not really interested in the last citizenship, as she doesn't want to live in that country.

For either, she'd have to gather paperwork, spend

money on an attorney, and then spend money on getting the passport issued. In the end, it's not worth it for her.

Another person who wants more options and more backup plans might make a different calculation.

The question about citizenship shouldn't be how many you can have... but rather how many would be useful for what you want to do.

# Epilogue

## From Pioneer To Jetsetter In Three Easy Steps

Over the years, I've met countless Americans who planned to move abroad because a particular president or a particular party was in office.

They didn't like that president or that party's politics and policies... and so they decided they were packing up and going somewhere else...

But creating a plan to internationalize your life isn't something you should do as a reaction to someone or something...

You should do it for yourself: to expand your wealth and your lifestyle... and to protect yourself, your family, and your assets.

## You're Not Running Away From Something...

The problem with reactionary "planning" based on the politics of the moment is that, by the time you get your plans in order, the president or party you hate could be gone and out of office.

What you need to consider, as I talked about in the introduction to this book, is the long-term trends...

Even if American Decline (and I believe it's real) is the reason for your move, you need more than that to motivate you... you want to make a positive decision to improve you and your family's lot.

This isn't about reacting to something or running away... but running towards all the opportunities the world has to offer...

Although it can happen quicker... it can also take years to get your affairs in order to effectuate a move from your home country to another one, especially if you're starting from ground zero.

Re-organizing your business affairs, shifting and structuring or re-structuring your assets, organizing residency, finding a place to live... all of these things take time.

They can be accomplished quickly if you're focused, but most people have other things going on in life that have to be managed as well, meaning these decisions and plans sometimes take a long time to come together.

The real point, however, isn't the time it takes to diversify your life internationally.

The real point is that you should be embarking on this path for yourself and your family because you want to take control of your future.

My other real point is that, whatever you're going to do, you need to get started today.

My goal is to help you create a diversified life that gives you the flexibility you need and deserve so that no matter what is going on in your home country, no matter what is going on in your current country of residence, and no matter what is going on in the world at large, you will be nimble enough to sail through unaffected.

Politicians will come and go. Currencies will rise and fall. Economies will grow and struggle. Values will appreciate and sometimes collapse.

But you won't have to worry about any of it. You won't be at the mercy of the bozos in power or of world events beyond your control. You won't be reduced to organizing your life as a reaction to other peoples' mistakes.

You'll be able to sit back, not worrying but watching for opportunity and your chance to seize it.

## You're In Control... Go As Far As Makes Sense For You

Once you get started, you'll eventually reach the point

where you'll ask yourself how much diversification is enough.

My real estate portfolio has included investments in more than two dozen countries over the years and currently holds twenty-four properties in eleven countries. For some, that might qualify as over-diversification. On the other hand, I invest when and where an opportunity I like presents itself.

If you're focused on this diversify offshore strategy, you'll likely make more than one investment, real estate or otherwise. Your non-investment offshore endeavors likely will be fewer, but you should still have multiples.

Any experience navigating the world of global diversification opportunities will teach you that you want more than one bank account offshore. However, few people consider multiple residencies.

I did know someone a few years ago who had established residency in three countries at the same time with the goal of attaining citizenship in at least one of the jurisdictions.

His premise was that everything in the offshore world doesn't work out as you plan, so he was getting as many residencies as he could in an effort to guarantee at least one second citizenship opportunity.

At the time, the idea seemed like overkill. Today, it seems like a prudent plan that I embrace and endorse.

In fact, more and more people I meet at conferences and while traveling are already pursuing this strategy and setting up residency in more than one other country beyond the one where they were born.

Legal residency often eventually leads to citizenship. Just because you're eligible for naturalization doesn't mean you have to apply. However, having the option should translate to peace of mind.

Maintaining multiple residencies at the same time can come with complications.

Some countries have no minimum requirement for how much time you must spend physically present in their country if you have residency. Other countries impose minimal stay requirements.

Those potential complications notwithstanding, I suggest that a second citizenship along with two alternative residencies makes for about as bulletproof a strategy as you could need.

This means four countries—the country of your original citizenship, the country of your second citizenship, and each of your two backup residency countries—where you would be able to legally reside indefinitely should you find the need.

Pick up an EU passport, and the number of countries where you could hang out indefinitely jumps to twenty-seven. Pick up a CARICOM passport, and you have many living options in the Caribbean.

**COWBOY MILLIONAIRE—THE NEW AMERICAN PIONEER**
*Epilogue: From Pioneer To Jet-Setter In Three Easy Steps*

## Taking The First Step On The Pioneer's Journey...

How should you get started? That's the question most often asked when I speak with people about going offshore. My answer is generally, "Do something."

That may seem unresponsive, but like in all things, you have to take that first step.

I wasn't a real estate investor until I bought my first property. Before that, I was a researcher. I had done due diligence on numerous buildings. I knew my target numbers for rental yield, price, mortgage payment, and more. However, to get started, I had to buy that first property.

For going offshore, you have more options for taking that first step, but my follow-up response to telling people to do something is to open a bank account. That's usually the simplest offshore "first step" and the least risky in that you can always close that first account and move your money back home or to another offshore bank that you find later that you prefer.

Of course, you have to take steps that fit your personal situation and ultimate goals. Fine-tuning your personal offshore infrastructure is an ongoing task. However, you can't course-correct unless you're already on your journey.

So, do something.

That said, don't spend money you don't need to. Maybe you don't need an offshore entity to achieve your offshore goals. That's OK.

Simply move on to the next step.

You'll find that once you take the first step, you'll be more comfortable taking the next one. And then the road ahead will become clearer...

## A Dream Life

Sitting on the porch of a friend's home on the water near Los Islotes, the coastal community I'm developing in Panama, looking out over the Pacific Ocean and listening to the surf... it struck me how different my life would have played out if I hadn't chosen to internationalize it early on.

The truth is, I could have taken an easier path.

The owners of the small CPA firm where I worked starting in high school and continuing through several years of college offered at one point to finish paying for my college education if I'd agree to major in accounting, get my CPA designation, and then commit to working for them full-time for some designated period.

It was an excellent offer for a kid struggling to pay his college fees semester by semester by working two jobs. Nevertheless, I declined. Sitting in an accounting office in Phoenix,

Arizona, every day for years to come didn't sound hugely appealing. I wanted to do something more interesting with my life... although at the time I didn't know specifically what that might be.

Today, nearly forty years later, I still couldn't tell you specifically what I'd like my end game to be... other than to say that a whole lot more of the same would be great.

I've found that moving myself and my money around the world to places where we're both treated well suits me. For me, diversification isn't a theoretical strategy; it's an organic reality.

How did I get from my working-class origins in Phoenix to living what many might describe as a jetset lifestyle a few decades later?

I think the answer comes down to not being afraid to take a chance and not being willing to settle for comfortable. You know, the American spirit. The pioneering spirit.

From an early age, I knew that I wanted to make money. However, an appetite for "outside the box" has always been equally important to me.

Since my first trips overseas when I was sixteen, every time I've discovered a place where I enjoyed spending time, I instinctively wanted to make an investment of my money in that place, as well.

Hence my position today... last week on Panama's Azuero

## COWBOY MILLIONAIRE—THE NEW AMERICAN PIONEER
*Epilogue: From Pioneer To Jet-Setter In Three Easy Steps*

Sunset Coast, meeting with my Los Islotes builder to check on the construction of my beach house... and this week on Mexico's Riviera Maya, meeting with colleagues about new investment opportunities in Mexico and Belize...

I came to the western coast of the Azuero Peninsula for the first time nearly twenty years ago. I knew right away it was a special place... a place I'd like a reason to return to... and, as well, a place presenting big upside investment potential. I decided to look for a way to invest my money on that coast that would translate to a reason to spend my time on it long-term.

From that agenda, Los Islotes was born.

The journey from struggling student to globetrotter hasn't been direct, easy, or without setbacks, but, sitting on my friend's porch, I realized that I'm sure glad I turned down my accounting firm bosses all those years ago.

In this book, I've shown you how to live the kind of life I do—the life of a "Millionaire Cowboy" or "New American Pioneer"—in three steps:

1. Creating your fortune on the international scene;
2. Securing it with offshore protection strategies; and
3. Giving yourself the ultimate Plan B for extra travel and residency freedom with a second passport.

It's a life offering more opportunity and independence

than you could ever imagine...

The journey can be wild and exciting, with lots of twists and turns (and a few obstacles in your way, of course)... but the list of steps themselves is simple.

You won't build this kind of life for yourself overnight. But you don't have to spend thirty years doing it, like I've done, either.

The reason why I wrote this book was to share with you all the lessons I've learned... so that you can take a much shorter route to success.

What you can do right now, today, is take a first step.

You can't imagine the opportunities that step or the next one will lead to...

But I guarantee that the ultimate outcome will be an adventure like no other.

## Take The First Step Towards International Diversification Today: Sign Up For Lief Simon's *Offshore Living Letter*

# OFFSHORE LIVING LETTER
### Diversify Or Die Broke

*Offshore Living Letter* is a publication of Live And Invest Overseas that comes straight from the desk of Lief Simon.

This is a top resource for anyone who wants to take control of their financial future. It offers tips and actionable information on asset protection, banking, diversification, forming a corporation, second citizenship, and much more.

Lief says, "You don't have to be a millionaire to take up the idea of banking, doing business, or investing offshore. There are different levels to this game. Only you will know what makes sense for your circumstances and what's within your comfort zone.

"Your strategy might be as simple as opening a bank account in another country... or you can get more complex and diversify into real estate or precious metals... form an offshore corporation... or move overseas and acquire second citizenship, as I have...

"Either way, *Offshore Living Letter* will help get you started on your path to relying on yourself for your future's prosperity."

Sign up for *Offshore Living Letter* at <u>offshorelivingletter.com</u> or by scanning the QR code below.

Made in United States
Orlando, FL
09 November 2024